# Women, Money, and Political Participation in the Middle East

Bozena C. Welborne

# Women, Money, and Political Participation in the Middle East

palgrave
macmillan

Bozena C. Welborne
Smith College
Northampton, MA, USA

ISBN 978-3-031-04876-0     ISBN 978-3-031-04877-7   (eBook)
https://doi.org/10.1007/978-3-031-04877-7

© The Editor(s) (if applicable) and The Author(s), under exclusive license to Springer
Nature Switzerland AG 2022
This work is subject to copyright. All rights are solely and exclusively licensed by the
Publisher, whether the whole or part of the material is concerned, specifically the rights
of translation, reprinting, reuse of illustrations, recitation, broadcasting, reproduction on
microfilms or in any other physical way, and transmission or information storage and
retrieval, electronic adaptation, computer software, or by similar or dissimilar methodology
now known or hereafter developed.
The use of general descriptive names, registered names, trademarks, service marks, etc.
in this publication does not imply, even in the absence of a specific statement, that such
names are exempt from the relevant protective laws and regulations and therefore free for
general use.
The publisher, the authors and the editors are safe to assume that the advice and information in this book are believed to be true and accurate at the date of publication. Neither
the publisher nor the authors or the editors give a warranty, expressed or implied, with
respect to the material contained herein or for any errors or omissions that may have been
made. The publisher remains neutral with regard to jurisdictional claims in published maps
and institutional affiliations.

Cover illustration: @ Alex Linch shutterstock.com

This Palgrave Macmillan imprint is published by the registered company Springer Nature
Switzerland AG
The registered company address is: Gewerbestrasse 11, 6330 Cham, Switzerland

# ACKNOWLEDGMENTS

To say that this manuscript has been a long-time coming would be an understatement. What started as a dissertation way back in 2011, has mutated into something more layered, hopefully offering new avenues for myself and others to explore the complex trajectory of women's political participation in the Middle East and North Africa (MENA). As so much of it was inspired by my fieldwork across Jordan, Morocco, and Bahrain from 2008 to 2009, I would be remiss in not thanking the granting agencies that backed my pilot work at the time, including the Institute of International Education's (IIE) Fulbright Fellowship for Jordan and the National Security Education Program's (NSEP) Boren Fellowship, which allowed me to extend my work to Morocco and Bahrain. Three individuals were instrumental in helping me obtain what at the time was remarkable access to the many key figures informing my findings: Hussain al-Shabib in Bahrain, Dr. Malika Bounfour in Morocco and, the sadly departed, Dr. Rula Quawas in Jordan. The latter was an amazingly generous scholar and unabashed feminist activist, who inspired multiple generations of Jordanian women (and beyond) to stand up for their rights. The world is a sadder place for her loss.

The University of Colorado at Boulder (CUB) was generous enough to fund my initial forays into exploring this topic and the requisite language training in first Yemen and later Morocco through the FLAS fellowship program as well a variety of university-wide grants (the

v

Dorothy Martin, Beverly Seers, and the Robert Vernon Stover fellowships). The political science department also bankrolled many a summer either studying Arabic or improving my data analysis skills. Most of all I am grateful for the tireless mentorship of my doctoral advisors David Brown and especially Susan Clarke. The latter is a dear friend and a source of continued counsel and inspiration. They don't come any classier than Susan.

The International Foundation for Electoral Systems (IFES) was the first post-graduate institution to take an interest in my work on electoral gender quotas in the MENA, which played a key role in my bigger understanding of women's political participation as outlined in this manuscript. The Project on Middle East Political Science (POMEPS) was the second such organization, which gave me the opportunity to brainstorm my ideas further at their Yale dissertation symposium. There I met Dr. Aili Tripp—a scholar who has continued to inspire me with her work and her willingness to push the envelope in terms of research interests and travels. Aili has remained a trusted source of wisdom and mirth across the multiple conferences and travels where we invariably encounter each other. POMEPS also funded research that introduced me to one of the research collaborators I cite heavily in this book—Nawra Al-Lawati. Nawra's energy and vision, as well as detailed knowledge of women's issues in the Arab Gulf states has been integral to much of this book.

Through Rice University's Baker Institute, the inimitable Dr. Marwa Shalaby offered me multiple opportunities to further refine preliminary insights on the concept of gender rentierism more broadly. I have also co-authored multiple policy briefs with my colleague and friend, Dr. Gail Buttorff, who helped flesh out the interaction between rent-seeking behavior and women's empowerment discussed in this manuscript, and is someone I know I can always refer to for sound advice and critique, dosed with warm support.

In 2017 a pilot scholarly exchange program between Smith College and Al-Akhawayne University (AUI) would afford me more time in Morocco, so allowing me to update findings from earlier fieldwork through further interviews and archival research. I am especially grateful to the Hillary Clinton Center for Women's Empowerment (HCC) and Drs. Doris Gray and Katya Zvan-Elliott for granting me a space to do my work, and offering insightful commentary on its content as well as ample opportunities to share it with other colleagues at AUI.

Through it all, my parents Bojana and Gerald Welborne, as well as my sister-friend, colleague, and co-author, Dr. Aubrey Westfall, have supported my research and occasionally off-the-wall musings with humor, quiet wisdom, and grounding feedback. Finally, I thank little Maja Florence for keeping her mother more or less on track with this book and my partner, Mike, for his love and encouragement throughout the writing process.

# CONTENTS

**1 An Introduction: Gendered Rentierism in the Arab World**    1
*Authoritarian Upgrading and State Feminism*    5
*Women's Empowerment as Virtue Signaling*    8
*Connecting Economics to Politics*    11
*Gendered Rentierism as an Analytical Tool*    15
*What to Expect from This Book*    18
*References*    20

**2 State Feminism and Gendered Rentierism**    27
*Upgrading Authoritarianism Through Women*    30
*Rentier-State Theory and Gender*    36
*Gendered Rentierism Revisited*    40
*References*    52

**3 Foreign Aid and Virtue Signaling**    59
*Foreign Aid Promotes Gender Equality*    63
*Virtue Signaling and Women's Representation*    71
*Foreign Aid and the Push to End Violence Against Women*    80
*Conclusion*    83
*References*    85

**4 The Gender Paradox of Remittances**    95
*Surveying Remittances in the MENA*    97
*Migrant Values and Social Change*    101

ix

x CONTENTS

| | | |
|---|---|---|
| *Promoting Old or New Gender Dynamics?* | | 103 |
| *Does Migration Lead to Emancipation?* | | 107 |
| *The Values of Remittance-Receiving Households* | | 109 |
| *The Indirect Political Effect of Remittances* | | 114 |
| *Conclusion* | | 120 |
| *References* | | 121 |
| **5** | **Independents, Women's Work, and Oil Rents** | **127** |
| | *The Emergence of Women Independents* | 130 |
| | *Gendered Rentierism in Oil-Dependent Versus* | |
| | *Oil-Abundant States* | 136 |
| | *The Political Economy of Women's Legislative Representation* | 140 |
| | *Conclusion* | 151 |
| | *References* | 154 |
| **6** | **Gendered Rentierism—A Curse or an Opportunity** | |
| | **for Women?** | **161** |
| | *Patriarchal Bargains Across Rentiers* | 164 |
| | *The Problem of Rents Depoliticizing Women's Empowerment* | 165 |
| | *References* | 167 |
| **Appendix** | | **169** |
| **Index** | | **173** |

# List of Figures

Fig. 2.1 Comparison of Rents for 2019, World vs. MENA* (*High-income countries excluded) (*Sources:* World Development Indicators, 2022)     40

Fig. 3.1 OECD-DAC Aid to Programs Targeting Gender Equality 2002–2020 (in millions of US Dollars) (*Sources:* OECD.Stat Database, 2022)     64

Fig. 4.1 Remittances as a percentage of GDP across the MENA, 2019 (*Sources:* World Development Indicators, 2022)     98

Fig. 4.2 Arab public opinion: Elected positions should be set aside for women (*Source:* Arab Barometer V [2018–2019], Q601A, categories collapsed)     113

Fig. 5.1 Women's labor force participation in the GCC, 2000–2019 (*Source:* World Development Indicators, 2022)     137

# LIST OF TABLES

| | | |
|---|---|---|
| Table 4.1 | Remittance recipients' attitudes toward women's rights in the MENA, 2018–2019 | 110 |
| Table 4.2 | The impact of remittances on women's labor force participation, world regions, 1994–2019 | 117 |
| Table 4.3 | The impact of remittances on women's political representation, world regions, 1994–2019 | 118 |
| Table 5.1 | Women independents in global assemblies, 2015–2018 | 131 |
| Table A.1 | Attitudes toward women among remittance receivers in MENA, 2010–2011 | 170 |
| Table A.2 | Attitudes toward women among remittance receivers in MENA, 2012–2014 | 171 |
| Table A.3 | Attitudes toward women among remittance receivers in MENA, 2016–2017 | 172 |

CHAPTER 1

# An Introduction: Gendered Rentierism in the Arab World

In 2015, Saudi Arabia hosted its first municipal elections featuring both male and female candidates.[1] It also allowed women to vote for the first time alongside men in *any* election in the kingdom. Nearly 1000 women ran for office, as did roughly 6000 men. Per Rasha Hefzi, one of the successful female candidates in the election: 'Any woman who won in this council is equal to ten men, because there is a wall that we [women] are trying to break'.[2] Unsurprisingly, these women often faced more scrutiny than their male counterparts (BBC, 2015), and, in a few cases, were barred from registering as candidates with no attendant explanation. Many suspected it was due to their being Shiite, as well as many of the female candidates' involvement in active lobbying for the expansion of women's rights in the kingdom (McDowall, 2015).

A fraction of the female population had registered to vote and, ultimately, only 20 women won office across the 2100 contested municipal

---

[1] The previous two municipal elections, in 2005 and 2011, had been open only to male candidates and male voters.

[2] Amos (2015).

---

© The Author(s), under exclusive license to Springer Nature Switzerland AG 2022
B. C. Welborne, *Women, Money, and Political Participation in the Middle East*,
https://doi.org/10.1007/978-3-031-04877-7_1

## 2 B. C. WELBORNE

seats.[3] However, 82 percent of registered women voted, compared to just 44 percent of registered men (Die Welt, 2015). The women who ran and won also represented a rarity in the kingdom, insofar as they were directly elected, rather than appointed to political posts as their predecessors in the Saudi Consultative Council.[4] Much like their counterparts in the rest of the Gulf Cooperation Council (GCC) states,[5] these women had all run without partisan support, winning barely one percent of municipal seats. Many of them complained about the high cost of running campaigns , even for local posts, and about insufficient support from the government (CBS News, 2015).

Alongside the sheer cost of running for office, these women also faced distinct challenges in campaigning in comparison to men, due to strict interpretations of Islamic guardianship laws in the kingdom. For example, female candidates were barred from speaking to male voters and forced to present their platforms behind screens and partitions. Others had to rely on their *walis* (male chaperones) and male relatives as campaign avatars (Worley, 2016).[6] A year after the elections, in fact, reports surfaced that the women who had won municipal seats were not allowed to sit side by side with their colleagues and had to participate remotely in council deliberations (Stancati & Al Omran, 2016).

A post-election NPR interview with a young female Saudi voter shed light on obstacles for women voters and candidates alike when navigating the public sphere without a chaperone:

[3] 1.5 million Saudis, from a population of 20 million, voted in the 2015 municipal elections with Saudi Arabia's General Election Commission proclaiming there were at least 5 million eligible voters. The female winners of the elections were Salma al-Oteibi in the Mecca region, Lama al-Suleiman and Rasha Hufaithi in Jeddah, Hanouf al-Hazimi in Al Jouf province, and Sanaa al-Hammam and Masoumah Abdelreda in the Ahsa region.

[4] The Consultative Council is an appointed national assembly with no powers. Whereas municipal councils in Saudi Arabia are elected, the 150 Consultative Council members—including 30 women—are appointed by the King.

[5] The Gulf Cooperation Council (GCC) is a political and economic alliance of six Persian Gulf monarchies founded in 1981. The following countries are member states: Saudi Arabia, Kuwait, the United Arab Emirates, Qatar, Bahrain, and Oman. Recently, there has been discussion of whether the GCC should be extended to include two monarchies outside of the Arabian Peninsula—Morocco and Jordan.

[6] Both genders were banned from using photographs of themselves to promote their campaigns, and women have been segregated from men at meetings of the official councils.

> I can't open a bank account for my children that takes money out of my paycheck and, like, for a savings account for them. I can't do that—their dad has to do that ... So it's like the whole guardianship issue. ... Even if my guardian tries to renew my passport, I can't pick it up. He has to pick it up for me. So I feel like these issues are more significant and more like they have influence on my daily life. (NPR, 2015)

Due to the intensity of Saudi segregation policies, many of the most successful female candidates were adept users of social media. Twitter, Facebook, and Instagram—as well as WhatsApp and YouTube, alongside local sites—gave them a way to contact and connect with male and female constituents without running afoul of religious authorities.

That the 20 Saudi women who succeeded in their municipal campaigns were well-connected 'elites' helped many of them overcome the financial barriers so many other female candidates who ran faced (Welborne, 2020). Lama al-Suleiman and the aforementioned Rasha Hefzi, both elected to municipal office in Jeddah, were prominent businesswomen who received roughly equal support from male and female voters. Suleiman, who served as vice president of the Jeddah Chamber of Commerce, was twice elected to the position by her (primarily male) peers, which speaks to her electability and experience in other desegregated contexts.

Suleiman also credited her performance to a savvy social media campaign targeting conservative men. Hefzi, on the other hand, touted her 'youth orientation' and hired male comedians to appeal to her male constituents. Both women also relied on more conventional tactics, such as organizing food-laden rallies. Needless to say, none of these strategies were cheap.

Surveying the successful female candidates of the 2010, 2013, 2016, and 2020 elections in the Kingdom of Jordan—a more 'liberal' context in comparison to Saudi Arabia—quickly reveals how many had ties to local and international businesses and organizations, similar to the Saudi municipal women. Furthermore, many acquired relevant experience in professions that allowed them to coordinate and fund their campaigns. What is more striking is how many of these women worked in the education sector, with more than 50 percent of women in the 18th Jordanian House of Representatives teaching at the secondary or university level, and eight out of 18 female parliamentarians possessing doctoral degrees—a much higher rate than their male counterparts in the assembly.

4   B. C. WELBORNE

Such intersecting ties to business and other local and international organizations, including the public and private sectors, are likely to be more salient for female candidates in countries where political parties are less established, weak, even banned, and thus cannot be relied on to fund expensive campaigns for women or other candidates deemed 'unelectable'. Dr. Nuha Maita, a former Jordanian Member of Parliament, spoke to me about the importance of women having their feet planted firmly in both the public and private sectors if they chose to run as political candidates:

> This is what we lack as women: that we didn't serve in public or in the army ... This is what women need. They need somebody to serve them there. There is not a political party to serve them ... If we serve in the army, if we serve in the ministry, and if she was good and serve in her area [tribal area or city] I think they will elect her.[7]

Dr. Maita was describing the key to the success of thrice-elected Jordanian representative, Dr. Falaak Jamani, who also happened to be the first Jordanian woman elected outside of the gender quota system (adopted in 2003). At the time, Dr. Jamani represented a departure from the trope of the 'tribal token' with her outright win of an electoral seat in 2007 and her unique background, which blended military and medical experience (she had been a dentist in the military's health division).[8] Her mixture of cross-cutting professional experience and social connections granted her the ability to place people in jobs across two key sectors and win the favor of local tribes to the point where they invited her to participate in their *diwans* (tribal councils) as a full member. This also occasionally invited ridicule that she was 'a man'.

The Jordanian and Saudi experiences both hint at the importance of access to campaign funds, income in general, and the 'right' social and economic networks for women to succeed in politics. Of course, women face other challenges in the Middle East and North Africa (MENA) when it comes to political participation. Getting on the ballot—much

[7] Interview with Nuha Maita in Amman, Jordan, November 2008.

[8] In this context, 'tribal token' refers to a female candidate fielded by smaller tribes or otherwise disadvantaged communities to take advantage of the Jordanian gender quota and so have a voice in the Lower House (see Bush & Gao, 2017). Dr. Jamani won her first mandate through the quota for governorate of Madaba in 2003 and was re-elected in a landslide victory in 2007.

less getting elected—is still no small feat, especially if there are no mechanisms already in place to bolster their campaigns, such as gender quotas or support from the women's nongovernmental organizations (NGOs) often associated with feminist social movements (Darhour & Dahlerup, 2013; Moghadam, 2012; Tripp, 2012).

One could, speciously, argue that because men and women face the same obstacles in authoritarian states, there should be nothing unique about women running for office. Yet, this logic ignores the immense challenges women face when participating in politics *on any level* in MENA states. In some cases, these states have only recently extended suffrage to both genders, have long infringed on women's mobility via antiquated personal status codes, and feature politics often driven by conservative and kin-based solidarities (Charrad, 2011).

My hope in sharing this research is to help demystify the economic challenges and the opportunities that women experience when opting to engage Arab regimes politically—whether through voting, mobilizing politically, running for office, or even by opting to join the workforce. The intersection of neoliberal capitalism and a state–society social contract, undergirded by *rentierism*, leads to distinct political-economic contexts for women in the MENA that are worth exploring in more depth, especially at a time when there is such a push—domestically and internationally—to empower women.

To do so, this book helps the reader unpack these contexts. We will discuss the gendered nature of authoritarian upgrading as a modern variant of state feminism and the international virtue signaling that arises from it. We will also move through a qualitative and quantitative exploration of how the global inflows of unearned rents to the MENA—in the guise of foreign aid, remittances, and oil revenues—generate specific dynamics women must reckon with in both economics and politics.

## Authoritarian Upgrading and State Feminism

The idea that women can 'authentically' contest politics in countries as conservative as Saudi Arabia often mystifies Western media outlets and political pundits.[9] When and why previously marginalized groups such as women are given purchase in a given political system—especially an

---

[9] Madawi Al-Rasheed's 2013 book 'A Most Masculine State' illustrates this vividly.

6    B. C. WELBORNE

autocratic one—is a perennial question in the scholarly literature. Yet, the last twenty years have seen extensive overtures from many an Arab state to its women—a trend that accelerated further in the aftermath of the Arab Spring protests.

These ostensive overtures to women and notions of inclusivity have often been part of fairly transparent bids for local autocrats to retrench their regimes—an approach that easily falls under the network of strategies coined as 'authoritarian upgrading' by Steven Heydemann (2007). Authoritarian upgrading manifests itself under the guise of 'political opening or liberalization', but is really about 'managing political contestation' and 'appropriating and containing civil society'—in particular, domestic social movements and NGOs (ibid.: 5). One of the most consistent strategies embraced in authoritarian upgrading over the past few decades has been the renewal of a more neoliberal variant of *state feminism* as national policy, especially in the Arab Levant and, more recently, the GCC.

Classical feminist literature may define state feminism as a concept capturing scenarios where women's movements and associated organizations *partner* with the state to craft and promote gender-related institutions and policy. However, the reality of state feminism in the Middle East has been very different (Mazur & McBride, 2008: 254). Laurie Brand's working definition of state feminism in the MENA is instructive. She notes the top-down nature of policies 'which aim at mobilizing or channeling women's (re)productive capabilities and coopting them into support for the state' through a variety of programs geared at increasing women's access to the public sector, whether political or economic, especially via state-sponsored women's organizations or government-sponsored NGOs, called GONGOs (Brand, 1998: 10). Brand continues,

> What needs to be understood, however, is the degree to which state feminist programs were not an end in themselves, but rather served as a part of broader regime consolidation activities. Women were instruments or tools, and their 'liberation' was part of a larger project of reinforcing control within a series of states that continued to be dominated by what are generically referred to as patriarchal structures. (ibid.)

Brand's definition is a 'feminist' precursor to Heydemann's notion of upgrading authoritarianism and the mechanisms by which Arab states co-opt civil society: 'In varying degrees, Arab regimes blended repression, regulation, cooptation and the appropriation of NGO [civil society] functions by the state to contain the deepening of civil societies and to erode their capacity to challenge political authority' (Heydemann, 2007: 6). And even Heydemann notes the role of state feminism in upgrading authoritarian regimes through his anecdotes on how often presidential first ladies (and royals) such as Basma al-Assad in Syria, Queen Rania in Jordan, and, previously, Suzanne Mubarak in Egypt were (and are) prominent sponsors of women's GONGOs and, more often than not, treat them as their own personal fiefdoms.

Importantly, the connection between authoritarian upgrading and state feminism in the MENA very much depends on the socioeconomic specificities of the patriarchal regimes in place in a given country. Deniz Kandiyoti's work illustrates the nature of this symbiotic relationship through the concept of 'patriarchal bargains'—an innovation that unveils the opportunities and pitfalls for women when Arab regimes embrace women's empowerment as a form of societal crisis management as well as international virtue signaling (Kandiyoti, 1988). Kandiyoti's pioneering work points us to a deeper exploration of how women strategize, respond to, and navigate discrimination and marginalization differently than other groups, striking these bargains depending on the type of paternalism present in a given world region. Effectively, patriarchal bargains reveal the set of options women have to actively (and passively) resist gender-based oppression, not to mention pro-actively engage in agenda-setting and policymaking. In a sense, it speaks to women's agency on a continuum, contingent on the geographic region they inhabit. As such, the scope and range of women's ability to 'bargain' unmistakably affects their access to socio-political institutions and capacity to garner any real influence over their own and others' private and public affairs.

State feminism and attendant women's social movements do not occur in a vacuum. As Mervat Hatem and others have demonstrated in their work on gender and the MENA states, Arab regimes promote women's education, work, and even political participation to signal modernity to the West—an oft-embraced strategy for the better part of the twentieth century and now the twenty-first (Hatem, 1992). In fact, current research has shown that many autocratic regimes have actually prioritized the advancement of women's rights for reputational benefit, but they can just as easily be attempting to secure the loyalty of a potentially restive female constituency (Donno & Kreft, 2019). Ann Towns (2010) vividly describes how international norms have shifted to include ideas of equality across genders as an important component of international 'civic virtue' over the last half century. The more recent work of Sarah Bush has explicitly shown how states signal their commitment to 'liberalization', if not actual democracy, by adopting gender quota laws with the intention of ensuring future aid flows from the West (Bush, 2011; Bush & Zetterberg, 2021; also Edgell, 2017).

Per Bush and Zetterberg, autocratic leaders, believe they can improve their international status and so secure their survival through embracing political gender equality (2021: 12). States' focus on improving their 'gender equality scorecard' is essentially geared at deflecting international and domestic pressures to substantively democratize, while still providing liberal autocratic regimes with reputational benefits from an international community that frames democracy as a core value, with women's legislative representation as a signature element of liberalism (Duque, 2018; Hyde, 2011; also Ottaway, 2005). It is no accident that Bush uses Jordan as her primary case to outline the perverse incentives undergirding the adoption of gender-related policy in low- and middle-income states and the financial windfalls often associated with it.

## Women's Empowerment as Virtue Signaling

No student of international relations will be surprised at the idea that states care about their international image (Kelley, 2017: 5), but it is arguably more salient in the new millennium in a socio-political world increasingly conditioned by the vicissitudes of social media. Judith Kelley's pioneering work on the importance of international reputation underscores this fact, documenting in particular the 'comparative scoring and grading' through indexes and other quantitative measures of state performance that have become ubiquitous in the international policy community (2017). This was something I noticed in my own initial fieldwork in the region back in 2008 and 2009, as I interviewed officials across Jordan, Morocco, and Bahrain—namely, their attention to gender indicators in extant reports compiled by international agencies. These officials, as well as the scholars and journalists I interviewed who were covering related issues, saw the state's embrace of indicator-based gender equality as an easy, if often disingenuous, mechanism to signal ongoing efforts to liberalize and commit, at least partially, to the conditions often associated with the disbursement of foreign aid. I was not shocked to hear this in my conversations in Jordan and Morocco, but it did take me aback in the context of Bahrain—a country less dependent on foreign aid.

The focus on 'grading' performance in gender equality as a mechanism to assess international civic virtue dovetails with Kelley's emphasis on how scorecard diplomacy is actively reshaping our world, with gender equality increasingly serving as a proxy for democracy and perhaps even civic conformity, if not stability. In fact, political gender equality is actively included as a variable in grading mechanisms assessing democracy such as Freedom House, the Varieties of Democracy measures, and those used by the Economist Intelligence Unit (Bush & Zetterberg, 2021: 4). Even the United States Agency for International Development (USAID) now includes a 'Gender Economic Gap' indicator as part of their current 'Journey to Self-Reliance' (J2SR) indicators. Furthermore, Kelley maintains, these scores 'take on symbolic value and can be employed by others as well as the creators', which also allows 'NGOs, IGOs, and the media to augment the effect of the scores' (2017: 12).

In a post-Arab Spring Middle East where social media still has a lot of pull, despite government efforts to clamp down on it, this trend in ensuring civic virtue through global policy scoring is not an unimportant one. Furthermore, the region has felt its outsize effects precisely because it has been historically so vulnerable to international influence and meddling. This is exemplified in the multiple regime-issued Vision 2020, 2025, and 2030 statements highlighting the importance of gender equality across the GCC states,[10] as well as the wholescale embrace of gender quotas in North Africa, the Levant, and female political appointments in the GCC as a way to jumpstart their international reputations. Some countries do so to secure financial investment, others to secure foreign aid. But, one way or the other, this is an updated modality of state feminism influenced by new forms of neoliberal dependency and Kelley's ideas of scorecard diplomacy.

Ironically, this updated state feminism is transpiring in a region where the majority of citizens remain deeply conflicted about women's 'proper'

---

[10] The Sultanate of Oman was the first to release Oman Vision 2020 in 1995, followed by Bahrain (The Economic Vision 2030) and Qatar (Qatar National Vision 2030) in 2008, Kuwait (Kuwait Vision 2035) and the United Arab Emirates (UAE Vision 2021) in 2010, and finally, Saudi Arabia' Vision 2030 in 2016. See Koch (2017).

role in the public sphere. If anything, until the last decade Arab public opinion was often seen as growing *more* conservative on women's issues.[11] Public opinion research released from the fifth wave of the Arab Barometer survey (2018–2019) reveals a mixed societal picture in which support for women's access to education and the halls of politics, not to mention economic opportunity, is still highly uneven across the twelve states surveyed.

Despite some progress on popular attitudes toward allowing women equal political and educational access, in fact, access to the workforce is still prioritized for men (Alayli, 2020; Alayli & Al-Shami, 2020). In previous waves of the Arab Barometer survey, two-thirds of respondents said men should be more entitled to jobs than women when work was scarce; this seemed to be a continuing trend in 2018–2019. Furthermore, there is little agreement on whether women should play an equal role to men in public and private life, and the question of employment is a consistently sticky one alongside questions pertaining to women's equal access to divorce and inheritance—the all-to-controversial province of personal status codes and family law, which are often governed by *Shari'ah* (Islamic law) and various other religious courts, and, of course, custom (Charrad, 2001, 2011; also Alayli & Al-Shami, 2020).

Thus, a puzzle emerges, since political elites seem ostensibly to be making overtures to women as political actors, while patriarchal MENA societies are still opposed to the idea of women's equal status in the public sphere. Cultural and institutional explanations can only go so far in elucidating this trend, although exploring the varying patriarchal bargains enacted across specific states represents a start (see Benstead, 2016). As we see in the public opinion surveys, the contention that a wholescale cultural

---

[11] For past statistics, see Amany (2010), Telhami (2006), and Zogby (2002). Also, refer to Benstead, L. J. (2016). Explaining egalitarian attitudes: The role of interests and exposure. In *Empowering Women after the Arab Spring* (pp. 119–146). New York: Palgrave Macmillan. Abbot, P. (2017). Gender Equality and MENA Women's Empowerment in the Aftermath of the 2011 Uprisings. Arab Transformations Working Paper 10. https://www.wilsoncenter.org/sites/default/files/media/uploads/documents/230130_Bleed_Rev%20%28LR-Proof%29%20%281%29.pdf. Newer statistics from the fifth wave of the Arabbarometer reflect uneven progress. For more current research, refer to Abbott, P., Teti, A., and Sapsford, R. (2020). The tide that failed to rise: Young people's politics and social values in and after the Arab uprisings. *Mediterranean Politics*, 25(1), 1–25; Glas, S., and Spierings, N. (2019). Support for feminism among highly religious Muslim citizens in the Arab region. *European Journal of Politics and Gender*, 2(2), 283–310.

and generational shift in attitudes is happening does not have conclusive support across the region, although there is certainly variation on gender-related issues among individual countries. And, of course, even where public opinion may be more progressive, there are still barriers to its enactment. Lebanese polls consistently reflect support for women in political office and in the workforce, yet the country persists in having some of the lowest numbers of female representatives in its national assembly, as well as hosting some of the lowest percentages of working women in the region—even in comparison to Saudi Arabia and other conservative Persian Gulf states.

Furthermore, any institutional effects from political innovations such as gender quotas are oftentimes constrained by the will of political elites and paternalistic leaders in what are by and large authoritarian, patronage-based regimes. So, we are left with the puzzle of what engenders social change if there are limited cultural drivers for these shifts in women's political participation—and, in many cases, if the domestic institutional infrastructure is too weak to encourage mobilization. Broad-based structural factors—economic factors in particular—could help shed light on this puzzle.

## Connecting Economics to Politics

Throughout the 1990s and the early 2000s, the United Nations (especially the United Nations Development Programme and UN Women) and the Bretton Woods institutions touted 'the potential multiplier effect of gender equality' as a key for achieving the targets in the Millennium Development Goals (MDGs) by 2015 (Bakker, 2007: 7). Women's empowerment became a *cause célèbre* for the international community, attracting global attention and significant private and public investment, with statements like this one from former U.S. Secretary of State Hillary Clinton in March 2009: 'Supporting women is a high-yield investment, resulting in stronger economies, more vibrant civil societies, healthier communities, and greater peace and stability'.[12]

USAID reflected this gender bias, openly stating on its website in 2009 that 67 percent of its basic education programs focused on girls' education, 60 percent of clients receiving loans from USAID-supported

[12] https://osce.usmission.gov/wp-content/uploads/sites/37/2016/03/MAR_12_09_womensday.pdf.

microfinance institutions were women, and a third of all clients receiving USAID-supported enterprise development services were also women.[13] As of August 2021, the revamped website touted that USAID was running some 78 activities in more than 60 countries in a bid to advance women's economic status worldwide.[14] Furthermore, current U.S. President Joseph Biden issued an Executive Order launching a White House Gender Policy Council with a view toward 'advancing gender equity and equality [as] a matter of human rights, justice, and fairness. It is also a strategic imperative that reduces poverty and promotes economic growth, increases access to education, improves health outcomes, advances political stability, and fosters democracy'.[15]

Over the last twenty to thirty years—the embrace of neoliberal economic policy across the majority of MENA states due to either rapid domestic economic transformation (as in the GCC) or structural adjustment measures (as seen in North Africa and the Levant) has increased pressures both from the outside and the inside to expand women's access to the workforce and to politics. Additionally, the template for 'modernity and development' has often included overtures to expand women's presence in the broader public arena. If there was a national push to get women into visible political office at the parliamentary, executive, and municipal level over the past 15 years, the focus has shifted since the 'conclusion' of the MDGs in 2015 toward 'women's economic empowerment'. Unsurprisingly, this has revealed itself to be a much more complicated venture, one that potentially *and controversially* invites many more women into the official public sphere.

By emphasizing women's empowerment as fundamental to development, the United Nations and the Bretton Woods institutions effectively aligned women's interests (certainly 'elite' women's interests) with the spread of neoliberalism (Prügl, 2017). As one of the largest sources of development project funding, the World Bank played a central role in popularizing development strategies that included women's empowerment from the 1990s onward, popularizing the term 'gender mainstreaming' (Finnemore, 1996). Close to $3.1 billion in aid had been

---

[13] http://www.usaid.gov/our_work/cross-cutting_programs/wid/ (website no longer operational).

[14] https://www.usaid.gov/what-we-do/gender-equality-and-womens-empowerment/womens-economic-empowerment.

[15] Ibid.

earmarked for gender-sensitive programming in 2007 alone via bilateral and multilateral donors (Williams, 2007). In the past, one of the largest charitable funds in the world, the Bill & Melinda Gates Foundation, highlighted gender as a 'grand challenge' in 2014, committing some $80 million to gender-related programming (Gates Foundation, 2016).

By 2016, the United States *alone* had distributed some $1.3 billion in foreign aid for women (Ser, 2016). And in 2017, G-20 leaders pledged $1 billion to the Women in Entrepreneurs Finance Initiative (We-Fi), the World Bank's newest gender initiative, notoriously linked to Ivanka Trump (MacBride, 2017). Even powerful consulting firms such as McKinsey are now openly touting the benefits of gender equality, forecasting how it could add some $12 trillion dollars to global economic growth (Woetzel et al., 2015). In line with this logic, we have even seen a number of states—notably Canada, France, and Sweden—embrace a 'feminist foreign policy'.

The legacy of September 11 is prominent in the popularity of the gender agenda in the MENA, specifically due to beliefs by Western donors that empowering women would temper Islamist sentiment and usher in more secular rule. Scholarship published at the time identified attitudes toward gender as the primary difference and potential point of contention between Muslim and Western societies, and partially motivated this trend of prioritizing gender as a security concern (Fish, 2002; Inglehart & Norris, 2003a, 2003b; Landes & Landes, 2001; Lewis, 2002). Many scholars ventured that resolving the 'gender gap' in Arab society was integral to the international community's efforts to democratize and moderate the region, with these selfsame efforts often promoted through conditional aid and development assistance (ibid.; also Bush, 2011; Carapico, 2002, 2013).

In the Middle East, such 'gendered' conditional aid packages encouraged an often-disingenuous government-sponsored renaissance of women's nonprofit organizations, with the state brokering women's access to the public sphere through dedicated institutions and the proliferation of GONGOs—their own variant of state feminism (Brand, 1998; Bush, 2011; Welborne, 2011). In fact, as we saw earlier, states heavily dependent on foreign aid—authoritarian regimes in particular—are often more likely to embrace gender quotas, and we definitely observe such patterns replicated in the MENA (Bush, 2011; Welborne, 2010).

But what about rich oil states, such as the United Arab Emirates (UAE) or Kuwait, that are unlikely to be pressured by aid but have made progress on a few key women's empowerment benchmarks—especially those related to women's access to the workforce? My work with Gail Buttorff and Nawra Al-Lawati tracked women's labor force participation rates across the Gulf countries over the last three decades and found that GCC women were employed at rates on par with those seen in Western Europe, and largely as professionals in the service sector (Buttorff & Welborne, 2015a, 2015b; Buttorff et al., 2018). With We-Fi and the increasing recognition by key players in global markets that investing in women could lead to trillion-dollar windfalls, women have been able to leverage more power in the region than they previously could (Mansour, 2020; Modern Diplomacy, 2020). An integral part of how this phenomenon came to be stems from states' reputational concerns surrounding foreign investment (Moghadam, 1999; Ross, 2008; Sapiro, 1983; Schlozman et al., 1999). Arab states are well-known recipients of foreign aid, but the region receives a relatively small share of global foreign direct investment outside of oil, so concerns related to attracting investment are very real—especially with limited intra-regional investment and trade.[16]

We have witnessed this neoliberal push for women in the workforce through copious regional and international gender-based conferences and workshops hosted across Arab states in the past two decades. The GCC, in particular, has touted its growing number of female entrepreneurs as part of a refashioned national identity for the new millennium. This was especially patent to me from focus group interviews conducted with my colleagues at Sultan Qaboos University in Oman in the summer of 2019. The majority of our subjects viewed the renewed focus on women in the workforce as a way for the Omani government to project an image of modernity, both domestically and internationally (Al-Lawati et al., 2019). As one subject stated,

> [T]his [is] part of the modernization and development of society to educate females. Part of the development is to increase the involvement of women in the society, in the politics, in the public jobs and so on.

---

[16] According to the World Bank's 2014 Development Indicators, foreign direct investment amounted to $54 billion, worker remittances received to $46 billion, and official development assistance to $25 billion in current U.S. dollars.

There is a great need, for example, for women in the medical jobs, in the education also. They need females for the public policy. They also want to show that, for example, Oman is a modern society.

All in all, women's changing status—whether as a byproduct of conditional aid pressures or of the changing labor requirements of states attempting to integrate with the global economy—is creating unprecedented opportunities for women in the MENA. It is also engendering problems common to states embracing neoliberal capitalism. This operational ecosystem for women is conditioned by the type of rentierism in place within a given state and, demarcated by externalities generated from oil, aid, or remittance-related foreign rents. The work of GCC scholar Crystal Ennis, on what she calls women's 'rentier-preneurship', speaks to this phenomenon. Ennis poignantly observes how the push for women's entry into the private workforce in the GCC states is a way to 'reify markets as the place of liberation ... while at the same time absolving the state from more impactful political reform' (2019: 64). This begs the question of whether decoupling women's empowerment from neoliberal mantras might lead to politically more substantive results for both women and men.

## Gendered Rentierism as an Analytical Tool

Macroeconomic factors have tended to draw less scholarly attention in explaining women's political fortunes in the MENA than have explanations centered on traditional values and Muslim religiosity (Charrad, 2001, 2011; Fish, 2002). Laurie Brand, Homa Hoodfar, Martha Posusney, Elizabeth Doumato, and Valentine Moghadam are some of the scholars who have directly addressed the macroeconomic underpinnings of women's political and social mobilization in the region, alongside more recent work by Sarah Bush and others.[17] An even smaller literature has explored how women's socioeconomic opportunity plays into their capacity and motivation to run for office—especially in authoritarian

---

[17] See Bush (2011), Jad (2003), Moghadam (1999), and Welborne (2010) for more on the impact of foreign aid on the adoption of gendered institutions, such as quotas in national parliaments.

16 B. C. WELBORNE

regimes—despite ample coverage of women's social and political incentives to join social movements from the early twentieth century onward (Arenfeldt & Golley, 2012; Robinson, 2015, 2016).

Women's uneven paths to power and participation in the MENA are commonly seen to be byproducts of stalled institutional reform and a weak party culture, coupled with the predominance of kinship ties and conservative religious mores.[18] Importantly, these paths are also often conditioned by unique forms of economic rentierism common to the region that also change the flavor of state feminism as a modernity project (Anderson, 1987; Beblawi, 1987; Herb, 2014; Ross, 2008; Richards & Waterbury, 2008). As Makio Yamada and Steffen Hertog (2020) observe in their survey of rentierism in the MENA, rentier-state theory has served as one of the dominant frames of reference for studies of resource-dependency in the region—a frame focusing on the negative impact of political and economic liberalization engendered by 'unearned' external income. While often related to states dependent on oil revenues, some of these same patterns apply to states whose livelihoods are tied to remittances and fungible foreign aid, which is why the region represents such a fascinating case for analysis. Most countries within the MENA depend on one of these streams of external finance—or a combination of all three streams.

The promotion of women's empowerment and women's rights is tied to the co-evolution of neoliberal capitalism and rentierism, creating a phenomenon unique to the region which I characterize as *gendered rentierism* (Benstead, 2020; Kantola & Squires, 2012). I have devised this term to help clarify the double-edged sword of the political, and occasionally economic and social, opportunities for women that the neoliberal commodification of women's empowerment has created when coupled with Arab states' efforts at signaling modernity and development domestically and abroad. In this context, the term 'gendered rentierism' captures the peculiar and often very gendered state–society relations that characterize countries which derive their income from externally driven rents. This creates what Ennis calls a marriage of convenience between rentierism and authoritarian neoliberalism (2019: 63).

---

[18] See Barnett et al. (2013), Buttorff and Welborne (2015a), and Jackson et al. (2019) on informal institutions such as *wasta* broadly defined as intercession or mediation on the part of an individual or specific community, usually as a way of wielding social influence. Also refer to Charrad (2001, 2011), on kinship ties.

1 AN INTRODUCTION: GENDERED RENTIERISM IN THE ARAB WORLD     17

Ennis and others have pointed out the problem of neglecting women's roles in rentier political economy, as well as the greater need to consider them as potential participants and agents within the template of economic development in the MENA. She continues,

> The utilization of both state feminism and market feminism to promote private sector growth, diversification, and women's advancement advances narratives of the state as a reformer and underlines how policy agendas can be co-constitutive and mutually beneficial. (ibid.)

Simply, women are part and parcel of how domestic and global-facing policies and social choices are made. And, how women and their families choose to spend money plays an integral role in shaping development outcomes in any given state.[19]

Unsurprisingly, gendered rentierism is tied to the neoliberal co-optation of social movements and the weaponization of women's issues by regimes in the Global South. No region has experienced this more than the MENA in the new millennium, with gender becoming a focal point in the battle against Islamic radicalism (Fish, 2002; Inglehart & Norris, 2003a, 2003b). In particular, whether the international and local promotion of women's empowerment creates meaningful opportunities for women is determined by pre-existing women's movements and the 'independent' (non-conditional) nature of the monies channeled into the region from foreign state and non-state actors. Most importantly, it is also conditioned by the brand of state feminism a given regime embraces and whether that brand links with pre-existing women's movements with their own well-defined agendas which are independent of the state, and with access to funds independent of the state (Arenfeldt & Golley, 2012; Moghadam, 2012; Tripp, 2019; Welborne, 2016).

This book explores how rentierism influences women's economic and political fortunes in a world where neoliberalism is the status quo. In particular, it considers how the spread of global financial linkages (Prasad et al., 2003) has interacted with rentier economies in the MENA and

---

[19] This is particularly clear in Chapter 4, where I address the question of remittance receiving households, a form of rent often neglected in the literature on gender and rentier political economy.

18    B. C. WELBORNE

created ripple effects across the political landscape of the Arab world that are often, unintentionally, transformational for women (Burkhart, 1998; Gray et al., 2006; Hafner-Burton, 2005; Henderson, 1996; McLaren, 1998; Meyer, 1996, 1998; Richards et al., 2001).

Many of the individuals I spoke with while conducting elite interviews for this book across Bahrain, Jordan, and Morocco in 2008 and 2009 surprisingly agreed that 'women's empowerment' was an idea recently imported from the West with defined neoliberal connotation, and had mixed feelings as to its underlying motivation and substance. In the intervening years, many of these same women and men would reclaim women's empowerment as *also* rooted in local traditions and rights afforded by the *Qur'an*—through Islamic feminism and a revived Arab nationalism. I use these past interviews, alongside insights from additional field research in Oman in 2016 and Morocco in 2017 as well as a combination of archival work, to track what has changed since 2008 for women when it comes to their political engagement, and how macroeconomic factors have affected women's socio-political fortunes overall. This allows the book to take a long view on the corresponding economic, political, and social changes alongside important technological shifts, that have shaped current gender issues and the gender revolutions to come in the MENA.

## WHAT TO EXPECT FROM THIS BOOK

This book is primarily interested in exploring how aspects of financial globalization as a key part of neoliberal capitalism have had transformational effects on the gendered development of Arab rentier states. Financial globalization, by definition, does not operate in a vacuum; its effects at best facilitate, if not determine, women's economic and political fate. However, the interaction between neoliberalism and rentierism has yielded a unique environment for Arab women—one that merits further exploration through the lens of gendered rentierism as a means of authoritarian upgrading.

In the ensuing chapters, I offer a comprehensive view of the impact of financial globalization and gendered rentierism on women's political participation across the MENA. In particular, I consider how neoliberal virtue signaling enables gendered rentierism in certain contexts. The second section (Chapters 3–5) explores the impact of specific types of

# 1 AN INTRODUCTION: GENDERED RENTIERISM IN THE ARAB WORLD    19

gendered rents and rentierism, and how they play out in the political and domestic sphere for women across the region.

In the third chapter, I consider foreign aid—one of the most notorious forms of 'rent' influencing gender relations in the MENA. I unpack how development assistance and finance create incentives for women's political participation in the Levant and North Africa, yet perhaps have only empowered a limited range of women. The chapter highlights the top-down nature of much of this empowerment and the underlying importance of 'international optics' in any agenda-setting women activists chose to embrace. Finally, the chapter outlines the role aid has played in incentivizing unpopular reforms, in particular, those related to the criminalization of rape, domestic violence, and sexual harassment from 2014 onward. It concludes with a discussion of the impact of aid-based agenda-setting on the framing of women's empowerment in states that are not aid-dependent in the MENA.

The fourth chapter grounds the analysis of foreign aid as a form of public money extended with conditional expectations, and provides a perspective on more individualized and fungible forms of funding: remittances. This chapter shows how monies sent home by diasporas living abroad incentivize important shifts in gender dynamics in the home, which also translate into the workplace, and ultimately into the political arena. I elaborate on the conservative mores directly and indirectly exported through remittances by Arab *diasporas* living abroad, using survey data and macroeconomic analysis to tease out the indirect effects of remittances on the likelihood of women entering the workforce and engaging with politics.

The fifth chapter explores how one of the most overt forms of rentierism—oil dependency and oil-dependent investment—plays into unexpected opportunities and pitfalls for women who choose to run for public office. This chapter explores the role of oil windfalls and foreign direct investment in creating high-paying job opportunities for female candidates—especially those who opt to run as independents for political office. I consider the case of female candidates in the GCC, where women enjoy some of the highest rates of citizen-based labor force participation across the MENA but simultaneously low rates of political representation short of government appointment, contrasting this discussion with an exploration of what it takes to campaign in a completely different setting: Morocco.

In the conclusion, I revisit the analytical utility of gendered rentierism as a concept that can illuminate new modalities of 'state to market feminism' in the MENA with possible implications for other countries in the Global South. I revisit the mixed impact of gender equality pursued through a neoliberal empowerment, also highlighting the importance of women's access to funds independent of the state that enable them to participate and agitate politically, even within autocratic regimes. The book closes with a discussion of the impact of COVID-19 on the fortunes of women residing in the MENA and how it may exacerbate current rent-dependencies and gender gaps.

Global financial integration has increased the amounts and types of private and public monies flowing into the MENA. Furthermore, it has also resulted in a substantial domestic social and political restructuring that has been responsible for deep-seated changes in women's political status. Using gendered rentierism as a lens, I integrate insights from rentier state theory in conjunction with the idea of rent-specific patriarchal bargains to shed light on the intersecting role of external and internal monies in shaping women's political opportunities in a specific type of authoritarian regime, demarcated by its dependency on rents derived from oil, foreign aid, and remittances. How Arab states navigate and adapt to changes at the intersection of macro- and microeconomics condition women's ability to effectively access and influence the political realm and, more importantly, prime the system itself for internal social change.

## References

Abbot, P. (2017). *Gender equality and MENA women's empowerment in the aftermath of the 2011 uprisings* (Arab transformations Working Paper 10).

Abbott, P., Teti, A., & Sapsford, R. (2020). The tide that failed to rise: Young people's politics and social values in and after the Arab uprisings. *Mediterranean Politics, 25*, 1–25.

Al Lawati, N., Welborne, B., & Buttorff, G. (2019). *Mind the gap: Lacking employment opportunities for female GCC University graduates.* Paper presented at the International Studies Association's Annual Conference, 27–31 March, Toronto, Canada.

Al-Rasheed, M. (2013). *A most masculine state: Gender, politics and religion in Saudi Arabia.* Cambridge University Press.

Alayli, A. (2020). *Gender dynamic: Examining public opinion data in light of Covid-19 crisis.* Arab Barometer V. https://www.arabbarometer.org/public ation/gender-dynamic-examining-public-opinion-data-in-light-of-covid-19-cri sis/

Alayli, A., & Al-Shami, S. (2020). *Women's agency & Economic mobility in MENA: Examining patterns & implications*. Arab-Barometer V. https://www.arabbarometer.org/publication/womens-agency-economic-mobility-in-mena-examining-patterns-implications/

Amany, J. (2010). *Democratic governance and women's rights in the Middle East and North Africa (MENA)*. Department of Politics, Princeton University. http://idl-bnc.idrc.ca/dspace/bitstream/10625/43867/1/130389.pdf

Amos, D. (2015, December 14). *Saudi women: Elections are one step forward on a long road*. NPR. https://www.npr.org/sections/parallels/2015/12/14/459683623/saudi-women-elections-are-one-step-forward-on-a-long-road

Anderson, L. (1987). The state in the Middle East and North Africa. *Comparative Politics, 20*(1), 1–18.

Arab Barometer. (2018–2019). *5th Wave of public opinion survey conducted in Algeria, Egypt, Iraq, Jordan, Kuwait, Lebanon, Libya, Morocco, Palestine, Sudan, Tunisia, and Yemen*. https://www.arabbarometer.org/surveys/arab-barometer-wave-v/

Arenfeldt, P., & Golley, N. A. H. (Eds.). (2012). *Mapping Arab women's movements: A century of transformations from within*. Oxford University Press.

Bakker, I. (2007). *Financing for gender equality and the empowerment of women: Paradoxes and possibilities*. Division for the Advancement of Women, Department of Economic and Social Affairs, United Nations. Expert group meeting on financing for gender equality and the empowerment of women. Oslo, Norway.

Barnett, A., Yandle, B., & Naufal, G. (2013). Regulation, trust, and cronyism in Middle Eastern societies: The simple economics of 'wasta.' *The Journal of Socio-Economics, 44*, 41–46.

BBC. (2015, December 12). *Saudi Arabia's women vote in election for first time*. https://www.bbc.com/news/world-middle-east-35075702

Beblawi, H. (1987). The rentier state in the Arab world. In H. Beblawi & G. Luciani (Eds.), *The rentier state*. Croom Helm.

Benstead, L. J. (2016). Explaining egalitarian attitudes: The role of interests and exposure. In M. Shalaby & V. Moghadam (Eds.), *Empowering women after the Arab Spring* (pp. 119–146). Palgrave Macmillan.

Benstead, L. J. (2020). Conceptualizing and measuring patriarchy: The importance of feminist theory. *Mediterranean Politics, 26*(3), 1–13.

Brand, L. (1998). *Women, the state, and political liberalization: Middle Eastern and North African experiences*. Columbia University Press.

Burkhart, R. E. (1998). *The capitalist political economy and human rights: Cross-national evidence*. State University of New York.

Bush, S. S. (2011). International politics and the spread of quotas for women in legislatures. *International Organization, 65*(1), 103–137.

Bush, S. S., & Gao, E. (2017). Small tribes, big gains: The strategic uses of gender quotas in the Middle East. *Comparative Politics, 49*(2), 149–167.

Bush, S. S., & Zetterberg, P. (2021). Gender quotas and international reputation. *American Journal of Political Science, 65*(2), 326–341.

Buttorff, G., & Welborne, B. (2015a). Working those connections: Exploring Arab women's differential access to opportunity in the Middle East and North Africa. *Baker Institute for Public Policy Issue Brief, 7*, 15.

Buttorff, G., & Welborne, B. (2015b). Rethinking economic rentierism and women's empowerment. *Baker Institute for Public Policy Issue Brief, 9*, 15.

Buttorff, G. J., Al Lawati, N., & Welborne, B. C. (2018). Cursed no more? The resource curse, gender, and labor nationalization policies in the GCC. *Journal of Arabian Studies, 8*(1), 65–86.

Carapico, S. (2002). Foreign aid for promoting democracy in the Arab world. *The Middle East Journal, 56*(3), 379–395.

Carapico, S. (2013). *Political aid and Arab activism: Democracy promotion, justice, and representation* (Vol. 44). Cambridge University Press.

CBS News. (2015, December 12). *Saudi women vote, run for office for the first time in history.* https://www.cbsnews.com/news/saudi-women-vote-run-for-office-for-first-time-in-history/

Charrad, M. M. (2001). *States and women's rights: The making of postcolonial Tunisia, Algeria, and Morocco.* University of California Press.

Charrad, M. M. (2011). Gender in the Middle East: Islam, state, agency. *Annual Review of Sociology, 37*, 417–437.

Darhour, H., & Dahlerup, D. (2013). Sustainable representation of women through gender quotas: A decade's experience in Morocco. *Women's Studies International Forum, 41*, 132–142.

Die Welt. (2015, December 14). *20 Frauen gewinnen Sitze bei Wahl in Saudi-Arabien* [20 women win seats in elections in Saudi Arabia]. https://www.welt.de/politik/ausland/article149921024/20-Frauen-gewinnen-Sitze-bei-Wahl-in-Saudi-Arabien.html

Donno, D., & Kreft, A. K. (2019). Authoritarian institutions and women's rights. *Comparative Political Studies, 52*(5), 720–753.

Duque, M. G. (2018). Recognizing international status: A relational approach. *International Studies Quarterly, 62*(3), 577–592.

Edgell, A. B. (2017). Foreign aid, democracy, and gender quota laws. *Democratization, 24*(6), 1103–1141.

Ennis, C. A. (2019). Rentier-preneurship: Dependence and autonomy in women's entrepreneurship in the Gulf: The politics of rentier states in the Gulf. *POMEPS Studies, 33*, 60–66.

Finnemore, M. (1996). *National interests in international society.* Cornell University Press.

Fish, S. (2002). Islam and authoritarianism. *World Politics, 55*(1), 4–37.

Gates Foundation. (2016, May). *The Bill & Melinda Gates Foundation announces $80 million commitment to close gender data gaps and accelerate progress for women and girls.* Media Center. https://www.gatesfoundation.org/Media-Center/Press-Releases/2016/05/Gates-Foundation-Announces-80-Mill-Doll-Comm-Closing-Gender-Data-Gaps-Acc-Progress-for-Women-Girls

Glas, S., & Spierings, N. (2019). Support for feminism among highly religious Muslim citizens in the Arab region. *European Journal of Politics and Gender, 2*(2), 283–310.

Gray, M. M., Caul-Kittilson, M., & Sandholtz, W. (2006). Women and globalization: A study of 180 nations, 1975–2000. *International Organization, 60*(2), 293–333.

Hafner-Burton, E. M. (2005). Right or robust? The sensitive nature of repression to globalization. *Journal of Peace Research, 42*(6), 679–698.

Hatem, M. (1992). Economic and political liberation in Egypt and the demise of state feminism. *International Journal of Middle East Studies, 24*(2), 231–251.

Henderson, C. (1996). Dependency and political repression: A caveat on research expectations. In D. L. Cingranelli (Ed.), *Human rights and developing countries.* JAI Press.

Herb, M. (2014). *The wages of oil: Parliaments and economic development in Kuwait and the UAE.* Cornell University Press.

Heydemann, S. (2007). Upgrading authoritarianism in the Arab world. *Brookings Paper, 13*(October), 1–40.

Hyde, S. D. (2011). *The pseudo-democrat's dilemma: Why election observation became an international porm.* Cornell University Press.

Inglehart, R., & Norris, P. (2003a). *Rising tide.* Cambridge University Press.

Inglehart, R., & Norris, P. (2003b). The true clash of civilizations. *Foreign Policy, 135*(9), 62–70. https://foreignpolicy.com/2009/11/04/the-true-clash-of-civilizations/

Jackson, D., Tobin, S. A., & Eggert, J. P. (2019). Women, corruption, and wasta in Jordan. In I. Kubbe & A. Varraich (Eds.), *Corruption and informal practices in the Middle East and North Africa* (pp. 172–187). Routledge.

Jad, I. (2003). The 'NGOization' of the Arab women's movements. *Al-Raida, 100*(20), 38–46.

Kandiyoti, D. (1988). Bargaining with patriarchy. *Gender & Society, 2*(3), 274–290.

Kantola, J., & Squires, J. (2012). From state feminism to market feminism? *International Political Science Review, 33*(4), 382–400.

Kelley, J. G. (2017). *Scorecard diplomacy: Grading states to influence their reputation and behavior.* Cambridge University Press.

Koch, C. (2017). *Success and shortcomings of GCC economic 'vision' documents.* Arab Development Portal (UNDP). https://www.arabdevelopmentportal.com/blog/success-and-shortcomings-gcc-economic-%E2%80%9Cvision%E2%80%9D-documents

## 24  B. C. WELBORNE

Landes, D., & Landes, R. (2001, October 8). Girl power: Do fundamentalists fear our women? *New Republic.*

Lewis, B. (2002). *What went wrong?* Oxford University Press.

MacBride, E. (2017, September 19). Ivanka Trump's We-Fi fund initiative could spark a $1.7 trillion market around the world. *CNBC.* https://www.cnbc.com/2017/09/19/ivanka-trumps-we-fi-fund-initiative-to-unlock-billions-for-women.html

Mansour, Z. (2020, February 16). UAE at the forefront of women empowerment in the region-Ivanka Trump. *Gulf Business.* https://gulfbusiness.com/uae-forefront-women-empowerment-region-ivanka-trump/

Mazur, A., & McBride, D. (2008). State feminism. In G. Goertz & A. Mazur (Eds.), *Politics, gender and concepts: Theory and methodology* (pp. 244–269). Cambridge University Press.

McDowall, A. (2015, December 12). *Saudi Arabian women vote for first time in local election.* Reuters. https://www.reuters.com/article/us-saudi-election-idUSKBN0TV0E520151212

McLaren, L. M. (1998). *The effect of IMF austerity programs on human rights violations: An exploratory analysis of Peru, Argentina, and Brazil.* Paper presented at the Annual Meeting of the Midwest Political Science Association, Chicago.

Meyer, W. H. (1996). Human rights and MNCs: Theory versus quantitative analysis. *Human Rights Quarterly, 18,* 368–397.

Meyer, W. H. (1998). *Human rights and international political economy in third world nations.* Praeger.

Modern Diplomacy. (2020, August 22). *Women entrepreneurs finance investments in over 15,000 women-led businesses.* https://moderndiplomacy.eu/2020/08/22/women-entrepreneurs-finance-initiative-invests-in-over-15000-women-led-businesses/

Moghadam, V. (1999). Gender and globalization: Female labor and women's movements. *Journal of World-Systems Research, 5*(2), 367–388.

Moghadam, V. (2012). *Globalization and social movements: Islamism, feminism, and the global justice movement* (2nd ed.). Rowman & Littlefield Publishers.

NPR. (2015, December 19). *After historic elections in Saudi Arabia, what's the future for women?* http://www.npr.org/2015/12/19/459491653/after-historic-elections-in-saudi-arabia-whats-the-future-for-women

Ottaway, M. (2005). The limits of women's rights. In T. Carothers & M. Ottaway (Eds.), *Uncharted journey: Promoting democracy in the Middle East* (pp. 115–130). Carnegie Endowment for International Peace.

Prasad, E., Rogoff, K., Shang-Jin, W., & Kose, M. A. (2003). *Effects of financial globalization on developing countries: Some empirical evidence* (IMF Working Paper: 1–84). https://www.imf.org/external/pubs/nft/op/220/index.htm

Prügl, E. (2017). Neoliberalism with a feminist face: Crafting a new hegemony at the World Bank. *Feminist Economics, 23*(1), 30–53.

Richards, A., & Waterbury, J. (2008). *A political economy of the Middle East* (3rd ed.). Westview.

Richards, D., Gelleny, R., & Sacko, D. (2001). Money with a mean streak? Foreign economic penetration and government espect for human rights in developing countries. *International Studies Quarterly, 45,* 219–239.

Robinson, N. (2015). *'Sisters of men': Syrian and Lebanese women's transnational campaigns for Arab independence and women's rights, 1910–1949* (Doctoral dissertation, Rutgers University–New Brunswick Graduate School).

Robinson, N. (2016). Arab internationalism and gender: Perspectives from the third session of the United Nations Commission on the status of women, 1949. *International Journal of Middle East Studies, 48*(3), 578–583.

Ross, M. L. (2008). Oil, Islam, and women. *American Political Science Review, 102*(1), 107–123.

Sapiro, V. (1983). *The political integration of women.* University of Illinois Press.

Schlozman, K., Burns, N., & Verba, S. (1999). What happened at work today? A multistage model of gender, employment, and political participation. *Journal of Politics, 61*(1), 29–53.

Ser, K. K. K. (2016, October 27). *How the US distributes $1.3 billion in aid for women around the world.* Public Radio International (PRI). https://www.pri.org/stories/2016-10-27/how-us-distributes-13-billion-aid-women-around-world

Stancati, M., & Al Omran, A. (2016, February 3). Saudi Arabia orders women segregated from men in council meetings. *Wall Street Journal.* https://www.wsj.com/articles/saudi-arabia-orders-women-segregated-from-men-in-council-meetings-1454522211

Telhami, S. (2006). *Anwar Sadat Chair for Peace and Development of University of Maryland/Zogby International 2006 Annual Arab Public Opinion Survey.* Saban Center for Middle East Policy at the Brookings Institution.

Thompson, L. (2019, May 20). *A French feminist foreign policy?* Foreign Policy: Argument. https://foreignpolicy.com/2019/05/20/g7-france-feminist-foreign-policy/

Towns, A. E. (2010). *Women and states: Norms and hierarchies in international society.* Cambridge University Press.

Tripp, A. (2012, January 19). *Do Arab women need electoral quotas?* Foreign Policy. https://foreignpolicy.com/2012/01/19/do-arab-women-need-electoral-quotas/

Tripp, A. M. (2019). *Seeking legitimacy: Why Arab autocracies adopt women's rights.* Cambridge University Press.

26    B. C. WELBORNE

USAID.   http://www.usaid.gov/our_work/cross-cutting_programs/wid/   (see https://osce.usmission.gov/wp-content/uploads/sites/37/2016/03/ MAR_12_09_womensday.pdf)

Welborne, B. C. (2010). *The strategic use of gender quotas in the Arab world*. William and Kathy Hybl Democracy Studies Fellowship Paper, International Foundation for Electoral Systems, Washington, DC. https://aceproject.org/ero-en/regions/africa/MZ/ifes-the-strategic-use-of-gender-quotas-in-the

Welborne, B. C. (2011). *Between the veil and the vote: Exploring incentives to politically incorporate women in the Arab world*. PhD presented to University of Colorado at Boulder.

Welborne, B. C. (2016). No agency without grassroots autonomy: A framework for evaluating women's political inclusion in Jordan, Bahrain, and Morocco. In M. Shalaby & V. Moghadam (Eds.), *Empowering women after the Arab Spring* (pp. 65–90). Palgrave Macmillan.

Welborne, B. C. (2020). On their own? Women running as independent candidates in the Middle East. *Middle East Law and Governance, 12*(3), 251–274.

Williams, M. (2007). *Gender and trade: Impacts and implications for financial resources for gender equality* (Commonwealth Secretariat, Background Paper WAMM (07)).

Woetzel, J., Madgavkar, A., Ellingrud, K., Labaya, E., Devillard, S., Kutcher, E., Manyika, J., Dobbs, R., & Krishnan, M. (2015, September 1). *How advancing women's equality can add $12 trillion to global growth* (McKinsey Global Institute Report). https://www.mckinsey.com/featured-insights/employment-and-growth/how-advancing-womens-equality-can-add-12-trillion-to-global-growth

Worley, W. (2016, February 5). Saudi Arabia women councillors segregated from men at meetings. *The Independent*. http://www.independent.co.uk/news/world/middle-east/saudi-arabia-women-councillors-segregated-from-men-at-meetings-a6855276.html

Yamada, M., & Hertog, S. (2020). Introduction: Revisiting rentierism—With a short note by Giacomo Luciani. *British Journal of Middle Eastern Studies, 47*(1), 1–5.

Zogby, J. J. (2002). *What Arabs think: Values, beliefs and concerns*. Zogby International/Arab Thought Foundation.

CHAPTER 2

# State Feminism and Gendered Rentierism

'This [women's empowerment] is all showmanship for the international community'.[1] These were the words uttered to me by a frustrated Moroccan NGO staff member in the summer of 2008. At the time, in my naivete, I registered shock at this sentiment. But I would hear variations on this theme over the next two years across Morocco, Jordan, Bahrain, and a few other countries. The cynicism surprised me less in Jordan and Morocco, since I knew aid agencies and foreign NGOs had a strong foothold in the secular women's movement, and vice versa. However, I was genuinely taken aback when I heard the same disillusionment in Bahrain and in the other GCC states—places that were, in my mind, much less susceptible to foreign pressure when it came to exporting 'democratic values' and where foreign organizations as well as local social movements were much more restricted in their activities. Quite simply I wondered: why would it matter? And, yet, by the end of my fieldwork, I was convinced that Judith Kelley's notion of *scorecard diplomacy* was very real, especially when it came to questions of pursuing gender equality in the MENA, and the aforementioned attitude pretty widespread across the region. If anything, traveling across North Africa, the Levant, and the Persian Gulf states back in 2008 convinced me that

---

[1] Interview with staff member at Subul Assalam Center, Fes, Morocco, June 2008.

© The Author(s), under exclusive license to Springer Nature     27
Switzerland AG 2022
B. C. Welborne, *Women, Money, and Political Participation in the Middle East,*
https://doi.org/10.1007/978-3-031-04877-7_2

'women's empowerment' had finally become a global buzzword, if not necessarily an actionable concept (Ababneh, 2018).

Fast forward to 2021, when 'women empowerment' and 'gender mainstreaming' are ubiquitous terms with real consequences in the region and beyond. Since 2000, women's legislative representation across the MENA has grown 300 percent (Welborne, 2020); every regional university worth its mettle has a program of gender studies with brisk enrollment rates, and even the uber-conservative GCC states have all issued vision statements for 2020, 2030, and 2035 with provisions for improving women's status economically—and even politically. Keep in mind, none of these latter countries extended real suffrage to women until the new millennium, in stark contrast with the rest of the MENA, where women had been voting for the better part of the twentieth century.[2]

Many GCC states had appointed women to ministerial positions around the time they extended suffrage, although in most cases the profile of these cabinet posts tended to be limited to the typical women's portfolios of social and cultural affairs, health, and education.[3] The Kuwaitis directly elected four female legislators in 2009, two of whom—Aseel al Awadhi and Rola Dashti—successfully pushed the Constitutional Court to rule that wearing the *hijab*, or headscarf, was optional for female parliamentarians, in direct defiance to Islamist opposition in the Parliament at the time. In 2013, Saudi Arabia appointed 30 women to the Consultative Council and allowed women to stand as candidates in the 2015 municipal elections as detailed in the introduction. Most notoriously, the kingdom finally repealed its 'ban' on women driving in 2018. The UAE, Qatar, and Kuwait have effectively adopted economic quotas to ensure more women in the private sphere, and have par numbers of men and women working in the financial sector (Buttorff et al., 2018). More recently, there has been discussion of adopting political quotas in Qatar and Kuwait—especially in the aftermath of the 2020 Kuwaiti elections where no female MPs won a seat in parliament (Deutsche Welle, 2020). And, as of 2019,

---

[2] Oman was the first GCC country to grant a limited number of women the right to vote in 1994, but did not grant universal suffrage until 2003. Qatar (1999), Bahrain (2002), Kuwait (2005), the UAE (2006), and finally Saudi Arabia (2015, but only at the municipal level), have largely extended universal suffrage in the 2000s. See Fadhel (2021).

[3] The exception is Bahrain, which appointed regime hard-liner Sameera Rajab as the Minister of State for Information Affairs in 2012 in a bid to thwart a restive media in the aftermath of the Arab Spring protests at Pearl Circle. See Shalaby and Elimam (2020: 142) for more info on legislative appointment trends.

the UAE ranks among the top three countries in the world in terms of gender representation due to a de facto quota requiring that 50 percent of its legislative assembly be composed of women (half are elected, half appointed).

At last count, twelve Arab countries have adopted meaningful gender quotas in their national parliaments, as well as at the local level.[4] Most Arab countries have even expanded the operations of their Ministries of Social Affairs or similar institutions to include women's units, if not already dedicating entire ministries to women—a move that is now seen as a silo-ing of women's interests more than a solution to the problem of gender equity across political institutions.[5] In 2012, Aili Tripp reported that Arab countries that had adopted quotas tended to have twice the rate of women's legislative representation of many of their Western counterparts (Tripp, 2012). In 2019, Tunisia (35.9 percent), Iraq (25.2 percent), Sudan (27.7 percent), Djibouti (26.2 percent) Algeria (25.8 percent), and Somalia (24.2 percent) had more female representatives in their national parliaments than the United States' Congress after the groundbreaking results of the 2018 mid-term elections (23.6 percent).

In the last two decades, outside of opportunities for women's political participation at the most basic level—such as voting or running for office—women's influence seems to have finally penetrated the upper echelons of Arab politics and engendered some substantive policy changes on issues ranging from combatting domestic violence to land use rights. For example, Morocco has seen poor women's access to housing and land rights pushed into the spotlight over the past decade by a group of illiterate women dubbed the '*Soulaliyate*', potentially representing a seminal achievement in terms of women's—especially marginalized women's—lobbying for policy change at the national level.[6] As mentioned earlier, parliamentary gender quotas are widespread in the region, but now even

---

[4] I am not including the UAE and Saudi Arabia in this count since a portion or all of the reserved seats dedicated to women are appointed.

[5] This kind of thinking is an artifact of 'women in development' rather than 'gender and development' thinking and reflects first and second-wave feminist interests rather than third wave feminism and beyond (Hafner-Burton & Pollak, 2002; Rathgeber, 1990; Razavi & Miller 1995).

[6] See Salime (2016: 35). Soulaliyate 'refers to "tribal" women, from both Arabic and Tamazight speaking collectivities that are demanding an equal share of land compared to men, when their land is privatized or divided'.

smaller conservative tribes are using them to access the political arena—a mainstreaming of sorts of the idea of women in political office, if not per se a substantive mainstreaming of women's issues (Bush & Gao, 2017). In 2017, Tunisia, Jordan, and Lebanon all repealed provisions in their penal code that allowed rapists to escape punishment by marrying their victims, and Morocco repealed similar provisions back in 2014 in response to the protests that erupted around the tragic suicide of Amina Filali in 2012—a victim of and martyr to this horrible practice (Begum, 2017).

## UPGRADING AUTHORITARIANISM THROUGH WOMEN

Certainly, the MENA of 2021 is a very different place from the region I encountered on the cusp of the new millennium. For better or worse, the upheaval of the Arab Spring has wrought significant changes across Arab states—empowering certain interest groups, while marginalizing others, and women are naturally caught in the crossfires of these processes. Many Arab states embarked on gender reforms in the aftermath of 2011 in a bid to secure their *status quo*. Multiple states either increased existing gender quotas or adopted new ones after an extended hiatus.[7] While these states were trying to mollify and co-opt an increasingly educated and informed female population during significant social upheaval, such political and social overtures to women in times of systemic crisis are not entirely new for the Middle East.

Laurie Brand details the recent past of this same strategy under former Tunisian President Habib Bourguiba . Tunisian women have long-enjoyed more political and economic opportunity than many of their counterparts in the Middle East owing to codified family laws that were reformed shortly after independence in 1956, but also *enforced* as Bourguiba looked to women as a bulwark again rising Islamism (Brand, 1998). His government drafted a personal status code that gave women almost full equality in marriage, which allowed for more advancement in terms of employment and education than in other parts of the MENA region at the time. In a similar vein, it is no accident that the *Moudawana* reforms of Morocco were passed in the wake of the Casablanca terrorist

---

[7] The Egyptian case is illustrative as the country has flirted with gender quotas for the assembly in 1979, 1984, 2010, and effective quotas in 2015. More recently in 2020, a new amendment was introduced to reserve 25 percent of parliamentary seats for women (Arab Euro-Mediterranean Women's Foundation, 2020; News, 2020).

bombing of 2003 with some scholars arguing that the then young king, Mohammad VI, hoped that by empowering women he could moderate Islamist factions within his society (Sadiqi, 2010b; Žvan Elliott, 2015). Nermin Allam's recent work exploring the role of Egyptian women in the Arab Spring protests also speaks to disingenuous attempts by Arab states to woo women in times of crisis. She outlines how the government of President Hosni Mubarak aimed to co-opt secular feminist activism in the face of perceived Islamist encroachment on public goodwill, as well as subsequent overtures to women from the current government of President Abdel Fatteh al-Sissi. Under al-Sissi the state has made a point of ostensibly issuing pro-women decrees on topics ranging from sexual harassment and domestic violence to the more recent re-instatement of a long-defunct parliamentary gender quota for the 2020 Egyptian parliamentary elections.

Such overtures speak to the Egyptian regime's strategic use of gender in times of crisis to shore up local, but, more importantly, international support while simultaneously jailing a record number of political prisoners (Mansour, 2021). Indeed, if current Secretary of State, Antony Blinken, is right about President Joe Biden's commitment to 'putting human rights back at the center of American foreign policy', al-Sissi's regime may face even more scrutiny on its human and women's rights record than it has in the four years under former President Donald Trump (U.S. Department of State, 2021). In the following section, I explore how we get to this 'modern' world in which gender has become part of brinkmanship in statecraft, and, in particular, what role financial neoliberalism has played in this turn of events within the MENA.

### Women's Movements Encounter State Feminism

The mechanisms through which women are integrated into political life in the MENA are necessarily distinct from those used in much of the West and demarcated by the experience of colonialism and the requirements of late-stage neoliberal capitalism. As intimated earlier, institutional change is still very much a top-down mandate in most Arab countries with the fledgling democracy of Tunisia as the lone exception. Thus, many of the policy changes associated with 'conventional notions' of state feminism are often top-down cosmetic ventures in Middle Eastern states, rather than a response to grassroots women's movements and mobilization. Not that the latter movements do not exist, but many of them have arguably

32    B. C. WELBORNE

not had 'transformative agendas' or have been successfully co-opted by Western-facing regimes (Arenfeldt & Golley, 2012).

Women's movements have a long pedigree in the Levant as well as in parts of North Africa. At the beginning of the twentieth century, appeals to greater women's rights and political access were often spearheaded by elite women akin to the famous Egyptian feminist and suffragette, Huda Sharawi, as well as others of her class—with these women often inspired by co-occurring international suffragette movements in the capitols of colonial empires (Arenfeldt & Golley, 2012; Sharawi & Badran, 2015). Scholars Mervat Hatem and Laurie Brand both trace this early historical bargaining between neophyte Arab states and their female elites across the twentieth and into the twenty-first century in the region. Hatem is evocative in her descriptions of how state feminism emerges as a conceit of modern Arab regimes—in particular, in the Levantine states as a response to colonial rulers who saw women's empowerment as an afterthought or even as a way to 'divide and conquer' deeply patriarchic traditional societies by 'liberating' their women via colonial decree (Hatem, 1987, 1992, 1994, 2018). Some of the first secular and also Islamic nationalists recognized the importance of women's status and even women's buy-in as a way of building international, if not always local, legitimacy for emerging nationalist movements (see Robinson, 2015, 2016). The first states to wrest their independence from colonial rule in some form or another—Egypt, Syria, and Lebanon—all had secular feminist movements agitating for change in women's status in newly sovereign nations, and in all cases, women were an indelible part of the early Arab nationalist struggles for independence. Later the rhetoric of these proto-movements would be co-opted into a top-down extension of full citizenship rights to women...however, women's domestic status would still too often fall under the religious domain of personal status codes and family law.

North Africa does not experience this same level of social change in women's status until the 1950s and 1960s with the overthrow of French colonial rule across Morocco, Algeria, and Tunisia, but its overtures to women wound up more durable and transformational in the aftermath of revolution.[8] In the heyday of Arab decolonization and the nationalist development projects of the 1940s, 1950s, and 1960s, mobilizing

---

[8] Charrad (2001); Tripp (2019).

both genders, especially with the requirements of increasing industrialization and modernization, would become a way for the state to extend its reach and consolidate its power—effectively undermining some of the traditional sources of control of the past—namely, local sheikhs and forms of religious leadership. With decolonization, nationalist leaders with a view toward modernizing their respective states would make women part of their citizenship template—including them into the social contracts formulated by new Arab states for the first time to varying degrees.[9]

This push for state-led modernization and development in the Levant and North Africa, and its requisite changes to gender roles at least in the public sphere—is often associated with countries that are embracing import substitution industrialization and later export-oriented industrialization.[10] In her work on state feminism, Hatem notes that the switch to market-oriented models changes the gender dynamics institutionalized during state-led nationalist decolonization and independence efforts. This neoliberal turn in the 1970s and 1980s somewhat loosens the state's grip on the women's agenda and introduces private actors into the promotion of women's rights, creating a gateway for what Johanna Kantola and Judith Squires' (2012) term *market feminism* and what has now been dubbed *neoliberal feminism* (Prügl, 2015).

Kantola and Squires also predict the NGO-ization of the women's movement more broadly across the world with the co-optation of feminism by market forces, and we see similar patterns in the MENA—especially from the 1990s onward. This NGO-ization (or privatization, if you will) of public services—which offers women *and* Islamists extended opportunities to enter and finally participate in the public realm—*also* gives Arab states a free pass to not engage in necessary reforms or enforcing those that have already been adopted related to women's issues since they can now claim they have been outsourced to private actors in a nod to neoliberalism.[11] Surprisingly, it also creates opportunities for the state to reassert its hold on these movements through NGO licensing and subsequent monitoring, while virtue signaling more inclusive practices to the international community in an age when both neoliberal development and women's empowerment are seen as trappings of modernity and

---

[9] Joseph (1996), Brand (1998), Arenfeldt and Golley (2012), Tripp (2019).

[10] Dildar 2021.

[11] Žvan Elliott 2015.

## 34    B. C. WELBORNE

stability. Eventually, this becomes a way to control both the public and private sector, and dictate the political agenda for women's groups as well as the restive religious community.[12]

In some of her most striking work, Hatem traces how even the institutionalization of the idea of a 'first lady' to the president in Egypt reflected this neoliberal shift, with the role directly imported from the United States in a bid to signal 'modernity' during the reign of President Anwar Sadat.[13] In fact, Sadat controversially ventured into changing personal status laws by presidential decree in 1979 to serve the societal ambitions of his spouse—Jehan Sadat—one of many moves that may have cost him his life at the hand of an Islamic militant. As sociologist Mounira Charrad and others poignantly attest to, revising family code and personal status laws has always been a consequential move in Muslim countries, and one not lightly received by Islamic clerics and affiliated social movements (Charrad, 2011).[14] The regime of President Hosni Mubarak also attempted to pass a revised personal status law in 1985, in anticipation of the United Nations women's conference in Nairobi, and later on yet another presidential decree was used by Mubarak to establish the National Council for Women—Egypt's first GONGO—chaired by his wife, Suzanne Mubarak. It is unsurprising that we have heard less from current President Sissi's spouse, Entissar Amer, as there has been significant public discontent with first ladies using women's rights as their personal political fiefdom, while appropriating the tireless and century-long work of Egyptian women's activists both on the Islamist and secular side (Brand et al., 2011; also Allam, 2018; Hatem, 2016).

Effectively, Middle Eastern women, have always been tied to the modernization templates of Arab states in the twentieth and, newly, in the twenty-first century. The most poignant example in the twenty-first century, is the refashioning of the welfare state in the GCC through the nationalization of the labor force in a bid to securitize the state from the dangerous 'other' of foreign (South Asian and European) labor (Buttorff et al., 2018). Such policies began absorbing a large pool of educated female university graduates that in the past had been more likely to go to

---

[12] Hatem 2016.

[13] In this case, this was also partially due to the mixed heritage of Sadat's wife and later even Susanne Mubarak (Hatem, 2016: 42).

[14] The High Constitutional Court struck down this decree in 1985.

university with a view toward finding a spouse than actually joining the workforce.[15] However, over the last three decades what has actually transpired is a slow, but steady penetration of the public sector and broader professional workforce by highly educated citizen women. This outcome was most likely unintended, but in many respects has tied the hands of Gulf rulers to the point where they have to provide their female citizens and their families with more economic opportunity than in the past. Some regimes have done this willingly, while others have embraced this as a *fait accompli* and post hoc spun it as part of a push to modernize their societies. These outcomes are particularly striking in the GCC states, because the motivation is internal and not necessarily galvanized by international pressures, nor the existence of longstanding women's movements. In countries where fledgling women's movements exist such as Kuwait or Bahrain, they are of a fairly recent vintage and thus haven't built the same base of support as in the North African and Levantine states (Al Mughni, 1993; Gonzales, 2013; Rizzo & Helen, 2005; Shalaby, 2015; Tétreault et al., 2012; Tripp, 2019).

What the previous paragraphs begin to illustrate is the mix of economic and security drivers that intentionally, but also unintentionally undergird the choice for a given country to embrace state feminism, as well neoliberal or market feminism, in a bid to signal modernity, but also ensure stability among what are often restive populations. These new versions of state feminism are demarcated by states operating in a neoliberal capitalist setting. Kantola and Squires clarify that global and local 'feminist engagements with public policy agendas are increasingly mediated via private sector organizations according to the logic of the market…this results in gender equality machineries in nation states becoming ever more embedded in neoliberal market reform'.[16] But this does not capture the

---

[15] There are a few choice exceptions to this in the women of Bahrain—especially Shiite women—who have been active participants in the workforce since the 1960s onward.

[16] Kantola, Johanna and Judith Squires (2012). From State Feminism to Market Feminism? *International Political Science Review*, 33(4), (383). 'We work with the assumption that both state feminism and market feminism are about substantive representation of women and constitutive representation of gender, which means, for example, that state feminist practices (as a form of representation) have been both enabling and constraining, constituting gender relations in particular ways. We suggest that market feminist practices make different sorts of representative claims, constituting gender relations in new ways – ways which erode the space for the types of representative claims-making pursued by an earlier generation of state feminists, but which also facilitate new forms of claim-making.'.

36   B. C. WELBORNE

full extent of the phenomenon we encounter in the MENA and many other liberal autocracies that have embraced 'women's empowerment' in the new millennium. As we see in the aforementioned anecdote about how measures undertaken in the GCC states to nationalize the workforce actually empowered educated women, many of these interventions were not intended to have gendered consequences—i.e. the state was not explicitly aiming to create more opportunities for women, rather it was securitizing itself. Simply, many of the adopted reforms are not as feminist in intent or execution as 'market feminism' implies, though neoliberal market logic definitely underpins them. Consequently, another useful way to think about the promotion of many a gender-related reform across the region is to contemplate its tie to the variant of *rentierism* present in a given Arab state and its impact on gender dynamics, or what I define as *gendered rentierism* in the next section.[17]

## RENTIER-STATE THEORY AND GENDER

In economics, 'rent' has been understood since the time of David Ricardo and Adam Smith as income or reward derived from the ownership of natural resources as well as any excess returns on a resource owner's transaction costs.[18] In the modern era, rentier states and rentierism or rent-seeking behavior are seen as leading to corrupt and economically unproductive practices where the majority of a given state's income is often derived from abroad and garnished by the state itself to serve its distributional interests and patronage networks. In his pioneering discussion of rentierism in the Arab world, Hazem Beblawi (1987), spoke to the importance of distinguishing between 'earned' income as opposed to 'effortlessly' accrued rent—in particular, the lacking productive outlook in the behavior of the rentier state. Beblawi highlighted the importance of rent derived from abroad as a defining characteristic of rentier economies in the MENA, illustrating its key role in sustaining economies that often

---

[17] Economic textbooks cite 'rent' as 'income derived from the gift of nature,' while the Oxford Dictionary sees it as 'the extra amount earned by an economic resource (e.g., land, capital, or labor) by virtue of its present use' (Marshall, 1890: 350). Fundamentally, economic rent is viewed by classical economics as income that is not subject to opportunity costs with the economist Robert Tomlinson defining it as 'a return in excess of the resource owner's opportunity cost.' (Tollison, 1982).

[18] Ricardo (1821: 53), Smith (1776: 181).

did not have strong productive domestic sectors.[19] For example, only a small fraction of the society—usually tied to the state—was actually involved in the generation of oil revenues, with the rest engaging in the use/distribution of said oil wealth, thereby creating the patron–client relationships that typify much of the region (1987:385).

As we shall see in this and ensuing chapters, the key rents driving political and economic as well as gender relationships in the MENA are largely external (foreign) in nature, which adds a distinct flavor to their impact on national societies at large. Arab governments are the most important recipients of this external rent in Beblawi's conception of rentierism, which further engenders an 'allocative' and dependent relationship rather than a productive one between the society and the state itself. This all-encompassing rentier mentality turns rewards into 'situational occurrences' rather than the product of concerted and independent economic processes and efforts (1987: 386). Adeel Malik (2017: 42) maintains that relying on these external windfalls is in reality 'the original sin of development in the Middle East and North Africa'—that the region is not so much plagued by a 'resource curse' as a 'rent curse'. The idea of a 'curse' builds on classical conceptions of Rentier-State Theory (RST) which expects distinct political, social, and economic effects from what is perceived as unearned income gleaned from the sale of oil and other commodities, which flood domestic markets with foreign exchange resulting in the resource curse and its associated misery, Dutch Disease. This disincentivizes the democratization of productive capacity and centralizes power in the rentier state, resulting in the bloating of state institutions, mono-economies, and even patriarchal political cultures.[20]

The variant of rentierism in the MENA also builds off of a unique type of social contract especially characteristic of the GCC states, which determines the relationship between the ruler and the ruled—essentially, the rulers provide their citizens with the trappings of oil and other income through guaranteed jobs and welfare, and, in exchange, the citizens offer their political quiescence, if not necessarily their unbridled loyalty to

---

[19] Mahdavi, H. (1970). The pattern and problems of economic development in rentier states: the case of Iran, in M. Cook (ed), Studies in the Economic History of the Middle East, Oxford University Press, London.

[20] Ross (2008).

the ruler.[21] The revenue from rents limits the need for taxation and government accountability to the governed, which also seems to engender limited demands for political participation beyond clientelism (Beblawi, 1987; 387). Yet, this is not the social contract present across all Arab states since the majority do not enjoy the same oil wealth coupled with smaller population as the GCC countries.

Most scholars of the region readily associate rentierism with the oil monarchies of the Gulf much as Beblawi does, as well as a few other oil-rich states across North Africa and the Levant. However, we do see other forms of clientelist relationships emerge due to state reliance on external rents such as foreign aid and remittances (Malik, 2017). Malik makes the case that these non-resource-based variants of rentierism are worth investigating, and categorizes all rentier states in the MENA into three types based on where they stand relative to capital vs. labor abundance: (1) capital-surplus oil exporting states (the GCC), (2) capital-deficient oil exporting states (Algeria, Iran, Sudan, Syria, and Iraq), and (3) oil-poor economies that derive rents from aid, remittances, and regulation (Jordan, Lebanon, Yemen, Morocco, and Tunisia). It is important to note that in the case of the Levant as well as few other states, remittances are *still* tied to oil rents (and oil prices) since many of the GCC members readily host migrant workers from other Arab countries. It is also noteworthy that the oil-exporting states are divided up into those with a labor surplus and those with small local workforces, creating distinct patronage and labor dynamics, where in many of the latter states the ex-pat community makes up the majority of the population, while the citizenry constitutes only a fraction of the demographics. Unsurprisingly, in such cases direct rents are distributed to the small citizen population, and it is not for nothing that the GCC countries have often been dubbed the 'welfare' states or 'Swedens' of the Arab world.

Jenkins et al (2011) would add an additional layer to this labor/capital taxonomy of rentierism, highlighting the importance of whether the dominant form of external rent is direct (oil and foreign aid) vs. indirect (remittances), since the former allows for greater centralization of the state's bureaucratic and social elites' power. Conversely, remittances

---

[21] Gengler, J., & Lambert, L. (2016). Renegotiating the ruling bargain: Selling fiscal reform in the GCC. *The Middle East Journal, 70*(2), 321–329; Mitchell, J. S., & Gengler, J. J. (2019). What money can't buy: Wealth, inequality, and economic satisfaction in the rentier state. *Political Research Quarterly, 72*(1), 75–89.

are much more dispersed and harder to control by the state and associated entities. Jenkins et al. found that the MENA region as a whole had the highest rate of rents as a percentage of Gross Domestic Product (GDP) at 32.6 percent relative to the global average of 18.4 percent from 2000 until 2008.[22] This is partially due to the very low taxation rates present in the region with the authors estimating that some 56.7 percent of state revenue came from non-taxable sources, whereas in the rest of the world that statistic was a much lower 13.9 percent for the aforementioned period. The implication here is the lack of accountability of the state to its citizens, when the revenue it needs to function comes from outside sources and not the citizens themselves. Certainly, with indirect rents such as remittances there is more scope for citizen agency as well as greater state vulnerability to challenges from the population, but this also explains why so many of these states are focused more on rent distribution and co-optation rather than leveraging rents toward increased economic growth. This phenomenon was somewhat born out during the Arab Spring where rentier states relying on indirect rents (i.e. foreign aid and remittances) such as Yemen, Tunisia, and Egypt were much more susceptible to popular mobilization and organized opposition than the classic oil rentier states of the GCC—of course with the notable exception of Bahrain.[23] Per Jenkins et al. (2011: 27):

> The major focus of rentier economic policy is how to distribute the revenues to insure stable rule and only secondarily to expand the rent stream. Focusing on the rent rates is, in this sense, secondary. More important is the organization of the rents and their centralization. Rentier elites are reluctant to launch initiatives that might create potential rivals.

Overall, scholars have shown that rent-seeking behavior negatively impacts democracy and the quality of institutions, engendering distinct elites and patronage coalitions.[24] Here is where we shift the discussion

---

[22] Jenkins et al., (2011: 25) created an index of direct and indirect rents flowing to the MENA and the world in the interest of evaluating whether rentierism in the region was much more prevalent than elsewhere.

[23] Yet, of all the GCC states, Bahrain relies most on a combination of indirect and direct rent due to its hosting of the U.S. military's fifth fleet and dwindling oil reserves.

[24] See Ross (2001), Chaudhry (1997), Isham et al. (2005), Hertog (2010).

to how rentierism impacts women and broader gender dynamics in Arab societies.

## Gendered Rentierism Revisited

As a concept, *gendered rentierism* captures the distinct gender dynamics created by rentier states and the warped social contract they forge with their female citizens in what are ostensibly liberal-facing autocracies. It is important to note that gendered rentierism operates differently depending on the type of rent that is dominant within a given country. The specific rent generates its own state–society dependencies and relations: in some cases the state depends on conservative migrants living abroad to send money back to the home-country as a welfare subsidy, in others on the international community promoting 'neoliberal conformity' through the commodification and depoliticization of gender equality. In particular, gendered rentierism encourages the reader and others to move beyond the role of oil as the sole economic pathology of the state with a gendered impact, and to recognize the centrality of other forms of 'unearned' revenue such as foreign aid, remittances, and even government regulation in having distinct effects on gender dynamics within a given society (Fig. 2.1).

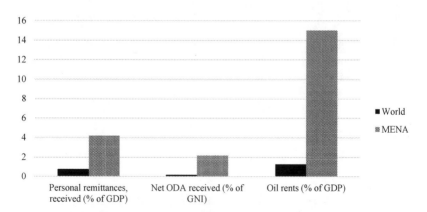

**Fig. 2.1** Comparison of Rents for 2019, World vs. MENA* (*High-income countries excluded) (*Sources:* World Development Indicators, 2022)

## 2 STATE FEMINISM AND GENDERED RENTIERISM 41

### *Oil, Investment, and Gender*

Michael Ross and others have already ventured into explaining the gendered effects of Dutch Disease, with Ross explicating that 'different types of economic growth have different consequences for gender relations'.[25] In Ross' mind, economic growth which encouraged women to join the labor market—in particular, in tradeable manufacturing jobs—ultimately resulted in more gender equality over time, while growth embedded in extractive oil and mineral industries seemed to discourage gender equality—roughly a comparison between North African and GCC states if translated directly into the MENA context.[26] In fact, Ross uses the MENA region to illustrate this point, focusing on oil-rich Algeria and oil-poor Morocco and Tunisia as his primary case studies, while also intimating that the GCC states are examples of the gender tax embedded in oil wealth.[27] In his work, Ross essentially finds that the patriarchal bargains engendered when oil is the dominant resource and rent of a respective country result in a type of deindustrialization that penalizes women from 'traditional' sources of work (tradable sectors such as agriculture and manufacturing), further locking them out of the halls of political power.[28] Essentially, he embraces and tests a quasi-Marxist argument where women's labor force participation determines their likelihood of political mobilization and participation. Per Ross, women's labor force participation amplifies their political influence on three levels: *the social level* via an increase in the likelihood of women's network formation by virtue of density of women in the labor market, *the individual level* through affecting their political views and identity, and, ultimately, on *the economic level* by highlighting their economic importance *to* the government giving them greater leverage over related policy.

However, the patterns Ross identifies hold less sway in the new millennium—especially with most GCC states extending suffrage to women in

---

[25] Ross (2008: 107).

[26] It is important to note that the data he used in his work largely predated the new millennium and is focused on women's legislative representation as a key way to measure gender equality.

[27] Though the latter definitely do not focus on agriculture or manufacturing as their primary streams of income as averse to parts of North Africa and the Levant.

[28] Musgrave and Liou (2015).

## 42    B. C. WELBORNE

the past twenty years as well as with higher rates of women's professional workforce participation in the GCC than the other states in the MENA.[29] Updated research from the International Labor Organization (ILO) and others reveals that most women in the MENA *are not* predominantly employed in manufacturing as we see in much of the Global South.[30] Furthermore, these insights barely apply to the GCC states, where professional women often benefit from the economic redistribution of oil-rentier welfare countries or what Michael Herb (2014) terms as resource-abundant oil regimes.[31] It is important to differentiate between what Herb calls resource-dependent vs. resource-abundant countries and their impact on the state's social contract with its citizens—in particular, with their women. Ross'[32] work captured the relationship between women's work and resource-dependence in the context of countries such as Iraq or Algeria, that are more vulnerable to the vicissitudes of international oil markets as well as the political machinations of the Organization for Petroleum Exporting Countries (OPEC). Both economies depend on receipts of foreign exchange from oil to fund their expansive public sectors, but also on foreign aid in the Iraqi case and remittances in the Algerian case—partially, because these two states are capital poor with larger populations (Malik, 2017). Thus, one would be hard-pressed to call them resource-abundant in Herb's parlance—rather, they are *dependent* on finding external markets for their resource to stave off domestic instability because of their labor surplus and high unemployment rates. Essentially, there is not enough money earned from external rents to engage in the kind of massive economic redistribution that we encounter in the GCC states, which only began to include female citizens in their patronage networks in the latter part of the twentieth century. Importantly, 'citizens' is the operative word here. In the 'extreme rentier' states

---

[29] Ross' data encapsulates the time period from 1960 until 2002, thus it is likely that much has changed in the intervening years, including the mainstreaming of women's empowerment as a desired social good in the international community.

[30] Buttorff, G., and Welborne, B. (2015). Rethinking Economic Rentierism and Women's Empowerment. Baker Institute *Issue Brief,* (09.25. 15).

[31] Ibid.; Buttorff, G. J., Al Lawati, N., and Welborne, B. C. (2018). Cursed No More? The Resource Curse, Gender, and Labor Nationalization Policies in the GCC. *Journal of Arabian Studies, 8*(1), 65–86.

[32] See Herb, M. (2014). *The wages of oil: Parliaments and economic development in Kuwait and the UAE.* Cornell University Press.

of Kuwait, Qatar, and the UAE we actually see women's labor force participation, and even ostensibly their political status, rising over the last two decades. One might argue these women have more employment opportunities precisely because such a robust service sector exists both in the public and private realm and, most importantly, because extreme rentiers can also afford to co-opt *everybody*. Essentially, in extreme rentier states women have been able to find jobs despite oil-driven development, and perhaps even because of it—especially since they are so heavily represented in the professional service sector economy.

Ultimately, there is evidence that despite Ross' argument of oil rents disincentivizing women's economic and political participation, the opposite is true and that there exists a state-led push to improve the optics of gender in what are largely muzzled GCC parliaments. Even the less oil-abundant Arab members of OPEC such as Iraq, Algeria, and Sudan exhibit similar patterns. Certainly, in the Iraqi case overbearing American influence and the push to 'liberalize' galvanized the adoption of a gender quota that keeps the Iraqi parliament at a steady 25 percent level of female representation—no more, no less (the quota itself is a 25 percent mandate). Algeria also hosts a gender quota, but is a more complicated story with its 'socialist' revolutionary past and present, and rabid bid to suppress any hints of Islamism. Sudan's oil wealth is relatively new and with the deposal of President Omar al-Bashir it is yet to be seen what this will bode for women. Ironically, it is rents from foreign aid that may be behind the push for women's legislative representation beyond the GCC—so a 'cosmetic' political equality may in fact still be rent-fueled, but by a different type of rent.

### *Foreign Aid and Gender*

The importance of foreign aid as a source of rent cannot be overstated as well as its impact on the burgeoning women's empowerment industry. Malik observes that 'by virtue of its strategic location, the average MENA state derives greater aid rents than the average low-income country or sub-Saharan African state' (2017: 48). He also notes how despite hosting more poor people than the MENA, South Asia only receives $6 per capita to the MENA region's $43 per capita in aid, revealing the strategic and ideological interests at play. In the new millennium a robust literature has emerged connecting conditional foreign aid to the promotion of gender equality across the Global South and the Middle East, in particular.[33] This literature arose at a time when bilateral and multilateral aid had moved beyond the safeguarding of women's rights within legal frameworks such as the Convention Against the Discrimination of Women (CEDAW) to encouraging developing countries to factor for endemic gender discrimination within their national budgets and political institutions—simply put, encouraging developing countries to embrace gender mainstreaming as standard practice.

The Fourth World Conference on Women (1995) which introduced the Beijing Platform for Action,[34] the 23rd special of the General Assembly (2000), the Millennium Summit (2000), and the 2005 World Summit, highlighted government and international organization's commitments to the financing of gender equality and women's empowerment to promote states' economic, as well as political interests. From 1999 until 2003 an Organization for Economic Cooperation and Development (OECD) DAC (Development Assistance Committee) study revealed that almost $3.1 billion dollars in aid targeted gender-sensitive programming.[35] With first the New Millennium Development Goals (MDGs) and later the Sustainable Development Goals (SDGs), the World Bank openly touted the importance of women's empowerment and gender mainstreaming existing political institutions for economic development. As one of the largest sources of external finance for development, the World Bank plays a central role in promoting the norms and

---

[33] Edgell (2017), Bush (2011), Baliamoune-Lutz (2013, 2016), Pickbourn, L., & Ndikumana, L. (2016). The impact of the sectoral allocation of foreign aid on gender inequality. *Journal of International Development, 28*(3), 396–411; Grown, Caren, Tony Addison, and Finn Tarp. (2016) Aid for gender equality and development: Lessons and challenges. *Journal of International Development, 28*(3), 311–319; Bali Swain, R., Garikipati, S., and Wallentin, F. Y. (2020). Does Foreign Aid Improve Gender Performance in Recipient Countries? *Journal of International Development, 32*(7) 1171–1193. Hicks, Daniel L., and Beatriz Maldonado. (2020) Do foreign aid donors reward recipients for improving gender outcomes? *Applied economics letters, 27* (1), 46–51.

[34] The Beijing Platform called for direct government participation in diverting resources to and creating a supportive environment for the complete inclusion of women into public society with the aid of women's NGOs, feminist groups, and the private sector—the first clear international promotion of gender mainstreaming. *Report of the Fourth World Conference on Women, Beijing, 4-15 September 1995* (United Nations publication, Sales No. E.96.IV.13), chap. I, resolution 1, annex II.

[35] Williams 2007.

imagery associated with progressive economic and political outcomes to the developing world as well as some countries in the 'developed' world.[36]

In the Arab world specifically, there has been a veritable wave of development programs focused on women's political inclusion since the 1990s. These initiatives at least partially contributed to increasing the regional average of female legislative representation through their explicit promotion of women-friendly institutional change, and through their *free* training of female political candidates and social organizers, thereby building a substantial technocratic elite with a vested interested in women's issues, but not necessarily interested in politicizing them.[37] This external push for women's empowerment in majority Muslim-Arab countries is also tied to the security environment in the aftermath of September 11th.[38] In the early 2000s, scholarship by prominent political scientists such as Steven Fish, Pippa Norris, and Ronald Ingelhart, identified attitudes toward gender as the primary difference and potential point of contention between Muslim and Western states, and this to no small degree, motivated American strategies for democracy promotion and deradicalization through women's empowerment in the Middle East (Fish, 2002; Inglehart & Norris, 2003, 2009; Landes & Landes, 2001; Lewis, 2002). Consequently, resolving the 'gender gap' through women's political inclusion became an integral talking point in the administration of former U.S. President George W. Bush and the broader international community's efforts to democratize the region. Essentially, bilateral donors in the West were gambling that the advent of women in politics would have a 'moderating' and 'secularizing' influence on local politics and so stem the perceived threat of Islamic fundamentalism. There are pretty clear state-based incentives in the western foreign aid community to promote women's political participation, but this same interest has not been extended to empowering them in the workforce—possibly because more women in an already saturated and public sector-dominated Arab workforce is seen as destabilizing already precarious employment opportunities for men. Women legislators do not pose similar threats and are

---

[36] Finnemore (1996).

[37] Officials with the International Republican Institute (IRI) and the National Democratic Institute (NDI) officials in Jordan in 2008 and Morocco in 2009 and 2017 emphasized the role they played in training female candidates to me in informal interviews.

[38] Abu-Lughod (2002).

## 46  B. C. WELBORNE

not necessarily even viewed by Arab leaders as really challenging the status quo of politics in what are effectively authoritarian regimes.

### Aid Conditionality to the Rescue?

The same kind of perverted incentives that oil engenders in the social contracts of GCC states with their citizens—namely lack of accountability and rampant clientelism—are also baked into the massive inflows of foreign aid coming into the MENA, especially in the aftermath of September 11th.[39] These financial windfalls allow certain regimes to forfeit on accountability to their citizens without necessarily having to engage in the massive welfare transfers typical of GCC states with oil money padding their coffers.

Many states that used to be more dependent on agriculture as a source of export such as those in the North Africa and the Levant, have recently shifted away from agriculture and are newly dependent on remittances and/or foreign aid, engendering a new type of rentier economy with distinct effects on women (Caraway, 2009; International Labor Organization, 2012). For women, the consequence of relying on foreign aid from neoliberal institutions such as the World Bank and its associated regional development banks, but also signing on to structural adjustment agreements with the International Monetary Fund (IMF) is that they are often the first to get trimmed from public sector work when inter-governmental organization (IGO) consultants invariably counsel Arab governments to reign in their bloated state sector. Furthermore, the region as a whole has a very high rate of women present in informal sectors (some 61.8 percent of workers) with many of these women embedded in informal work within the agricultural sector in oil-poor states (UN Women, 2020). With the shift away from agriculture to relying on rents from foreign aid or even remittances—especially with increasingly unpredictable weather patterns, women are yet again more likely to get kicked out of the very sectors that are most likely to employ them in oil-poor states.

---

[39] Some might argue that this is not completely true since a portion of the development assistance flowing into the region is conditional on performance centered around 'deradicalization' and 'liberalization' of domestic society, but typically the most popular aid recipients such as Jordan, Egypt, Iraq, and, newly, Sudan have faced no real penalties for non-compliance with associated conditionalities.

Perhaps one of the most striking features of gendered rentierism as encapsulated by aid-dependent rentier states pursuing state feminism is that it effectively depoliticizes gender equality and women's rights in curious, and often counterproductive, ways. Sara Ababneh speaks to this depoliticization poignantly in the Jordanian context (Ababneh, 2020). One of the key features of Jordan's experiences with gendered rentierism is the influx of foreign aid—especially development assistance geared at women's empowerment—often seen as a mechanism to deradicalize Islamic fundamentalists. A striking aspect of the Jordanian experience with IMF structural adjustment agreements of the late twentieth century as well as aid-sponsored democracy promotion efforts in the new millennium has been the proliferation of NGOs.[40] This certainly echoes the shift away from the public sector to the private sector of community development we see in other states bound by structural adjustment agreements, keen on embracing neoliberal development strategies. Yet, this shift has a very specific impact on women's NGOs in particular with Ababneh documenting how such organizations transitioned from being registered at the Ministry of Interior to the Ministry of Social Development in Jordan, hinting at the successful '(re)conceptualization of women's activism from being political (similarly to political parties) to becoming social', and thus in many ways less threatening to the state. She continues,

> It is ironic that this increased interest in women nationally and internationally, depoliticized women's activism; that as international and national interest in 'women's issues' increased, women's rights were depoliticized. This depoliticization is also connected to women's work being seen as development work, and women's rights organizations becoming women's NGOs. (Ababneh, 2020: 277)

An academic I interviewed at the University of Bahrain back in 2009 struck a similar chord:

> I think most of the [gender-related] changes are galvanized by national reports. They take international ratings very seriously. They [the government] use amendments to cover things; they try to make up positions

---

[40] There was an increase of some 67 percent from 1989 until 1994 alone in the number of women's NGOs operating in the kingdom. See Harmsen (2008).

48 B. C. WELBORNE

for women; but many ministries that women belong to are of secondary importance. The ministry of interior, finance, etc. these will affect government decisions.[41]

In promoting the NGO-ization of women's issues, oftentimes through conditional aid agreements, the state outsources the concern, activism, and responsibility for gender equality and ensuring women's rights from the public to the private sector, while still giving the regime gross oversight through existence of GONGOs. As Ababneh further attests, in the aftermath of the UN World Conference in Beijing 'it was no longer the states, the structures it had put in place, or the lack of rights that needed to be addressed or were considered as the root of the problem [of gender inequality]. Rather, it was the communities from which these women came'.[42] Ironically, the famous 1995 UN conference on women in Beijing incentivized the creation of many of the GONGOs and RONGOs (royally sponsored NGOs) that now dot the MENA and effectively muzzle women's grassroots activism.[43] And these institutions have often been exceedingly good at divorcing women's struggle from larger issues facing the state and nation as a whole.

My interviews with government officials in Jordan, Bahrain, and Morocco revealed that many Arab leaders viewed women's empowerment as a way to improve their 'image' abroad in the interest of attracting more financial investment alongside foreign aid. They also believed resolving the 'cosmetic' issues of women's legislative representation was a quick way to conciliate donors as well as investors requesting concrete signs of progress in democracy and development. Importantly, the incentive structure is different in Gulf countries since they receive low levels of development assistance, but attract substantial often oil-related investment in comparison to other Arab countries. That said, many GCC states still wish to portray themselves as investment-friendly and non-threatening nations, and see women's political inclusion as a ready message to the outside world of their 'progressive' environment.

Photos of women cloaked in black *abayas* are easily the first visual most people associate with the Gulf outside of looming oil rigs nestled in a sea

---

[41] Author interview in Manama, Bahrain. June 2009.

[42] Ababneh 2020: 278.

[43] States hoping to send envoys to the seminal UN conference in Beijing in 1995 were required to form national councils on women's affairs as a precondition for participation.

of sand. Certainly, movies such as *Sex and the City 2* have furthered this image. Unsurprisingly, the former is an unsettling image and one, for all attempts to romanticize it, that the Gulf actively attempts to dispel for fear of alienating investors, tourists, and white-collar foreign labor. Today that visual can be supplemented with images of women within almost every legislative assembly of the GCC and even some ministerial appointments. It may not be an accident that much of this 'New Arabia' came into being with suffrage hastily implemented from 2002 onward in the wake of the September 11th attacks. In this respect, while conditional aid may directly mandate that Arab leaders show evidence of progress on gender and 'democracy' indicators, foreign investment seems to have also created incentives for the political inclusion of women in countries where aid conditionality is moot.

### Remittances and Gender

While foreign aid and its associated conditionalities may represent state and intergovernmental pressures on Arab countries to exhibit or 'perform' certain gender dynamics within their societies, remittances as a form of rent play a much more individualized, private role in determining emergent gender relations. And per the work of Faisal Ahmed (2012), remittances can also in some cases weaken patron–client linkages, affording recipients opportunities for political agency and the creation of independent political space. As private monies sent back home by *Diasporas* living abroad, on the surface many may not see remittances as eliciting any impact on gender relations at the domestic, much less national level. In this they would be wrong. More often than not, remittance recipients are 'left-behind' women family members who take charge of household finances. As a region, the MENA states have the largest average share of remittances as a percent of GDP in the world.[44] And as, Chapter 4 will show, they too impact gender relations in Arab states albeit not as directly as foreign aid or oil revenues.

Since the early 2000s remittances have overshadowed both foreign direct investment (FDI) and development assistance flows into the region in terms of volume. As early as 2001, there were some $15 billion

---

[44] 5.6 percent of GDP on average relative to the 0.8 percent overall of the rest of the world. Only the islands of Oceania have a similar rate.

worth of remittances flowing into the MENA in comparison to approximately $3 billion in FDI and $6 billion in official development assistance (ODA)—keeping in mind a portion of this money is flowing into MENA economies from the GCC alongside monies coming in from Western Europe (Kapur, 2005). Egypt, Lebanon, Jordan, and Morocco represent countries with the world's largest influx of remittances from their citizens working abroad. These nations receive in excess of two billion dollars a year to supplement the government's coffers—a number which significantly rivals or is equal to other sources of foreign exchange and has been shown to deteriorate governance and government accountability in states that rely on it (Ahmed, 2012, 2013; Singer, 2010). In effect, the sheer level of remittances flowing into the region might give at least some of these states the opportunity to thumb their noses at a donor community intent on promoting gender reforms alongside a slew of other democratizing policy measures.

More fascinating, however, is the effect of remittances on household dynamics, dependent on whether their receipt allows female-headed households to flourish due to absentee male breadwinners or whether they disincentivize women from working since the home now enjoys an effective welfare subsidy from abroad. As Ross himself posits (2008: 117), 'Labor remittances tend to have the same economic effects as oil: they constitute a large influx of foreign exchange, which raises the real exchange rate, hence making it harder for countries to develop low-wage, export-oriented manufacturing; and they increase household incomes, giving women less incentive to work outside the home'.He cites the cases of Yemen, Egypt, and Jordan as examples of states where we would expect higher levels of women's labor force participation and speaks to the possibility that labor remittances from the conservative GCC states stifled incentives to include women in the workforce—especially since these three countries were responsible for the majority of labor migrants sent to the Persian Gulf from 1970 until 1990. *Where* the money is coming from can also impact how the values of the sender country influence the primary male breadwinner in sending money back to his family and the distributional preferences he passes on to the household. Furthermore, the incentives behind whether women work or not are *also* contingent on the kinds of values households exhibit in the first place. The potential ideological changes in the preferences of the primary breadwinner from his experience living abroad may shift and evolve domestic gender relations into something completely new (oftentimes either more or less conservative than was the case originally).

Importantly, by virtue of so many Arab ex-patriates living and working in the GCC states from North Africa and the Levant, remittances are often highly correlated with oil prices and, therefore, oil rents. Effectively, oil rents are recycled into the rest of the oil-poor Arab countries through both oil subsidies and money sent by migrants back to their home-country. Hameed (2020) highlights this connection revealing that from 2000 until 2014 remittances very much tracked the increase in oil prices, as did the aid and regional investment flowing into the rest of the Arab world from the GCC states. Steffen Hertog (2017: 52–53) notes that a 'significant outflow of [oil] rents' exists to 'appease strategically important external constituencies' and 'align their interests with domestic political continuity', demonstrating how the local cycling of rents is not the only distributional mechanism scholars should be paying attention to in the MENA states. There are also intra-regional coalitions that are built through rent-cycling in the interest of propping up national regimes. Per Hertog,

> Resource-rich Arab states face the imperative of sharing their resource wealth, not just with their citizens, but also with key external constituencies. In fact, the resource-rich countries of the Gulf are effectively financing the social contracts of Yemen, Egypt and Jordan. (2017: 53)

### *A Rent Curse?*

Essentially, all of the MENA states suffer from some form of 'rent curse', where foreign capital inflows either from oil exports, foreign aid, or remittances engender dynamics that can shift the economy away from productive, 'tradeable' sectors and so effectively de-industrialize the economy (Ross, 2008; Corden & Neary, 1982; Karl, 1997, 1999, 2007; Majed, 2021). The question becomes whether a service sector economy in the information age is really as much of a liability as the 'resource curse' logic would predict and what that entails for the women often employed within it. Ironically, as we shall see in the ensuing chapters the social outcomes created by gendered rentierism can be a blessing as well as a curse for women, depending on the type of rent-dependencies predominant in a given country. Gendered rentierism has both increased women's political participation by virtue of foreign aid conditionalities as well as increased women's economic participation through distributional incentives generated by oil rents in a portion of oil-rich states. Yet, the ultimate outcome for women is not so clear-cut, nor are the gains for what is often only a subset of elite or middle-class, educated women. Their less-educated and globally connected sisters are often unable to tap into the opportunities engendered by the coalitional and patronage interests of the rentier state. Consequently, it is worth asking whether any of these gendered effects are ultimately positive, substantive, and sustainable in the long run.

## References

Ababneh, S. (2018, June 30). Do you know who governs us? The damned monetary fund. Middle East Report Online. https://merip.org/2018/06/do-you-know-who-governs-us-the-damned-monetary-fund/

Ababneh, S. (2020). The time to question, rethink and popularize the notion of 'women's issues': Lessons from Jordan's popular and labor movements from 2006 to Now. *Journal of International Women's Studies, 21*(1), 271–288.

Abu-Lughod, L. (2002). Do muslim women really need saving? Anthropological reflections on cultural relativism and its others. *American Anthropologist, 104*(3), 783–790.

Ahmed, F. Z. (2012). The perils of unearned foreign income: Aid, remittances, and government survival. *American Political Science Review, 106*(1), 146–165.

Ahmed, F. Z. (2013). Remittances deteriorate governance. *Review of Economics and Statistics, 95*(4), 1166–1182.

Al-, H. (1993). *Women in Kuwait: The politics of gender*. Saqi Books.

Allam, N. (2018). *Women and the Egyptian revolution: Engagement and activism during the 2011 Arab uprisings*. Cambridge University Press.

Arab News, (2020, July 2). Egypt parliament allocates 25% of seats to women. https://www.arabnews.com/node/1690091/middle-east

Arenfeldt, P., & Golley, N. A. H. (Eds.). (2012). *Mapping Arab women's movements: A century of transformations from within*. American University in Cairo Press.

Bali, S. R., Garikipati, S., & Wallentin, F. Y. (2020). Does foreign aid improve gender performance in recipient countries? *Journal of International Development, 32*(7), 1171–1193.

Baliamoune-Lutz, M. (2013). The effectiveness of foreign aid to women's equality organizations in the MENA: Does aid promote women's political participation? (No. 2013/074). WIDER Working Paper.

Baliamoune, M. (2016). The effectiveness of foreign aid to women's equality organisations in the MENA. *Journal of International Development, 28*(3), 320–341.

Beblawi, H. (1987). The rentier state in the Arab world. *Arab Studies Quarterly,* 383–398.

Begum, R. (2017, August 24). Middle east on a roll to repeal 'Marry the Rapist' laws. human rights watch. https://www.hrw.org/news/2017/08/24/middle-east-roll-repeal-marry-rapist-laws

Brand, L. (1998). *Women, the state, and political liberalization: Middle Eastern and North African experiences.* Columbia University Press.

Brand, L. Kaki, R., & Stacher, J. (2011, February 16). First ladies as focal points for discontent, foreign policy. https://foreignpolicy.com/2011/02/16/first-ladies-as-focal-points-for-discontent/

Bush, S. S. (2011). International politics and the spread of quotas for women in legislatures. *International Organization, 65*(1), 103–137.

Bush, S. S., & Gao, E. (2017). Small tribes, big gains: The strategic uses of gender quotas in the middle east. *Comparative Politics, 49*(2), 149–167.

Buttorff, G. J., Al, N., & Welborne, B. C. (2018). Cursed no more? The resource curse, gender, and labor nationalization policies in the GCC. *Journal of Arabian Studies, 8*(1), 65–86.

Buttorff, G., and Welborne, B. (2015, September 25). Rethinking economic rentierism and women's empowerment. Baker Institute Issue Brief 1. https://scholarship.rice.edu/bitstream/handle/1911/91825/BI-Brief-092515-WRME_FemaleLaborForce.pdf

Caraway, T. L. (2009). Comparative political economy, gender, and labor markets. *Politics & Gender, 5*(4), 568–575.

Charrad, M. M. (2001). *States and women's rights: The making of postcolonial Tunisia, Algeria, and Morocco.* University of California Press.

Charrad, M. M. (2011). Gender in the Middle East: Islam, State, Agency. *Annual Review of Sociology, 37,* 417–437.

Corden, W. M., & Neary, J. P. (1982). Booming sector and de-industrialisation in a small open economy. *The Economic Journal, 92*(368), 825–848.

Deutsche Welle (2020, October 12). Kuwait's new all-male parliament is a blow to women's rights. https://www.dw.com/en/kuwaits-new-all-male-parliament-is-a-blow-for-womens-rights/a-55897172

Dildar, Y. (2021). Gendered patterns of industrialization in MENA. *Middle East Development Journal, 13*(1), 128–149.

Edgell, A. B. (2017). Foreign aid, democracy, and gender quota laws. *Democratization, 24*(6), 1103–1141.

Euro-Mediterranean Women's Foundation (2020, August 31). Women's political participation in Egypt: The 2020 Senate Elections. https://www.euromedwomen.foundation/pg/en/documents/view/9248/womens-political-representation-in-egypt-the-2020-senate-elections

Fadhel, S. (2021, February 1). Kuwaiti women's political experience: A Khaleeji affair. London School of Economics Blog. https://blogs.lse.ac.uk/mec/2021/02/01/kuwaiti-womens-political-experience-a-khaleeji-affair/

Finnemore, M. (1996). *National interests in international society.* Cornell University Press.

Fish, S. (2002). Islam and authoritarianism. *World Politics, 55*(1), 4–37.

Gengler, J., & Lambert, L. (2016). Renegotiating the ruling bargain: Selling fiscal reform in the GCC. *The Middle East Journal, 70*(2), 321–329.

Gonzales, A. (2013) Islamic feminism in Kuwait: The politics and paradoxes. Palgrave.

Grown, C., Addison, T., & Tarp, F. (2016). Aid for gender equality and development: Lessons and challenges. *Journal of International Development, 28*(3), 311–319.

Hafner, E., & Pollack, M. A. (2002). Mainstreaming gender in global governance. *European Journal of International Relations, 8*(3), 339–373.

Hameed, S. (2020). Political economy of rentierism in the middle east and disruptions from the digital space. *Contemporary Review of the Middle East, 7*(1), 54–89.

Harmsen, E. (2008). *Islam, civil society and social work: Muslim voluntary welfare associations in Jordan between patronage and empowerment.* Amsterdam University Press.

Hatem, M. (1987). Class and patriarchy as competing paradigms for the study of Middle Eastern women. *Comparative Studies in Society and History, 29*(4), 811–818.

Hatem, M. F. (1992). Economic and political liberation in Egypt and the demise of state feminism. *International Journal of Middle East Studies, 24*(2), 231–251.

Hatem, M. F. (1994). Egyptian discourses on gender and political liberalization: Do secularist and Islamist views really differ? *Middle East Journal, 48*(4), 661–676.

Hatem, M. F. (2016). First ladies and the (re)definition of the authoritarian state in Egypt. *Women and Gender in Middle East Politics, POMEPS Studies, 19,* 42–45.

Hatem, M. F. (2018). Modernization, the state, and the family in middle east women's studies. *Social History of Women and Gender in the Modern Middle East* (pp. 63–87). Routledge.

Herb, M. (2014). *The wages of oil: Parliaments and economic development in Kuwait and the UAE.* Cornell University Press.

Hertog, S. (2010). The sociology of the Gulf Rentier systems: Societies of intermediaries. *Comparative Studies in Society and History, 52*(2), 1–37.

Hertog, S. (2017). The political economy of distribution in the middle east: Is there scope for a new social contract? In G. Luciani (Ed.), *Combining economic and political development*, Brill Nijhoff, pp. 88–113.

Hicks, D. L., & Maldonado, B. (2020). Do foreign aid donors reward recipients for improving gender outcomes? *Applied Economics Letters, 27*(1), 46–51.

Inglehart, R., & Norris, P. (2003). *Rising tide.* Cambridge University Press.

Inglehart, R., and Norris, P. (2009, November 9). The True Clash of Civilizations. Foreign Policy 135. https://foreignpolicy.com/2009/11/04/the-true-clash-of-civilizations/

ILO. (2012). Global employment trends for women report. International labour organization (ILO). http://www.ilo.org/wcmsp5/groups/public/---dgrepo rts/---dcomm/documents/publication/wcms_195447.pdf

Isham, J., Woolcock, M., Pritchett, L., & Busby, G. (2005). The varieties of resource experience: Natural resource export structures and the political economy of economic growth. *The World Bank Economic Review, 19*(2), 141–174.

Jenkins, J. C., Meyer, K., Costello, M., & Aly, H. (2011). International rentierism in the Middle East Africa, 1971–2008. *International Area Studies Review, 14*(3), 3–31.

Joseph, S. (1996). *Gender and citizenship in Middle Eastern states.* Middle East Report, 4–10.

Kantola, J., & Squires, J. (2012). From state feminism to market feminism? *International Political Science Review, 33*(4), 382–400.

Kapur, D. (2005). Remittances: The new development mantra? *Remittances: Development Impact and Future Prospects 2*(1), 331–360.

Karl, T. L. (1997). *The paradox of plenty.* University of California Press.

Karl, T. L. (1999). The perils of the petro-state: Reflections on the paradox of plenty. *Journal of International Affairs, 53*(1), 31–48.

Karl, T. L. (2007). Oil-led development: social, political, and economic consequences. *Encyclopedia of Energy, 4*(8), 661–672.

Landes, D., & Landes, R. (2001, October 8). Girl power: Do fundamentalists fear our women? *New Republic.*

Lewis, B. (2002). *What went wrong?* Oxford University Press.

Liou, Y.-M., & Musgrave, P. (2016). Oil, autocratic survival, and the gendered resource curse: when inefficient policy is politically expedient. *International Studies Quarterly, 60*(3), 440–456.

Mahdavi, H. (1970). The pattern and problems of economic development in rentier states: The case of Iran. In M. Cook (Ed.), *Studies in the Economic History of the Middle East* (pp. 428–467). Oxford University Press.

Majed, R. (2021, January 27). Towards a feminist political economy in the MENA region. Women's International League for Peace and Freedom.

https://www.wilpf.org/towards-a-feminist-political-economy-in-the-mena-region/

Malik, A. (2017) Rethinking the rentier curse. International development policy, *Revue Internationale de Politique de Développement, 7.*

Mansour, A. (2021, January 27). Sisi's last stand. *Foreign Policy.* https://foreignpolicy.com/2021/01/27/egypt-sisi-human-rights-protests-detention-terrorism-biden-trump/

Marshall, A. (1890). *Principles of economics* (8th ed. [1920]). Mcmillan.

Mitchell, J. S., & Gengler, J. J. (2019). What money can't buy: Wealth, inequality, and economic satisfaction in the rentier state. *Political Research Quarterly, 72*(1), 75–89.

Pickbourn, L., & Ndikumana, L. (2016). The impact of the sectoral allocation of foreign aid on gender inequality. *Journal of International Development, 28*(3), 396–411.

Prügl, E. (2015). Neoliberalizing feminism. *New Political Economy, 20*(4), 614–631.

Rathgeber, E. M. (1990). WID, WAD, GAD: Trends in research and practice. *The Journal of Developing Areas, 24,* 489–502.

Razavi, S., and Miller, C. (1995). From WID to GAD: Conceptual shifts in the women and development discourse. United Nations Research Institute for Social Development (UNRISD) Occasional Paper No. 1, United Nations Fourth World Conference on Women, http://www.unicc.org/unrisd/html/op/opb/opb1/op1_gop.txt

Rizzo, H. M., and Helen, M. (2005). Islam, democracy, and the status of women: The case of Kuwait. Psychology Press.

Robinson, N. (2015). 'Sisters of men': Syrian and Lebanese women's transnational campaigns for Arab independence and women's rights, 1910–1949 (Doctoral dissertation, Rutgers University–New Brunswick Graduate School).

Robinson, N. (1949). (2016) Arab internationalism and gender: Perspectives from the third session of the United Nations Commission on the status of women. *International Journal of Middle East Studies, 48*(3), 578–583.

Ross, M. L. (2001). Does oil hinder democracy? *World Politics, 53*(3), 325–361.

Ross, M. L. (2008). Oil, Islam, and women. *American Political Science Review, 102*(1), 107–123.

Sadiqi, F. (2010a). A theoretical framework for research on gender/women issues in the Maghrib and North Africa. http://www.ucy.ac.cy/unesco/documents/unesco/Articles_2010a-2010a_conference/Sadiqi_paper.pdf

Sadiqi, F. (2010b). *Special report on women's rights in morocco. Women's rights in the Middle East and North Africa: Progress amid resistance.* Freedom House.

Salime, Z. (2016). Women and the right to land in Morocco: The Sulaliyyates movement. In women and gender in Middle East politics. *POMEPS Studies,* 19, https://pomeps.org/wpcontent/uploads/2016/05/POMEPS_Studies_19_Gender_Web.pdf

Shalaby, M. (2015). Women's political representation in Kuwait: An untold story. Rice University's Baker Institute of Public Policy, https://scholarship.rice.edu/bitstream/handle/1911/91824/WRME-pub-PoliRep-Kuwait-091515.pdf

Shalaby, M. M., & Elimam, L. (2020). Women in legislative committees in Arab parliaments. *Comparative Politics, 53*(1), 142.

Sharawi, M., & Badran, M. (2015). *Harem years: The memoirs of an Egyptian feminist 1879–1924.* The Feminist Press.

Singer, D. A. (2010). Migrant remittances and exchange rate regimes in the developing world. *American Political Science Review, 104*(2), 307–323.

Tétreault, M. A., Rizzo, H., & Shultziner, D. (2012). Fashioning the future: The women's movement in Kuwait. In Arenfeldt and Golly (Eds.). *Mapping Arab Women's Movements* (pp. 253–280). AUC Press.

Tollison, R. D. (1982). Rent seeking: A survey. *Kyklos, 35*(4), 575–602.

Tripp, A.M. (2012, January 19). Do Arab women need electoral Quotas? *Foreign Policy,* http://foreignpolicy.com/2012/01/19/do-arab-women-need-electoral-quotas/

Tripp, A. M. (2019). *Seeking legitimacy: Why Arab autocracies adopt women's rights.* Cambridge University Press.

United Nations. (1995). Report of the fourth world conference on women, Beijing, 4–15 September (United Nations publication, Sales No. E.96.IV.13), chap. I, resolution 1, annex II.

UN Women. (2020). The impact of COVID-19 on gender equality in the Arab region. ESCWA Policy Brief 4, https://www2.unwomen.org/-/media/field%20office%20arab%20states/attachments/publications/2020/04/impact%20of%20covid%20on%20gender%20equality%20-%20policy%20brief.pdf

U.S. Department of State. (2021). Secretary Antony J. Blinken on Release of the 2020 Country Reports on Human Rights Practices: Remarks to the Press, 30 March, https://www.state.gov/secretary-antony-j-blinken-on-release-of-the-2020-country-reports-on-human-rights-practices/

Welborne, B.C. (2010). The strategic use of gender quotas in the Arab World. William and Kathy Hybl Democracy Studies Fellowship Paper, International Foundation for Electoral Systems. https://aceproject.org/ero-en/regions/africa/MZ/ifes-the-strategic-use-of-gender-quotas-in-the

Welborne, B. C. (2020). On their own? Women running as independent candidates in the Middle East. *Middle East Law and Governance, 12*(3), 251–274.

Williams, M. (2007). Gender and trade: Impacts and implications for financial resources for gender equality. *Commonwealth Secretariat, Background Paper WAMM, 07,* 10.

Žvan Elliott, K. (2015). *Modernizing patriarchy: The politics of women's rights in Morocco.* University of Texas Press.

CHAPTER 3

# Foreign Aid and Virtue Signaling

When I started working on this book in 2008, much of the scholarly literature on foreign aid and the Middle East focused on aid's use in enhancing international security following the September 11th terrorist attacks (see Carapico, 2002, 2013; Schwedler, 2002). This re-animated post-Cold-War militarism coincided with the emergence of rights-based approaches to economic development, pioneered by Nobel-Prize-winner Amartya Sen.[1] Sen raised the question of whether aid could be used for more than strengthening flagging economies or bolstering state militaries.

In the early 2000s, a duo of economists, Craig Burnside and David Dollar (2000a, 2000b), had begun to lay the groundwork for a rich literature investigating how aid could be harnessed for democracy promotion (effectively a revamped form of state engineering)—a body of academic work that was cited and used actively in attempts at democratizing and 'deradicalizing' the Arab states.[2] Aid monies also often served as a fungible subsidy for the brutal security apparatus of U.S. allies such as

---

[1] Sen (1990) borrows heavily from the capabilities framework introduced by the philosopher Martha Nussbaum (1988, 1995, 2000).

[2] Conversely, David Collier (2008), William Easterly (2002, 2007), and many other development economists—Jeffrey Sachs (2006, 2014) notwithstanding—see aid and aid conditionality as incentivizing corruption and rentier behavior.

© The Author(s), under exclusive license to Springer Nature Switzerland AG 2022
B. C. Welborne, *Women, Money, and Political Participation in the Middle East,*
https://doi.org/10.1007/978-3-031-04877-7_3

60    B. C. WELBORNE

Egypt, Jordan, and Morocco in a bid to ensure regional stability and the *status quo*.

While the language of popular electoral reform was readily embraced as a stepping-stone to ideally more democratic, less 'radical' (read: 'Islamist') societies,[3] another idea increasingly cropped up among academics and pundits alike: how could empowering women in Muslim countries help foster democratization and deradicalization efforts through the pursuit of gender equality. This logic emerged from the writings of non-regional specialists such as Steven Fish, Ronald Inglehart, and Pippa Norris, who actively connected the persistence of authoritarianism and instability in the region to the embrace of conservative, patriarchic values—particularly the subjugation of women and an intolerance toward other religions—in the Muslim world (Fish, 2002; Inglehart & Norris, 2003, 2009; Landes, 2001; Lewis, 2002). These lines of reasoning also identified attitudes toward gender as the primary difference and potential point of contention between Muslim and Western societies.

Consequently, resolving the 'gender gap' through women's greater social and political inclusion became integral to the international community's efforts at democratizing the Arab world. Western donors gambled that the advent of women in politics would have a 'moderating' and 'secularizing' influence on national and local politics. Following this intuition, foreign aid was increasingly earmarked for projects promoting women's activism across the region and became a standard part of American democracy promotion efforts from President George W. Bush's administration to that of Presidents Barack Obama, and even Donald Trump.[4] Examples of this ranged from the Millennium Challenge Corporation's strong-arming Jordan to adopt municipal level gender quotas in exchange for $10 million in international aid in 2006 to a $9.6 million grant extended to Morocco for programs geared at preventing gender-based violence more recently (Assaf & Nanes, 2011; Baliamoune-Lutz, 2016).

These monies have spurred and reinvigorated a veritable cottage industry of NGOs promoting women's rights and empowerment-related 'capacity building'—one that many local and international critics have claimed is more interested in the cosmetics and commercial value of

---

[3] A traditional pathway, following Sam Huntington's ideas of democratic consolidation as discussed in his book, *The Third Wave* (1993).

[4] Few regions in the U.S. Department of State's aid portfolio have received as much money for 'women's empowerment' as the MENA.

women's empowerment than any substantive change for actual women on the ground (see Ababneh, 2020; Prügl, 2015). Even the United Nations' 2005 Arab Human Development Report implied that aid-induced democratization efforts condoned Arab states' passing of gender-related reforms in place of more hard-hitting policy changes that would curb the power of the executive (UNDP, 2006). Many argue that it has, unfortunately, also further widened the chasm between the experiences of elite women versus lower-class and 'traditional' women.

The story of foreign aid's use in promoting women's rights and gender-related reforms in the MENA is neither simple nor transparent. Yet, one thing is clear: It has significantly changed the landscape of women's opportunities in many of the states receiving such aid, as well as those who are merely onlookers, as is the case with the GCC. Importantly, research over the past two decades has shown that gender-related development assistance seems to be less fungible than other types of foreign aid, meaning it is more likely to be earmarked for women and less likely to be pocketed by corrupt government officials.[5]

One of the most striking aspects of this scholarship is its implication that the fungibility of foreign aid might also be contingent on whether grassroots movements can serve as guarantors that the monies in question achieve goals through their ability to hold authoritarian states accountable to international scrutiny. For example, a wide array of research has demonstrated that a state's dependence on foreign aid increases its likelihood of adopting parliamentary gender quotas, with the MENA region as a primary case evoking this pattern (Bush, 2011; Welborne, 2010). In fact, much of the progress we have seen in the MENA in terms of raising women's presence in legislative assemblies is due to Arab states' active adoption of gender quotas (Assaf & Nanes, 2011; Welborne, 2010). The success and widespread nature of gender quotas can be laid squarely at the foot of binding foreign aid initiatives in the last two decades.

---

[5] An interesting line of research might emerge from these findings if we chose to explore how transnational feminism and associated feminist organizations have established fairly effective institutions to ensure this earmarking does, in fact, work for women—although it is an imperfect solution for women from lower-middle-class and impoverished backgrounds (see Baliamoune-Lutz, 2013, 2016; Bush, 2011; Moghadam, 2012; Welborne, 2010).

Indeed, the robustness of findings supporting the positive impact of foreign assistance aimed at increasing women's representation in the Middle East is surprising, since the mainstream Western press frequently excoriates this region for its patriarchic norms. This chapter examines why such assumptions are misguided, using an in-depth exploration of the historical connections between official development assistance (ODA), women's formal and informal activism, and gendered institutional change across the Middle East.

It is important to keep in mind as we begin this discussion that foreign aid in authoritarian regimes behaves as a type of rent, or unearned income, for the government (Ahmed, 2012; Bauer, 1972). It functions this way because aid essentially comprises slack resources that states can use at will—and often do—to develop patronage networks within *aid-rentier states*, as with oil. This is especially true when foreign aid is more fungible, as with much of the concessional and multilateral funds distributed through Bretton Woods institutions. Some of this patronage is now happening through individual women and through local and transnational women's organizations that bring in money, but are also tapped to enhance the reputation of the state—in other words, for states to use gender in 'virtue signaling' to the international political and economic community.

There is some evidence that the outcomes generated by aid conditionality in North Africa and the Levant have emboldened women in less aid-dependent states, such as those of the GCC, to lobby for enhanced rights, as well. This is a byproduct of the increasing trend of virtue signaling across Arab regimes, whether motivated by the need to signal state stability or compliance with neoliberal norms. Put more simply, the progress on gender issues we have seen in the UAE, Saudi Arabia, and Kuwait would have been less likely if Jordan, Egypt, and Morocco had not piloted women's empowerment as a form of virtue and stability signaling to the West in hope of obtaining development financing and attracting renewed investment and interest.

This chapter relies on insights from interviews I conducted in Morocco, Jordan, Bahrain, Yemen, and Oman over a ten-year period from 2007 until 2017. We will explore virtue signaling as an important concept for rentier (or rentier-like) states when rents are derived from aid and consider why the language of pursuing gender equality and women's empowerment has become one of the prime tools for doing this in the MENA.

## Foreign Aid Promotes Gender Equality

In 2002, the United Nations' Arab Human Development Report observed that 'no society can achieve the desired state of well-being and human development, or compete in a globalizing world, if half its people remain marginalized and disempowered'.[6] This effectively launched a more formal external intervention on issues related to women's empowerment across the MENA region from intergovernmental organizations (IGOs) and the bilateral donor community—a phenomenon that was not exclusive to the Arab world. The Fourth World Conference on Women (1995) that introduced the Beijing Platform for Action,[7] the 23rd special of the United Nations General Assembly (2000), the Millennium Summit (2000), and the 2005 World Summit all highlighted emerging commitments from states and IGOs alike to combat gender inequality and promote women's empowerment in the interest of promoting economic and political interests.

The World Bank, openly touting the importance of women's empowerment for economic development, popularized gender mainstreaming as a viable national strategy, as did the increasing amount of gender-related bilateral aid coming from the 30 OECD-DAC countries. From 1999 through 2003, a DAC study revealed, almost $3.1 billion in aid had targeted gender-sensitive programming (Williams, 2007). The DAC has spent billions on gender equality and women's empowerment, from between $11 billion and $14 billion in 2005–2006 to $24.8 billion in 2009–2010. In 2016–2017, that amount rose again to $44.8 billion—representing fully 38 percent of allocable bilateral aid (Baliamoune-Lutz, 2016; OECD, 2019). And in 2017–2018, some 42 percent of bilateral aid from OECD-DAC, roughly $48.7 billion, focused on gender equality and women's empowerment. Slightly less than $4 billion was dedicated to the MENA region in 2018 (OECD, 2020a) (Fig. 3.1).

As one of the largest sources of external development financing, the World Bank and Bretton Woods institutions as well as regional development banks play a central role in promoting the norms and imagery

---

[6] As quoted by Inglehart and Norris (2009: 65).

[7] The Beijing Platform called for direct government participation in diverting resources to and creating a supportive environment for the complete inclusion of women into public society with the aid of women's NGOs, feminist groups, and the private sector—the first clear international promotion of gender mainstreaming (United Nations, 1995).

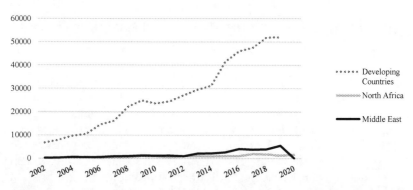

**Fig. 3.1** OECD-DAC Aid to Programs Targeting Gender Equality 2002–2020 (in millions of US Dollars) (*Sources:* OECD.Stat Database, 2022)

associated with progressive economic and political outcomes in the 'developing' world (Finnemore, 1996). The World Bank's focus on building 'human capital' through the Millennium Development Goals, and later through the Sustainable Development Goals, benefited the promotion of women and standardized gender mainstreaming as a best practice in much of the MENA and beyond (Finnemore, 1996). Today, the World Bank's portal actively touts the expected monetary benefits of improving gender equality: 'Women in all countries face earnings gaps. If women could have the same lifetime earnings as men, global wealth could increase by $172 trillion, and human capital wealth could increase by about one fifth globally' (Wodon et al., 2020; World Bank, 2020).

A quick look at women-specific projects coordinated by the IGO from the early 2000s through 2013 shows significant programming in the Arab world. Since the 1990s and especially in the new millennium, there has been a veritable wave of gender-related funding flooding the MENA. Jordanian scholar and women's activist Amal Sabbagh was more direct in her assessment of how such initiatives have shifted the attentions of Arab governments toward women's issues:

> [T]hey are being told, bluntly [by multilateral agencies to focus on women] … Jordan always likes to say that we are a modern Arab state. We are saying that to the West again, not just to get the money. We like to think

of ourselves as such, but you just scratch the surface ... [for example] with the infamous Middle East Partnership Initiative, with one of its main pillars as women's rights, the whole world changes.[8]

When I interviewed Sabbagh in 2008, we were discussing questions of women's political participation in Jordan. Sabbagh was fairly skeptical about the substance of women's entry into the political arena, especially considering the weak institutionalization of parties in Jordan. Our conversation was very much in line with earlier work she had published in which she excoriates political parties for being worse at female tokenism than even the Jordanian state (Sabbagh, 2005).

Sabbagh's words regarding the Middle East Partnership Initiative (MEPI), and aid-sponsored gender initiatives more broadly, reflect the power and reach of these measures at the time, and their role in externally pushing for more women's representation at the national and local levels. In Jordan and elsewhere, this was often done through encouraging the adoption of gender quotas and by training female political candidates and social organizers, thereby building a substantial technocratic 'women's empowerment' elite across a slew of states that included Morocco, Egypt, Yemen, Lebanon, the Palestinian Territories, and even Bahrain at the time (Bush, 2011; Welborne, 2010).[9] The National Democratic Institute (NDI) and the International Republican Institute (IRI), American development contractors ubiquitous in the region, were both active in offering services and workshops to professionalize elected female parliamentarians in Jordan and Morocco, and consulting on the electoral campaigns of female candidates. The United Nations Development Programme (UNDP) purportedly even dedicated some 600,000 Bahraini dinars ($1.6 million) to sponsoring women's political campaigns in the 2003 parliamentary election—the first to feature women as candidates (Sidhu & Meena, 2007; UNDP, 2014).

The international development community and the Moroccan government were so close that back in 2009, a gender-mainstreaming coordinator for the German GONGO, die Gemeinschaft fur Technische Entwicklung (GTZ), said that the organization's Moroccan satellite office was housed *inside* the Moroccan Ministry of Solidarity, Women, Family,

---

[8] Author interview, Amman, Jordan. December 2008.

[9] In the last two decades, NDI has expanded its operations to Saudi Arabia, Libya, Syria, and Tunisia.

## 66    B. C. WELBORNE

and Social Development in Rabat.[10] At the time, the ministry was run by Nouzha Skalli, a Socialist Union of Political Forces (USFP) stalwart and well-known women's activist. A roughly similar arrangement existed in Jordan between the UNDP and the *Majles al-Nawab* (House of Representatives) with the Parliament building effectively hosting an in-house UNDP office. In the words of a local civil servant I interviewed in Amman at the time:

> Yeah, the UNDP contacted the speaker [of the Parliament] and the secretary general and they offered some programs or something like that to the parliament and the speaker ... they [the UNDP] talked to the speaker about their target and he agreed to give them an office here.[11]

When I observed that there might be a conflict of interest when housing an IGO with a dedicated national agenda within the Parliament building, my respondent ventured:

> You know, because they [are] coming from the UNDP, not a private organization, the UNDP [is allowed to have an] office in the parliament. And specialize on the women's issue and the NGOs issue ... it seems there's some sort of agreement for the UN to coordinate with the parliament activities, for the deputies, there are funds provided by the UN to carry out training workshops, to upgrade the level of deputies and stuff like that in various ways. Um, women's participation, blah blah blah ...

Another Jordanian official working with the House of Representative's unit for parliamentary affairs observed that USAID also had offices in the parliamentary building at the time.[12]

In the Moroccan case, my GTZ contact mentioned how other ministries were actively contacting her office in the Ministry of Solidarity, Women, Family, and Social Development to enquire how their own departments could be more women-friendly and perhaps attract some external financial support. At the time, these ministries were populated by socialist party acolytes from the Party of Progress and Socialism (PSS) and the USFP. Today, the Islamist Party of Justice and Development (PJD)

---

[10] Author interview, Rabat, Morocco. November 2009.

[11] Author interview, Amman, Jordan. April 2009.

[12] Author interview, Amman, Jordan. April 2009.

rules the roost. Interestingly, my GTZ counterpart somewhat predicted this turn of events, observing how only PJD women showed up to the candidate-training workshops the ministry hosted in partnership with Western development contractors and GONGOs. Then-minister Nouzha Skalli had requested that GTZ, along with NDI and IRI, hold campaign workshops for women running for municipal office in 2009.[13] None of the female candidates from the reigning USFP or the PSS showed up to the training sessions, but the PJD was there in full force and parlayed these strategies into success, winning a parliamentary mandate in 2011 and continuing to dominate politics until this day. This is likely due in no small part to the PJD women's taking advantage of municipal and national gender quotas that initially gave the party a foothold in parliamentary politics, relative to the more established USFP and the republican *Istiqlal* parties.

A Moroccan interview subject who ran an NGO in Fes posited, 'The government is conforming to U.S. and E.U. pressure as a means [a guarantor] to overcoming terrorism; it's a way to control Islam in Morocco'.[14] These close ties have often cost women parliamentarians— and the political parties that affiliate with international organizations and Western development contractors—their public audience. Sabbagh mentioned how the Islamic Action Front (IAF) in Jordan had been skewered in the Jordanian press when it turned out they had been cooperating with NDI on the campaign trail, despite their denial of close ties to foreign organizations: 'The newspapers really ripped the IAF apart, look at them ... they make themselves look like they don't deal with the Americans and now they cooperate with the NDI. ... it was a big scandal'.

If the push by foreign donors has led to more Arab regimes' embracing a new variant of aid-dependent state feminism by hook or by crook, it

---

[13] A sub-national gender quota, introduced in 2008 in anticipation of the local elections, created a 12 percent quota for communal elections through 'additional electoral constituencies' in urban and rural communities and districts (Articles 204[1] and [2] of the electoral code) and a 'support fund for the promotion of women representativeness' (Article 288). Although not explicit in the electoral law, there was a national consensus that these seats would be reserved for women. As a result, women's representation increased from 0.6 percent to 12.3 percent in the 2009 local government elections. In the next local elections, the 2011 law on the election of council members of local authorities—reserving seats for women in regional, communal and district councils—was applied (IDEA, n.d.).

[14] Author interview, Fes, Morocco. July 2008.

has also galvanized an 'NGO-ization' of women's movements across the entire MENA region, and it is not altogether clear that this is a positive development. There has been a state-backed push to standardize this type of lucrative gender advocacy, whether through the creation of umbrella organizations (the ubiquitous GONGOs and RONGOs common in the region) regulating women's activism and agency, or by instituting ministries for women's and/or social affairs to co-opt and steer this advocacy. These institutions are often led by women who have experience in civil society organizations (CSOs) and ties to the international community, either through work with development contractors or through other foreign development agencies that play (intentional and unintentional) roles in 'corporatizing'—but also professionalizing—this kind of work.

Sabbagh, who is also the former general secretary of a prominent GONGO—the Jordanian National Commission for Women (JNCW)—spoke to the perverse incentives galvanized by donor interests in the women's NGO community: 'If there is money, of course all of them [women's NGOs] will jump to that. Some of them even change their bio to include new areas of interest, just to be able to get some funding'. Many of my interview subjects noted that there was a substantial amount of duplication of development projects, a critique often lobbed by William Easterly and other scholars critical of foreign aid (Easterly & Williamson, 2011). Essentially, the complaint states that the lack of donor specialization impedes effectiveness at the ground level and leads the NGO community to focus its programming on whatever agenda the donor community is promoting at a given moment, neglecting other much-needed interventions. This results in a multiplicity of redundant projects, and was very common in the women's CSO and NGO community. In 2008, this redundant programming in Jordan centered around the issue of combating breast cancer, which affected a relatively small section of the population but dominated much of the rhetoric surrounding women's empowerment (Abdel-Razeq et al., 2020).

When it came to aid disbursement, Sabbagh commented, donors were not innocent, and would often reify existing practices through blatant favoritism of certain women's NGOs:

> They [foreign donors] were very selective in overseeing. Some of them would accept anything from them. Others, they would really go with them

3 FOREIGN AID AND VIRTUE SIGNALING 69

> to get [the last] 0.00000001 cent in the financial report ... I'm not saying that the donors are angels. The donors have the dirty games too ... They talk about our government being full of favoritism, you just look at their systems!

She elaborated on how this applied to the female parliamentarians that Western donors endorsed:

> Some of them come with romantic ideas ... for many people in the West they have this romantic ideal, for example they never could think that Toujan[15] had her own drawbacks when she was in parliament. Me, being a Jordanian, I could see both aspects. So you have the same thing applying to women's NGOs.

Alongside the drive to cater to foreign donors' agendas, the incentives to duplicate projects and programming also spurred a substantial amount of competition among the women's NGOs—a narrative that my interview subjects in Bahrain and Morocco also shared. Sabbagh mentioned this in our conversation, but also highlighted that most of the Jordanian women's NGOs did not directly view the JNCW as their primary competitor—more as their patron.

> Yes, [there is] unhealthy competitiveness, absolutely. However, I would say at least during my eight years at JNCW I never thought of the women NGOs as competitors, honestly, because the JNCW is different. We don't have any grassroots, we just have our board and secretariat, and we have to work with everybody. Otherwise, we should not exist. Of course, some of them, maybe the Jordanian Women's Union, thought we were cooperating with everybody. I have to say with everybody across the board. I never considered that they were competitors, [but] I could see the competition between them ...

The Jordanian parliamentary affairs official I interviewed highlighted how the parliamentary representatives, especially the men, distrusted women's NGOs they saw as being 'owned by foreign interests'[16]:

---

[15] Toujan Faisal was the first woman to be elected to the Jordanian parliament after it resumed operations in 1993. She was elected through the Circassian quota.

[16] Author interview, Amman, Jordan. April 2009.

> [T]he parliamentarians in Jordan until now, they don't have good idea about the NGOs. They thought the NGOs have the financial aid from outside, they have their own agenda, you know, it's difficult for the people who don't know about the NGOs and about how they are working ... I have to clarify the NGOs' work to the parliamentarian.

This same individual ventured that some of the distrust between the parliamentarians and women's NGOs at the time might have stemmed from the fact that most well-known NGOs and CSOs were housed in Amman at the expense of other communities.

> ... all the women organizations working in Jordan are working in Amman, they are sent [to] Amman and the women who work for this organization are from Amman. So [there is] nobody from outside of Amman ... But the women who are elected to be a member of the parliament are [from] outside of Amman. There is no communication ... between them.

This official also noted common complaints by parliamentarians that NGOs, and even women parliamentarians' agendas, 'came from the outside', with many male representatives opining that they 'want to change our customs, they want to change our community, because they have the money from outside, they want to make our community like the European or American or Australian ... They are like the enemy'.

The recent work of Marwa Shalaby and Sarah Elimam (2020a, 2020b) on bias against women parliamentarians in legislative committee assignments speaks to some of the formal and informal prejudices elected women face when trying to influence politics. They show that across Algeria, Morocco, Tunisia, and Jordan, women have been systematically excluded from influential legislative committees dealing with security, financial, or technical issues, but meanwhile are often over-represented in committees focused around social issues—particularly those dealing with women and the family. They also find that the adoption of gender quotas has resulted in a durable increase in the number of women legislators, including more women in influential committees, over time. These findings indicate the institutional mechanisms necessary to overcome some of the biases against women reflected in the interview excerpts I have presented here. Shalaby and Elimam also show that women are often excluded from committees with an international focus, which may speak to some male legislators' underlying fears that women are stooges, or worse, of the international community.

## Virtue Signaling and Women's Representation

When I conducted interviews in Jordan back in 2008 and 2009, as with Morocco and elsewhere, aid-galvanized *state feminism* was in full force. This was evident in conversations with another foreign NGO official I spoke with, who was working with the World Bank and the Jordanian government on a three-year project to increase women's presence in the Jordanian workforce.[17] It was telling that in a discussion of the groups involved, my interview subject neglected to mention the 'targeted' community of college-attending women as *key* to the project, alongside the requisite 'representatives from government ministries, ... JNCW, various NGOs'.[18] Sometimes it felt like the women's empowerment 'machinery' in Jordan—and in Morocco—had a life of its own, beyond the women who were supposed to benefit from these interventions. Certainly, many educated, middle-class women obtained jobs and, of course, there were the ubiquitous hires across multiple government agencies engaged in the country's vision to 'operationalize' gender mainstreaming in all ministries.

There has always been a question of what motivation underlies these sweeping interventions. As many of the comments from NGO and state officials hint at, even the people involved in adopting gender-related reforms often felt they were disingenuous and driven by reputational concerns. It is fascinating that gender has been incorporated into so much of the 'branding' of the modern state in the post-Cold-War world—especially as a potential indicator of stability and democratization. As we saw earlier in this book, Judith Kelley's work on 'scorecard diplomacy' illuminates the importance of international reputation for electoral autocracies and highlights some of the more tangible, and often financial, benefits available to regimes that engage in institutional virtue signaling—especially surrounding elections and electoral outcomes.

Gender-focused researchers such as Drude Dahlerup and Yuree Noh have also shown autocracies to be more likely to adopt gender quotas

---

[17] Author interview, Amman, Jordan. April 2009.

[18] This is very much a sore spot for the Jordanian government in terms of its achievements related to women's empowerment. In 2019, Jordan's rate of women's labor force participation was the world's fourth lowest, holding fast at 15 percent since 1990. See Kasoolu et al. (2019) and ILO (n.d.).

more so than other regime types, while Sarah Bush and Par Zetterburg directly unpack the link between the adoption of gender quotas and tangible benefits from 'enhanced international reputation'—namely, a greater likelihood of obtaining foreign aid from major donor states such as Sweden and the United States (Bush & Zetterberg, 2021; Dahlerup, 2007; Hughes et al., 2015; Noh, 2019). Bush and Zetterburg's findings suggest that 'some citizens view women's representation as a necessary condition for democracy in other countries', which by extension could influence the foreign aid regime prevalent in a donor country. Extant research has shown similar logic and outcomes for electoral autocracies embracing women's rights more broadly (Htun & Weldon, 2018; Tripp, 2019). All in all, this scholarship hints at 'sympathy' extended to electoral autocracies' embracing what are often seen initially as cosmetic changes, driven by gender rentierism as a variant of market feminism, if you will.

That said, there is some evidence that gender reform measures seem to be yielding substantive changes, largely because of pre-existing women's movements that can directly benefit from them or leverage international contacts for agenda-setting and to hold governments accountable. Aili Tripp's (2019) latest research showcases the powerful role of the long-standing and tireless mobilizing of regional and international women's advocacy networks and the changes they have brought about for the women of the MENA—first, in creating fertile opportunities for legislative reforms that create space for women to join the electoral arena, and second, in pushing for gender-related reforms such as changes to family codes and criminalizing sexual harassment, domestic violence, and rape. Many of these changes have been contingent on an increase in the number of women representatives in national parliaments, with 30 percent female representation ostensibly connoting somewhat of a tipping point in women's ability to present relevant legislation on the parliamentary floor (see Dahlerup, 1988; Kanter, 1977).[19] On the flip side, many have argued the importance of considering 'who is composing' that 30 percent and whether they are, in fact, introducing women-friendly legislation (Childs & Krook, 2008).

---

[19] In 1995, the UN Economic and Social Council (ECOSOC) endorsed a 30 percent target of women participation at decision-making levels, while in 1997 the Southern African Development Community (SADC) formulated and adopted the 'Declaration on Gender and Development', which included a commitment to a 30 percent quota of women in political decision-making bodies by 2005.

I want to qualify that a *tipping point* in the context of authoritarian regimes in the Middle East is a tricky proposition, especially when it comes to women's mobilization for enhanced parliamentary access and substantive change. Lisa Baldez's (2002) work on women's mobilization in Chile, at a time when the regime was transitioning to democracy, can be instructive in this case. I invoke the idea of a tipping point here as a moment when 'political entrepreneurs frame the need for mobilization in terms that resonate with an array of people, at a particular point in time' (Baldez, 2002: 6).

Following Thomas Schelling (1978), the Nobel-prize-winning economist behind the conceit of the tipping point, the probability that individuals—in this case parliamentary representatives—would participate in promoting a certain piece of legislation is contingent on the likelihood that the Member of Parliament (MP) in question would perceive others as likely or ready to participate. Essentially, the tipping point occurs when people—in this case, male representatives—are likely to perceive their action as necessary or even 'required, driven by the notion of how their position or decision to participate hinges on their beliefs about what others expect' (Baldez, 2002; Chong, 1991). Increasingly, international norms promoting gender equality are part of that calculation, even for a tribal elected body dominated by patron–client relationships, as in the case of Jordan. These MPs can still appreciate Jordan's importance as an aid-rentier state. Gender quotas are one such example of the tipping-point logic working in the context of a legislature's decision-making.

Civil society, the state, and international as well as transnational organizations—usually working in tandem—tend to be the primary actors conditioning gender quota adoption (Krook & Hall, 2009). Grassroots women's organizations often see quotas as a mechanism to increase and institutionalize gender representation. Certainly, political elites recognize the strategic value of quotas for inter-party or coalition advantage (Tripp, 2003). Quotas are also promulgated through international norms and transnational sharing of ideas and information (True & Mintrom, 2001). Similar factors influence quota adoption in the Arab world, with some important nuances. Islam and conservative tribal culture have a role in conditioning the acceptance of women in the political arena and any associated institutional changes (Donno & Russett, 2004; Fish, 2002; Lewis, 2002). Yet opposition to gender quotas comes from secular feminists and Islamists alike, the first criticizing the policy as cosmetic, and the latter

## 74    B. C. WELBORNE

tending to attack the injustice of quotas as privileging a specific group, especially when that group represents women.

Finally, gender quotas have often been inspired or at least sanctioned by Arab monarchs, such as King Abdullah of Jordan or King Mohammad VI of Morocco, or dictators, such as Tunisian President Zine el Abidine Ben Ali, who are interested in currying favor with international donors and investors by showcasing their 'progressive' values. Consequently, this policy usually represents a top-down decision brokered by the state (*state feminism*), rather than a response to legitimate social pressures (Brand, 1998; Sabbagh, 2007).

David Assaf and Stephanie Nanes (2011) investigated the Millennium Challenge Corporation's (MCC) pressuring of the Jordanian government to adopt municipal gender quotas back in 2007, in exchange for $25 million in aid, showcasing the powerful sway of foreign donors. They detail how a USAID official acknowledged that the municipal gender quota was a 'conditioned precedent' for Jordan to qualify for the MCC's Threshold program, which would offer up even more promised financial disbursements, including a possibility to qualify for the Compact program, a goal which Jordan ultimately achieved (ibid.: 285). At that time as today, the country was the fourth largest recipient of U.S. foreign aid, to the tune of about $1.6 billion per year—roughly four percent of Jordan's GDP. These and other funds have had a none-too-subtle impact, not only on the Jordanian government's ability to keep the country financially and politically stable (Peters & Moore, 2009),[20] but also on its ability to slowly change the social fabric from the top-down through GONGOs, RONGOs, and CSOs gunning for women's rights.

Laurie Brand's (1998) work introduces us to this newer neoliberal variant of state feminism emerging in Jordan and Morocco during the early 2000s—a variant in which top-down changes in gender relations are often galvanized by international pressure and foreign conditional aid. Mervat Hatem's (1992, 1994) scholarship, in contrast, highlights the state feminisms of yore, in which the audience was equal parts local and international—with the 'virtue' signaling largely from states (such as Egypt, Algeria, and Tunisia) to their own populations, who were newly decolonized and looking for some semblance of a 'modern' and 'industrialized' identity. The changing of gender relations fit this goal, as it had

---

[20] Princess Basma's many charitable enterprises come to mind.

with the president Mustapha Kemal Ataturk in re-conceptualizing and re-institutionalizing gender relations in a newly formed Turkish Republic back in the 1920s.

We really see the impact of foreign aid as part of *a new brand of state feminism* when we compare women's status in Morocco and Lebanon. Morocco has always had more female political representation and gender-related policy reform, despite Lebanon's media image of being more urbane. Until recently, Lebanon has had the reputation for being one of the few transitioning or quasi-democratic regimes in the MENA alongside Tunisia, and Lebanese women won the right to vote and participated in national elections as early as 1952, a decade before Morocco (1963). Even public awareness of gender-related issues was substantially higher in Lebanon than in Morocco up until the last ten years (Abdul-Latif & Serpe, 2010). However, only 17 women had *ever* served in Lebanon's parliament before the 2018 elections (ibid.).

Morocco, conversely, is a constitutional monarchy with some of the world's highest rates of illiteracy across genders, yet it has experienced greater levels of women's political representation and economic participation over the last two decades, especially compared with Lebanon (Tripp, 2019). Currently, Morocco has 34 women parliamentarians out of a total of 325, 30 of whom were elected via a legislated gender quota adopted in 2002. Furthermore, Morocco's *Moudawana* reforms have been hailed as a landmark example of gender policy reform because of their progressive content and the grassroots nature of the movements that put the proposal on the government's agenda.[21]

Certainly, international pressures for 'reform' exerted through the higher levels of conditional aid present in Morocco relative to Lebanon have played a seminal role in upholding this progress.[22] Morocco has received much greater levels of targeted development assistance from the multilateral community than Lebanon over the past two decades.

---

[21] The *Moudawana* law is a revision of Morocco's family code passed by the Moroccan Parliament in 2004 granting women substantial rights vis-à-vis their spouses. Women are now allowed to obtain and dispute a divorce on equal terms in civil courts, polygamy has been circumscribed, the legal age of marriage was raised to 18 from 15, sexual harassment is now an offense punishable by law, and so on.

[22] These strategies can also be seen as byproducts of Arab governments' attempts to attain 'democracy' benchmarks set by the World Bank, the United Nations, and other high-profile international organizations, as well as donor governments, rather than bids to truly enfranchise women.

Lebanon's insulation from such pressures—whether through GCC-backed investments and substantial remittances from its more affluent diaspora community in the West—may have inured it somewhat from following global trends related to women's empowerment (Welborne, 2010). These aid disbursement patterns remained steady until 2004, when foreign aid to both countries rose. Shortly thereafter, in 2005, the idea of implementing a gender quota emerged as a central topic of Lebanese parliamentary and cabinet debate. That year, a national commission drafted a new electoral law recommending a 20 percent gender quota for the legislative assembly, which was subsequently rejected by the legislative and executive offices. Considering Lebanon's current financial crisis and the greater role IGOs are likely to play in bailing it out financially, it will be interesting to see whether gender equality gets put on the agenda of the Lebanese regime yet again, but more forcefully.

The renewed discussion of a gender quota following Lebanon's 2018 elections and Morocco's decision to adopt a legislated quota were not accidental developments. These significant shifts in election policy are motivated by the increasing financial pressures from abroad, requiring ostensibly credible commitments to democratization, in some cases via women's empowerment.[23] As I intimated earlier, there is some evidence that this external pressure to improve gender equality at least in the political realm works. Mina Baliamoune-Lutz (2016) finds that ODA sent to women's organizations was effective, overall, at increasing women's legislative representation from 2000 through 2010 across the MENA region, highlighting the independent effect of an increase of $200 in ODA per 1000 people, which raised the percentage of women in office by three points.[24] Baliamoune-Lutz is likely also capturing the independent effect of gender quotas in bumping up women's representation, as documented in Bush's (2011) work. Between Baliamoune-Lutz's results

[23] These relationships reverse when considering ODA on a per capita basis, with Lebanon receiving substantially more aid per person than Morocco due to its smaller population. However, the aid that is disbursed in Morocco goes a lot further, considering the relative per capita incomes adjusted for purchasing power parity (PPP) in each country (Morocco's ranges from $3000 to $5000, on average, while Lebanon's from $11,000 to $15,000 according to the most recent data from the IMF). Still, that the overall rising patterns strategically convene around the 2000s, when the global gender agenda comes into its own, hints that these results are not accidental.

[24] She uses an interaction term between ODA and the presence of a women's organization to capture this.

and Bush's scholarship on gender quotas, there is some reason for optimism about the potential positive impact of ODA on women's political empowerment in the MENA region specifically.

Krook and O'Brien (2010) ventured that more than three quarters of proposals to adopt gender quotas in the early years of the new millennium directly followed the rise of *gender mainstreaming* that began with the United Nations' Fourth World Conference for Women in 1995 through to the Millennium Summit in 2000 (Hafner-Burton & Pollack, 2002; Krook & True, 2008). Noted quota scholar Drude Dahlerup (2003) believes a country's international image has become more important across international and national contexts, pushing countries to market themselves as modern and innovative, with women's empowerment quickly becoming a popular and timely way to promote just such an image to the world. Furthermore, the Beijing Conference goals (1995) and the Millennium Development Goals (2000) explicitly promoted the idea of women's importance for economic development. This new rhetoric rapidly created an economic incentive to institutionally incorporate women into the political systems of countries with less than stellar reputations for upholding women's rights. *The Economist* pointed this out in the early 2000s with a tongue-in-cheek observation: 'Around 110 countries have rules helping women get elected, joined in recent years by such feminist-friendly places as Afghanistan, Iraq and Sudan' (*The Economist*, 2008).

Ironically, these demands to signal a commitment to democratization through gender equality via the adoption of gender quotas and increases in women's political participation come at a time when many authoritarian regimes have better records, numerically, in promoting women's representation than quite a few Western democracies (see Jamal, 2010; Mervis & Nyemba, 2013; Noh, 2019; Tripp, 2019). Democracy is not synonymous with women's equal representation in political institutions, nor has it translated into women's equal participation (Mervis & Nyemba, 2013: 174). And although foreign aid is not usually allocated to women's electoral campaigns , it does finance the structural support that allows them to overcome some of the biggest obstacles to running for office, especially when the aid funds women's organizations focused on political participation.

## 78    B. C. WELBORNE

We see similar 'coincidences' across the entire region over the past two decades, as women's empowerment and gender-related reforms are seen as a 'low political cost' formula to satisfy donors eager to deradicalize and democratize states without initiating the political reforms that might destabilize a regime (such as widely unpopular gender-related reforms to family code, personal status laws, and nationality laws). Essentially, adopting gender quotas appeared to be the least costly measure to satisfy many a donor's notion of reform (Assaf & Nanes, 2011: 286).

Grassroots promotion of gender quotas does exist. Local women's organizations partnering with transnational women's networks have promoted legislative gender quotas in Morocco, Egypt, Tunisia, Lebanon, Jordan, Sudan, and even Yemen. Unsurprisingly, these countries all receive significant levels of ODA, but are also heavy remittance recipients.[25] Party elites often promote quotas to expand voter share in a bid for earmarked funding from international NGOs and national governments, to bandwagon with other parties once such reforms are implemented, or to revamp a stale image, as was the case in Morocco and Algeria. Where prominent left-wing parties exist (Algeria, Yemen, and Morocco), they have promoted gender quotas as measures to attain social equality both within the party apparatus and beyond, as in the West.[26]

Regimes often use women's quotas to sideline Islamist interests (Tripp & Kang, 2008). Despite initial opposition, Islamic parties tend to be some of the most successful actors in parlaying gender quotas toward greater Islamist representation in legislative assemblies, as in the case of the Jordanian Islamic Action Front, with MP Hayat Massimi and the Moroccan Parti de la Justice et du Développement and their most notorious MP, Bassima Hakaoui (Shitrit, 2016). In Iraq, we saw gender quotas institutionally imposed by international actors; however, women rose to the occasion, actively campaigned, and won seats even beyond the quota in some districts during the 2010 parliamentary elections.

As Stephanie Nanes (2010) showcases in her work, the ability to engage in 'public service provision' is the gold standard of politics and political influence in many Arab countries. In Nanes' interview with

---

[25] For development assistance, see Carapico (2002, 2013) and Schwedler (2002).

[26] The *Union Socialiste des Forces Populaires* of Morocco has five women on its 21-member central board via an internal quota. The Yemeni Socialist Party has an internal quota mandating 30 percent of candidates must be women. *Front de Llibération Nationale* of Algeria mandates two out of the first five names on a candidate list must be women.

municipal councilors at the time one council member aptly described women as being part of *qarda wa dayn*, which literally translates as 'loan and debt'. This is the set of exchange relations that define local politics in Jordan. Women were increasingly seen as capable political agents, since male and female constituents come to female councilors to get help with municipal business (Nanes, 2010: 12). In my own experience in Jordan, this talent was duly rewarded in women and men. Falaak Jamani, the first woman directly elected to the Jordanian Lower House, was adept at taking care of her constituents, helping build a new school here and a hospital there, ensuring someone's education was paid for or their unemployed status resolved. She won her first mandate for the district of Kerak in 2003 and was re-elected in a landslide victory in 2007. Integral to her skill were her status as a general in the military's health division and her ability to place people in jobs in the military and the health sector. She had the support of her tribe and was even invited to a sitting of the all-male tribal *diwan* (council) as a full-fledged member and contributor. During my interview with her, I was amazed at the diversity of individuals lined up outside of her office in the Parliament, hoping she would intercede on their behalf.[27] Invariably many requests were private and direct, from helping a son get into university or attain a military post to directly paying off hospital bills.

Yet, it is questionable whether Jamani would have gotten her foot in the door without King Abdullah's pushing for the adoption of a legislative quota for women in 2003. The measure was extremely unpopular at the time and commonly seen as being foisted on the king from abroad. With this in mind, it becomes even more curious from where the incentives to integrate women into politics arose at the time, since they represented a controversial issue for an often restive and deeply conservative public. In my interview with a female Islamist politician in Bahrain, she ventured, 'The West is pushing this agenda [women's empowerment], not the Arabs'.[28]

---

[27] Author interview, Amman, Jordan. September 2008. I recall it being a longer line than those outside other parliamentarians' offices, but perhaps it was a slow day for the other MPs.

[28] Author interview, Manama, Bahrain. July 2009.

# Foreign Aid and the Push to End Violence Against Women

*We are facing a phenomenon [sexual harassment] that is limiting women's right to move ... and is threatening women's participation in all walks of life.*

In the quote above, Neda Khomsan—an Egyptian activist—is speaking to the problem of *taharrush* (sexual harassment) in her home country, linking it eloquently to the political (Abdelmonem, 2015; Deeb, 2009). Sexual harassment is so pervasive in Egypt that some see it as having single-handedly reinvigorated the Egyptian feminist movement in the wake of the Arab Spring (Al-Ali, 2014; Moghadam, 2012). Reported sexual assaults during Arab Spring protests further highlighted the problem of violence against women, even spurring the formation of vigilante groups aimed at punishing street harassers in Egypt and the creation of the HarassMap app to track the whereabouts of offenders (Abdelmonem, 2015; Fadel, 2012; Human Rights Watch, 2013).

Although studies have hinted at the alarming scale of sexual harassment, sexual assault, and intimate partner violence in the MENA, exhaustive regional studies are few and far between (Boy & Kulcyzcki, 2008; Khomsan, 2009). Still, countrywide surveys in the last decade revealed that some 90 percent of Yemeni women, 83 percent of Egyptian women, and 30 percent of Lebanese women had reported being harassed in the street (Deeb, 2009). In more recent surveys conducted by the United Nations, some 33.7 percent of Egyptian women respondents claimed they had been victims of intimate partner violence, while 47.4 percent claimed they had been victims of physical violence over their lifetime (UN Women, 2011). In Jordan, 32 percent of women reported having been exposed to physical violence over their lifetime, while an astonishing 62.8 percent of Moroccan women maintained they had been victims of physical and/or sexual violence (UN Women, 2011). According to Žvan Elliott (2015) and Yassine (2009), the majority of Moroccan women filing for divorce cited domestic violence as the primary reason, partially in a bid to avoid reporting intimate partner violence as a crime, which would come with additional social stigma.

For all the complaints about gender quotas and accusations that elected women are therefore status quo operators at best, there is some evidence that the increase in women's legislative representation has spurred more opportunities for agenda-setting on women's issues in Arab parliaments, particularly around violence against women. Contemporary changes pertaining to 'rape laws' in a number of countries are partially attributed to the increasing number of women representatives in the national assemblies of Jordan, Tunisia, and Morocco, in conjunction with decades of lobbying by local women's NGOs and pressure from the international aid community.[29] Essentially, these 'marry your rapist' laws state that an individual convicted of rape can be acquitted if he marries the presumably female victim.[30] Extant research has shown that in most cases, these laws are actually colonial artifacts of either the French Napoleonic Code of 1810 or the Ottoman Code of 1911, rather than Islamic laws per se (Begum, 2017).

Consequently, a key argument of critics has been that the laws are not even 'indigenous' to the region. Jordan, Lebanon, and Tunisia made news in 2017 with parliamentary decisions to amend or fully repeal such laws, with Iraq recently announcing it would follow suit.[31] Even though Egypt fully repealed its own controversial rape law in 1999 and passed laws criminalizing sexual harassment in 2014,[32] it still has a reputation for ubiquitous sexual harassment for both local and foreign women (Al Jazeera, 2014b).[33]

The recent push by IGOs to highlight domestic or intimate partner violence has further bolstered this agenda and put some real (foreign) financial incentives behind it. For example, a few of my interlocutors in Morocco cited the multi-year Spotlight Initiative—launched in 2017

---

[29] Lebanon is the outlier here, since its national assembly hosts only four female MPs—the lowest percentage in the Levant—despite a reputation for progressivism and innovation in the region (Luck, 2017).

[30] If an underage male is abducted or raped, the offense is punishable by a fine and two to five years in prison. In the case where a female minor is abducted, raped, and/or married without the consent of her parents, the perpetrator cannot be prosecuted unless the courts annul the marriage with the consent of the parents (Mesbahi, 2018: 53).

[31] Article 308, 98 in Jordan was repealed in 2017. Article 522 was repealed in Lebanon in 2017. Tunisia repealed article 227 in 2017 and Morocco took steps to amend article 475 in 2014.

[32] Article 291 of the Egyptian penal code.

[33] The U.S. State Department issues special travel warnings for women visiting Egypt and Morocco, warning them against the likelihood of sexual harassment and physical assault, especially when traveling alone. See Thomas (2018).

by the United Nations and the European Union to eliminate violence against women worldwide—as partially inspiring greater efforts to legislate against domestic violence and sexual harassment in the kingdom (United Nations, 2017).[34] Some 500 million euros have already been committed to projects geared at raising awareness and combating factors that contribute to such violence, especially in the Global South. The initiative is also seen as contributing to the agenda of the 2030 Sustainable Development Goals.

In Morocco, alongside the push from IGOs, the galvanizing event to change the existing rape law was the suicide of Moroccan teenager, Amina Filali, in 2012 (Mesbahi, 2018). Filali killed herself by ingesting rat poison after the judge presiding over her case ruled that per clause 475 of the Moroccan criminal code, she would have to marry the man she alleged to have raped her. As a minor, Filali might have refused this outcome, but her father or guardian would have been entitled to accept the ruling on her behalf. She rejected this fate and took matters into her own hands. Morocco amended its rapist amnesty law in 2014 in the wake of her tragic death after public pressure and protests, coordinated by feminist organizations, to repeal the antiquated legislation (Al Jazeera, 2014a).

That said, at last reading only a handful of Arab states had criminalized sexual harassment. Many have recently looked to criminalize domestic violence, and the majority of states do explicitly outlaw sexual assault and rape. Yet rape is often treated as a private offense (meaning the state cannot act without the consent of the complainant or her legal guardian) or an 'honor crime', and not as a violent crime in which the state is legally obligated to intervene. Furthermore, spousal rape is still not criminalized in any penal code in the region except Tunisia's (Kassem et al., 2014). Among the 22 Arab League member states, only Jordan, Tunisia, and Saudi Arabia offer specific legal protection for women against domestic violence (Al Jazeera, 2013; Roberts, 2017).

This raises the questions of how meaningful laws criminalizing violence against women are in the MENA states and whether their lack of 'teeth' is a byproduct of newer pedigree or problematic enforcement.[35] Although most Arab states have ratified or at least signed the Convention on the

---

[34] Informal author interview, Ifrane, Morocco. November, 2017.

[35] See the work of Žvan Elliott (2014) for the Moroccan case. The competing legal jurisdictions in terms of civil, shar'iah, and customary law represent an additional difficulty.

Elimination of Discrimination Against Women (CEDAW), most of these states also have reservations on family law, nationality law, and labor law, as well as 'suggested' levels for women's political participation claiming that related provisions in CEDAW challenge and marginalize local cultural mores.[36] The result of this combination of social mores, fears of compromising family honor, and a recalcitrant legal system choppily enforcing women's rights to legal protection is an environment that ultimately reduces women's outward mobility and sense of personal security, which has also been shown to result in electoral demobilization (Abdo-Katsipis, 2018).

## Conclusion

Foreign aid is often conceptualized as a coercive mechanism, more than a constructive one, for promoting desired policy outcomes outside of the fiscal and monetary realms in the Global South (Addison et al., 2005; Baliamoune-Lutz, 2013; Baliamoune-Lutz & Mavrotas, 2009; Dalgaard et al., 2004; Wright & Winters, 2010). The extensive literature chronicling the effect of external finance on reforms to public expenditures and even legal codes hints that conditionality could, and indeed does, partially extend to gender-related policy. Importantly, this is highly contingent on the type of monies in question and the level of conditionality. We must also consider the difference between aid coming from bilateral donors relative to multilateral donors, and whether donors are from the OECD-DAC or from elsewhere, even the Arab world.[37]

Conditional aid has been shown to have constructive effects in some cases, especially for increasing social expenditure relative to other types of public spending in recipient countries (Bienen & Gersovitz, 1985; Collier et al., 1997; Marchesi & Thomas, 1999; Przeworski & Vreeland, 2000; Williamson, 1983).ODA certainly has been cited as promoting the spread

---

[36] The exceptions are Sudan and Somalia.

[37] OECD-DAC now comprises 22 countries, namely the 15 member-countries of the European Union plus Norway, Switzerland, the United States, Canada, Japan, Australia, and New Zealand. The lead donors for the MENA are Kuwait, Saudi Arabia, and the UAE, with smaller donors such as Algeria, Libya, Iraq, and Qatar also hosting national aid agencies. Importantly, these national agencies may not be the ones through which Arab aid is actually channeled, but rather the national ministries of finance (Neumeyer, 2002).

of gender quotas, and has been associated with other measures encouraging women's empowerment.[38] Other types of external funding, such as multilateral loans or structural adjustment agreements from the International Monetary Fund (IMF), have a mixed legacy, often resulting in outcomes that constrained and compromised women's economic opportunities. This is not surprising, since one of the primary stipulations of IMF structural adjustment agreements was to cut public expenditures, and women are often disproportionately employed in the public sector—especially in MENA countries (Detraz & Peksen, 2016).

With the global economic fallout delivered by the 2008 financial crisis, the IMF revisited its prior advice on market regulation and capital controls to endorse these politics to a more limited extent (Chwieroth, 2013; Gallagher, 2014; Gallagher & Tian, 2014; Grabel, 2011). The COVID-19 pandemic has also galvanized a rethinking of the importance of public investment spending, especially in health, which could yet again shift structural adjustment agreement priorities in a direction that might benefit women in the long term (Tandberg & Allen, 2020). During the pandemic, however, we have seen the income vulnerabilities of MENA women in stark relief; it is questionable whether regional governments alone will be able to address those vulnerabilities (OECD, 2020b). With disproportionate numbers of women employed in the health sector and engaged in informal work, we can anticipate ever more women bumped out of the economy due to health complications related to COVID-19 and/or due to the prioritization of men as breadwinners, especially in the public sector.

Yet, this crisis offers an opportunity for the MENA to reimagine women's roles in society and the economy—especially with so many working as primary caregivers—and perhaps play an integral role in crafting post-COVID health and societal infrastructure. This will happen with or without aid, but with many foreign bilateral donors focused on their own domestic pandemic issues, MENA countries may have no choice but to turn inward and tap their skilled workforce, which in many parts of the region is increasingly female.

In the next chapter, we will explore how remittances as another form of rent with gendered effects impact the likelihood of that female workforce increasing, much less politically mobilizing. As we saw in Chapter 2,

---

[38] ODA is defined as loans that are at least 25 percent grant-based (OECD 2020b: 294).

the conventional wisdom is that the path to women's political participation flows from their economic participation. The adoption of gender quotas across the MENA, where women still comprise a small share of the formal workforce, turns that logic on its head. And although foreign aid as a form of conditional rent can accelerate cosmetic changes in political participation, women's access to the workforce is another matter entirely—delimited by official, market, and cultural interests. As we are about to see, remittances can play a not insubstantial role in mediating women's presence in the labor force.

## REFERENCES

Ababneh, S. (2020). The time to question, rethink and popularize the notion of 'Women's Issues': Lessons from Jordan's popular and labor movements from 2006 to now. *Journal of International Women's Studies, 21*(1), 271–288.

Abdo-Katsipis, C. B. (2018). Personal security and electoral demobilization: A comparative analysis. *Digest of Middle East Studies, 27*(1), 53–78.

Abdelmonem, A. (2015). Reconceptualizing sexual harassment in Egypt: A longitudinal assessment of el-Taharrush el-Ginsy in Arabic Online Forums and anti-sexual harassment activism. *Kohl: A Journal for Body and Gender Research, 1*(1), 24–41.

Abdel-Razeq, H., Mansour, A., & Jaddan, D. (2020). Breast cancer care in Jordan. *JCO Global Oncology, 6.* https://www.ncbi.nlm.nih.gov/pmc/art icles/PMC7051801/

Abdul-Latif, R., & Serpe, L. (2010). The status of women in the Middle East and North Africa: A grassroots research and advocacy approach. Preliminary findings from surveys in Lebanon and Morocco. Presented for the International Foundation for Electoral Systems at the WAPOR Conference 2010.

Addison, T., Mavrotas, G., & McGillivray, M. (2005). Development assistance and development finance: Evidence and global policy agendas. *Journal of International Development: The Journal of the Development Studies Association, 17*(6), 819–836.

Ahmed, F. Z. (2012). The perils of unearned foreign income: Aid, remittances, and government survival. *American Political Science Review, 106*(1), 146–165.

Al-Ali, N. (2014, February 14). Egyptian sexual harassment activists battle growing acceptance of violence. *The Conversation.* https://theconversation. com/egyptian-sexual-harassment-activists-battle-growing-acceptance-of-vio lence-23264

Al Jazeera. (2013, August 30). Saudi Arabia outlaws domestic violence. https://www.aljazeera.com/news/2013/8/30/saudi-arabia-outlaws-domestic-violence

Al Jazeera. (2014a, January 23). Morocco repeals 'rape marriage law'. https://www.aljazeera.com/news/2014/1/23/morocco-repeals-rape-marriage-law

Al Jazeera. (2014b, June 12). New law to end sexual harassment in Egypt. https://www.aljazeera.com/news/2014/6/12/new-law-to-end-sexual-harassment-in-egypt

Assaf, D., & Nanes, S. (2011). The women's quota in Jordan's municipal councils: International and domestic dimensions. *Journal of Women, Politics & Policy, 32*(4), 275–304.

Baldez, L. (2002). *Why women protest: Women's movements in Chile*. Cambridge University Press.

Baliamoune-Lutz, M. (2013). *The effectiveness of foreign aid to women's equality organizations in the MENA: Does aid promote women's political participation?* (WIDER Working Paper No. 2013/074).

Baliamoune-Lutz, M. (2016). The effectiveness of foreign aid to women's equality organisations in the MENA. *Journal of International Development, 28*(3), 320–341.

Baliamoune-Lutz, M., & Mavrotas, G. (2009). Aid effectiveness: Looking at the aid–social capital–growth nexus. *Review of Development Economics, 13*(3), 510–525.

Bauer, P. T. (1972). *Dissent on development: Studies and debates in development economics*. Harvard University Press.

Begum, R. (2017, August 24). *Middle East on a roll to repeal 'marry the rapist' laws*. Human Rights Watch. https://www.hrw.org/news/2017/08/24/middle-east-roll-repeal-marry-rapist-laws

Bienen, H. S., & Gersovitz, M. (1985). Economic stabilization, conditionality, and political stability. *International Organization, 39*(4), 729–754.

Boy, A., & Kulcyzcki, A. (2008). What we know about intimate partner violence in the Middle East and North Africa. *Violence Against Women, 14*(7), 53–70.

Brand, L. (1998). *Women, the state, and political liberalization: Middle Eastern and North African experiences*. Columbia University Press.

Burnside, C., & Dollar, D. (2000a). Aid, policies, and growth. *American Economic Review, 90*(4), 847–868.

Burnside, C., & Dollar, D. (2000b). Aid, growth, the incentive regime, and poverty reduction. *The World Bank: Structure and Policies, 3*(2), 200–227.

Bush, S. S. (2011). International politics and the spread of quotas for women in legislatures. *International Organization, 65*(1), 103–137.

Bush, S. S., & Zetterberg, P. (2021). Gender quotas and international reputation. *American Journal of Political Science, 65*(2), 326–341.

Carapico, S. (2002). Foreign aid for promoting democracy in the Arab world. *The Middle East Journal, 56*(3), 379–395.

Carapico, S. (2013). *Political aid and Arab activism: Democracy promotion, justice, and representation* (Vol. 44). Cambridge University Press.

Childs, S., & Krook, M. L. (2008). Theorizing women's political representation: Debates and innovations in empirical research. *Femina Politica–Zeitschrift für feministische Politikwissenschaft, 17*(2), 7–8.

Chong, D. (1991). *Collective action and the civil rights movement.* University of Chicago Press.

Chwieroth, J. M. (2013). Controlling capital: The IMF and transformational incremental change from within international organizations. *New Political Economy, 19*(3), 445–469.

Collier, P. (2008). *The bottom billion: Why the poorest countries are failing and what can be done about it.* Oxford University Press.

Collier, P., Guillamont, P., Guillamont, S., & Gunning, J. W. (1997). Redesigning conditionality. *World Development, 25*(9), 1399–1407.

Dahlerup, D. (1988). From a small to a large minority: Women in Scandinavian politics. *Scandinavian Political Studies, 11*(4), 275–298.

Dahlerup, D. (2003, November). Quotas are changing the history of women. In ponencia presentada en International Institute for Democracy and Electoral Assistance (IDEA)/Electoral Institute of Southern Africa (EISA)/Southern African Development Community (SADC), Parliamentary Forum Conference "*The Implementation of Quotas. African Experiences*". Pretoria, Sudáfrica (pp. 11–12).

Dahlerup, D. (2007). Electoral gender quotas: Between equality of opportunity and equality of result. *Representation, 43*(2), 73–92.

Dalgaard, C. J., Hansen, H., & Tarp, F. (2004). On the empirics of foreign aid and growth. *The Economic Journal, 114*(496), 191–216.

Deeb, S. (2009, December 17). *Sexual harassment across Arab world drives women inside.* http://www.cleveland.com/world/index.ssf/2009/12/sexual_harassment_across_arab.html

Detraz, N., & Peksen, D. (2016). The effect of IMF programs on women's economic and political rights. *International Interactions, 42*(1), 81–105.

Donno, D., & Russett, B. (2004). Islam, authoritarianism, and female empowerment: What are the linkages? *World Politics, 56*(4), 582–607.

Easterly, W. (2002). The cartel of good intentions: The problem of bureaucracy in foreign aid. *The Journal of Policy Reform, 5*(4), 223–250.

Easterly, W. (2007). *The white man's burden: Why the west's efforts to aid the rest have done so much ill and so little good.* OUP Catalogue.

Easterly, W., & Williamson, C. (2011). Rhetoric vs. reality: The best and the worst of aid agency practices. *World Development 39*(11): 1930–1949.

88    B. C. WELBORNE

*The Economist.* (2008, September 18). Women rising. Quotas to help women reach power are spreading. https://www.economist.com/internati onal/2008/09/18/women-rising

Fadel, L. (2012). *Vigilantes spray-paint sexual harassers in Cairo.* http://m.npr. org/story/164099058 (Published November 1, 2012).

Finnemore, M. (1996). *National interests in international society.* Cornell University Press.

Fish, S. (2002). Islam and authoritarianism. *World Politics, 55*(1), 4–37.

Gallagher, K. P. (2014). *Ruling capital: Emerging markets and the reregulation of cross-border finance.* Cornell University Press.

Gallagher, K., & Tian, Y. (2014). *Regulating capital flows in emerging markets: The IMF and the Global Financial Crisis* (GEGI Working Paper). https://www.bu.edu/pardeeschool/files/2014/11/Regulating-Cap ital-Flows-Working-Paper.pdf

Grabel, I. (2011). Not your grandfather's IMF: Global crisis, 'productive incoherence' and developmental policy space. *Cambridge Journal of Economics, 35*(5), 805–830.

Hafner-Burton, E., & Pollack, M. A. (2002). Mainstreaming gender in global governance. *European Journal of International Relations, 8*(3), 339–373.

Hatem, M. F. (1992). Economic and political liberation in Egypt and the demise of state feminism. *International Journal of Middle East Studies, 24*(2), 231–251.

Hatem, M. F. (1994). Egyptian discourses on gender and political liberalization: Do secularist and Islamist views really differ? *Middle East Journal, 48*(4), 661–676.

Htun, M., & Weldon, L. S. (2018). *The logics of gender justice: State action on women's rights around the world.* Cambridge University Press.

Hughes, M., Krook, M. L., & Paxton, P. (2015). Transnational women's activism and the global diffusion of gender quotas. *International Studies Quarterly, 59*(2), 357–372.

Human Rights Watch. (2013). *Egypt: Epidemic of sexual violence.* http://www. hrw.org/news/2013/07/03/egypt-epidemic-sexual-violence

Huntington, S. P. (1993). *The third wave: Democratization in the late twentieth century* (Vol. 4). University of Oklahoma Press.

IDEA. (n.d.). Gender quotas database: Morocco. Stockholm: International Institute for Democracy and Electoral Assistance (IDEA). https://www.idea.int/data-tools/data/gender-quotas/country-view/200/35

Inglehart, R., & Norris, P. (2003). *Rising tide.* Cambridge University Press.

Inglehart, R., & Norris, P. (2009, November 9). The True clash of civilizations. *Foreign Policy, 135.* https://foreignpolicy.com/2009/11/04/the-true-clash-of-civilizations/

ILO. (n.d.). *ILOSTAT database: The leading source of labour statistics. International Labor Organization*. Retrieved September 18, 2020, from https://ilo stat.ilo.org/

Jamal, A. (2010). Democratic Governance and Women's Rights in the Middle East and North Africa (MENA). White Paper for Department for International Development (DFID) and the International Development Research Centre (IDRC).

Kanter, R. M. (1977). Some effects of proportions on group life: Skewed sex ratios and responses to token women. *American Journal of Sociology, 82*, 965–990.

Kassem, L. M., al-Malek, T. S., & Ali, F. M. (2014). *Domestic violence legislation and reform efforts in Qatar—Conflict & Intl. Politics*. Heinrich Böll Stiftung. https://lb.boell.org/en/2014/03/03/domestic-violence-legislation-and-reform-efforts-qatar-conflict-intl-politics

Kasoolu, S., Hausmann, R., O'Brien, T., & Santos, M. A. (2019, October). *Female labor in Jordan: A systematic approach to the exclusion puzzle* (CID Faculty Working Paper No. 365). Center for International Development (CID) at Harvard University. Retrieved September 18, 2020, from https://growthlab.cid.harvard.edu/files/growthlab/files/2019-10-cid-wp-365-female-labor-jordan.pdf

Khomsan, N. (Ed.). (2009, December 13–14). Sexual harassment in the Arab Region: Cultural challenges and legal gaps. In *Findings from the Conference on 'Sexual Harassment as Social Violence, and its Effect on Women'*. The Egyptian Center for Women's Rights.

Krook, M., & True, J. (2008, March). Global strategies for gender equality: The United Nations before and after Beijing. In *Annual International Studies Association Conference*.

Krook, M. L., & O'Brien, D. Z. (2010). The politics of group representation: Quotas for women and minorities worldwide. *Comparative Politics, 42*(3), 253–272.

Krook, M. L., & Hall, B. (2009, April 14). *The diffusion of electoral reform: Gender quotas in global perspective*. European Consortium for Political Research.

Landes, D. (2001, October 8). Girl power: Do fundamentalists fear our women? *The New Republic*.

Lewis, B. (2002). *What went wrong?* Oxford University Press.

Luck, T. (2017, August 9). Across the Arab world, a 'Women's Spring' comes into view. *The Christian Science Monitor*. https://www.csmonitor.com/World/Middle-East/2017/0809/Across-the-Arab-world-a-Women-s-Spring-comes-into-view

Marchesi, S., & Thomas, J. P. (1999). IMF conditionality as a screening device. *The Economic Journal, 109*(454), 111–125.

90   B. C. WELBORNE

Mervis, Z., & Nyemba, E. (2013). The implications of the quota system in promoting gender equality in Zimbabwean politics. *International Journal of Humanities and Social Science, 3*(2), 204–212.

Mesbahi, N. (2018). The victimization of the 'Muslim Woman': The case of Amina Filali Morocco. *Journal of International Women's Studies, 19*(3), 49–59.

Moghadam, V. M. (2012). *Globalization and social movements: Islamism, feminism, and the global justice movement.* Rowman & Littlefield (Proquest/Ebrary).

Morocco Ministry of Justice. http://www.justice.gov.ma/MOUDAWANA/Cod efamille.pdf

Nanes, S. (2010). *Regime stability in the face of global economic crisis: Cosmetic reform and a municipal quota for women.* Paper presented at Annual Meeting of the American Political Science Association.

Neumeyer, E. (2002). *Arab-related bilateral and multilateral sources of development and finance* (Working Paper No. 2002/96). WIDER.

Noh, Y. (2019). *Why do dictatorships bother adopting gender quotas? Co-optation as electoral strategy* (Workshop Paper for New England Middle East Politics Working Group).

Nussbaum, M. (1988). Nature, functioning and capability: Aristotle on political distribution. *Oxford studies in ancient philosophy, supplementary volume* (pp. 145–184).

Nussbaum, M. (1995). Human capabilities, female human beings. In M. Nussbaum & J. Glover (Eds.), *Women, culture and development* (pp. 61–104). Clarendon Press.

Nussbaum, M. (2000). *Women and human development: The capabilities approach.* Cambridge University Press.

OECD. (2019). *Development finance for gender equality and women's empowerment: A snapshot.* Organisation for Economic Co-operation and Development (OECD) Development Co-operation Directorate, DAC Network on Gender Equality. http://www.oecd.org/development/gender-development/Dev-fin ance-for-gender-equality-and-womens-economic-empowerment-2019.pdf

OECD. (2020a). *Aid focussed on gender equality and women's empowerment: A snapshot of current funding and trends over time in support of the implementation of the Beijing Declaration and Platform for Action.* Organisation for Economic Co-operation and Development (OECD), DAC Network on Gender Equality. https://www.oecd.org/development/gender-development/ Aid-Focussed-on-Gender-Equality-and-Women-s-Empowerment-2020a.pdf

OECD. (2020b, June 11). *Covid-19 crisis in the MENA region: Impact on gender equality and policy responses.* OECD Policy Responses to Coronavirus (COVID-19). https://www.oecd.org/coronavirus/policy-responses/covid-19-crisis-in-the-mena-region-impact-on-gender-equality-and-policy-responses-ee4cd4f4/

Peters, A. M., & Moore, P. W. (2009). Beyond boom and bust: External rents, durable authoritarianism, and institutional adaptation in the Hashemite Kingdom of Jordan. *Studies in Comparative International Development, 44*(3), 256–285.

Prügl, E. (2015). Neoliberalizing feminism. *New Political Economy, 20*(4), 614–631.

Przeworski, A., & Vreeland, J. R. (2000). The effect of IMF programs on economic growth. *Journal of Development Economics, 62*(2), 385–421.

Roberts, R. (2017, July 28). Tunisia: 'Landmark' New Law Gives Women Protection from Rape and Domestic Violence. Independent. https://www.independent.co.uk/news/world/tunisia-law-women-protect-rape-domestic-violence-north-africa-landmark-rights-abuse-sexual-a7864846.html

Sabbagh, A. (2005). The Arab states: Enhancing women's political participation. In J. Ballington & A. Karam (Eds.), *Women in parliament: Beyond numbers.* International IDEA Handbook Series.

Sabbagh, A. (2007). Overview of women's political representation in the Arab Region: Opportunities and challenges. In *The Arab Quota report: Selected case studies* (pp. 7–18). IDEA—International Institute for Democracy and Electoral Assistance.

Sachs, J. D. (2006). *The end of poverty: Economic possibilities for our time.* Penguin.

Sachs, J. (2014, January 21). The case for aid. *Foreign Policy.* https://foreignpolicy.com/2014/01/21/the-case-for-aid/

Schelling, T. C. (1978). *Micromotives and macrobehavior.* Norton.

Schwedler, J. (2002). Democratization in the Arab world? Yemen's Aborted Opening. *Journal of Democracy, 13*(4), 48–55.

Sen, A. (1990). Development as capability expansion. *The Community Development Reader,* 41–58.

Shalaby, M. M., & Elimam, L. (2020a). Women in legislative committees in Arab parliaments. *Comparative Politics, 53*(1), 139–167.

Shalaby, M. M., & Elimam, L. (2020b). Examining female membership and leadership of legislative committees in Jordan. In H. Darhour & D. Dahlerup (Eds.), *Double-edged politics on women's rights in the MENA region* (pp. 231–255). Palgrave Macmillan.

Shitrit, L. B. (2016). Authenticating representation: Women's Quotas and Islamist Parties. *Politics & Gender, 12*(4), 781–806.

Sidhu, G. L., & Meena, R. (2007, January 1). *Electoral financing to advance women's political participation: A guide for UNDP support.* Primers in Gender and Democratic Governance #3. United Nations Development Programme (UNDP). http://iknowpolitics.org/sites/default/files/electoral_financing-en-ebook.pdf

Tandberg, E., & Allen, R. (2020, May 11). Managing public investment spending during the crisis. IMF Covid Series. https://www.imf.org/~/media/Files/Publications/covid19-special-notes/en-special-series-on-covid-19-managing-public-investment-spending-during-the-crisis.ashx

Thomas, J. (2018, March 15). Travel tips: Comparison between Morocco & Egypt for tourists. *USA Today*. https://traveltips.usatoday.com/comparison-between-morocco-egypt-tourists-57041.html

Tripp, A. M. (2003). *The changing face of Africa's legislatures: Women and quotas*. International Institute for Development and Electoral Assistance (IDEA).

Tripp, A. M. (2019). *Seeking legitimacy: Why Arab autocracies adopt women's rights*. Cambridge University Press.

Tripp, A. M., & Kang, A. (2008). The global impact of quotas: On the fast track to increased female legislative representation. *Comparative Political Studies, 41*, 338–361.

True, J., & Mintrom, M. (2001). Transnational networks and policy diffusion: The case of gender mainstreaming. *International Studies Quarterly, 45*, 22–57.

United Nations. (1995, September 4–15). *Report of the Fourth World Conference on Women*. United Nations publication, Sales No. E.96.IV.13, Chap. I, Resolution 1, Annex II.

United Nations. (2017). *The spotlight initiative to eliminate violence against women and girls*. https://www.un.org/en/spotlight-initiative/

UNDP. (2006). *The Arab human development report 2005: Towards the rise of women in the Arab world*. United Nations Development Programme (UNDP). Regional Bureau for Arab States.

UNDP. (2014). *The future we want: Rights and empowerment: UNDP gender equality strategy 2014–2017*. United Nations Development Programme (UNDP). https://www.undp.org/publications/gender-equality-strategy-2014-2017

United Nations Women. (2011). *Violence against women prevalence data: Surveys by country*. http://www.endvawnow.org/uploads/browser/files/vaw_prevalence_matrix_15april_2011.pdf

Welborne, B. C. (2010). *The strategic use of gender quotas in the Arab world*. William and Kathy Hybl Democracy Studies Fellowship Paper, International Foundation for Electoral Systems. https://aceproject.org/ero-en/regions/africa/MZ/ifes-the-strategic-use-of-gender-quotas-in-the

Williams, M. (2007). *Gender and trade: Impacts and implications for financial resources for gender equality*. Commonwealth Secretariat, Background Paper WAMM (07)10.

Williamson, J. (1983). On seeking to improve IMF conditionality. *The American Economic Review, 73*, 354–358.

Wodon, Q., Onagoruwa, A., Malé, C., Montenegro, C., Nguyen, H., & De La Brière, B. (2020). *How large is the gender dividend? Measuring selected impacts and costs of gender inequality.* The Cost of Gender Inequality Notes Series. World Bank Group. https://openknowledge.worldbank.org/handle/10986/33396

World Bank. (2020). *The World Bank in gender: Overview.* https://www.worldbank.org/en/topic/gender/overview

Wright, J., & Winters, M. (2010). The politics of effective foreign aid. *Annual Review of Political Science, 13*, 61–80.

Yassine, N. (2009). Modernity, Muslim women, and politics in the mediterranean. In R. L. Euben & M. Q. Zaman (Eds.), *Princeton readings in Islamist thought: Texts and contexts from Al-Banna to Bin Laden* (pp. 302–311). Princeton University Press.

Žvan Elliott, K. (2014). Morocco and it's women's rights struggles: A failure to live up to its progressive image. *Journal of Middle East Women's Studies, 10*(2), 1–30.

Žvan Elliott, K. (2015). *Modernizing patriarchy: The politics of women's rights in Morocco.* University of Texas Press.

CHAPTER 4

# The Gender Paradox of Remittances

Back in 2009, when I was conducting interviews in the Atlas mountains of Morocco, I had the pleasure of chatting with an activist for local Amazigh ('Berber') and women's rights. My counterpart, then employed in the Ministry of Agriculture, had originally worked on imparting sustainable agricultural practices to rural women outside of Marrakesh and had recently decided to hitch her wagon to the activism of La Ligue Democratique pour les Droits de la Femme (LDDF)—an association focusing on educating rural women on their legal rights and entitlements. LDDF was especially active in the aftermath of the *Moudawana* reforms of 2004.[1]

As we spoke, this activist shared stories on how the Amazigh diasporas in France and Spain were financing Amazigh identity movements within Morocco by wiring funds from abroad.[2] She highlighted the successes

[1] The *Moudawana*, a new family code adopted unanimously by the Moroccan Parliament in 2004, included a series of reforms that equalized women's status in matters of marriage and family. Some of the key reforms were the abrogation of male guardianship, raising the minimum age of marriage to 18 for women; mandating property sharing between couples, regulation of polygamy, changing child custody to give more opportunities to women, improvements in women's inheritance rights, a recognition of children born out of wedlock, simplification of procedures to establish paternity, and an enhancement of children's rights according to international law.

[2] Author interview, Marrakesh, Morocco. December 2009.

© The Author(s), under exclusive license to Springer Nature Switzerland AG 2022
B. C. Welborne, *Women, Money, and Political Participation in the Middle East*,
https://doi.org/10.1007/978-3-031-04877-7_4

95

96    B. C. WELBORNE

of local Amazigh organizations in partnering with diaspora organizations to push for the kingdom to initiate school instruction and television programming in one of the Amazigh languages, Tamazight, and to officially recognize Amazigh names given to newborns. Until the 2000s, all Moroccan children's names had to be Arabized (Human Rights Watch, 2009, 2010). With the constitutional reforms of 2011, a standardized single version of three native Amazigh languages—Tachelhit, Tamazight, and Tarifit—was recognized as an official language in Morocco. And, Amazigh rights activists transitioned from being political dissidents to actively participating in the *Majles al-Nawab*—the Moroccan House of Representatives.

The constitutional reforms were certainly a byproduct of diaspora activism, since international aid geared at the Amazigh population was highly restricted before 2011. Yet, these same movements were successful at agenda-setting despite heavy constraints from the Arab-dominated state. Of course, none of this would have transpired without simultaneous pressures from foreign donors on the state to include its largest non-Arab minority group. As Chapter 3 showed, foreign aid is often the necessary, if not the sufficient, condition for initiating domestic reforms to incorporate marginalized groups into existing power structures in many transitioning autocracies in the Arab world. The successes of the activist Amazigh diaspora raise the question of whether other MENA diasporas are as effective at rallying around political and social issues beyond irredentism.[3]

In the following pages, we will consider the impact remittances— funds migrants send back to their relatives or others in their countries of origin—have had on changing gender relations in the MENA, particularly whether and how they have created opportunities for women to participate in the workforce and, by extension, the politics of Arab regimes. Scholarship on the gendered effects of remittances is still very much in its infancy, despite the donor community's two-decade embrace of remittances as a tool for economic development (Kunz, 2008; Ramírez et al., 2005; Sorensen, 2004). Rachel Kunz attributes some of this lack of interest to the pervasive 'gender blindness' in the policy and academic communities, especially because remittances are so often presumed and loudly proclaimed to be a net positive for development, so possible externalities are not interrogated as exhaustively. Kunz believes this is due to

---

[3] Of course, the Palestinian diaspora has been very successful.

the financial rather than social ways remittances are defined in current development discourse. Consequently, surrounding rhetoric is better able to evade 'delving into the complex and varied human, social, political, and economic realities, within which remittances are embedded' (2008: 1398).

The effect of remittances is less direct than that of official development assistance (ODA) and other forms of conditional aid. However, remittances play an important role in incentivizing what kinds of work women engage in and whether they pursue education, and, increasingly, in conditioning the gender dynamics within migrant households, broader families, and local communities (Buvinic, 2009). More importantly, do these emergent patterns scale to the national level?

As we shall see, there is evidence that remittances actually have a more progressive effect on attitudes toward women's most basic rights than may be expected given the fairly critical sociological literature on the subject. None of this is surprising when we consider the demographics of some of the individuals who migrate from the MENA, where they end up, and how their experiences influence the values they send back home alongside those monies. But it is worth asking whether we are seeing a permanent shift in gender relations and how changing migration patterns may further affect them.

## Surveying Remittances in the MENA

Over the past three decades, a vibrant field of research has emerged on the multifaceted impact of remittances on domestic development in the Global South. This literature has focused largely on the economic consequences of private transfers or their use in funding civil conflicts.[4] But, remittances have been shown to have an impact on a wider array of social phenomena.[5] Less attention has been paid to their impact on domestic gender dynamics. There are reasons to believe that impact is substantial, but also distinct, in the context of the MENA.

[4] See Adams (2009), Adams and Page (2005), Kapur (2003), Singer (2010), and Newland and Patrick (2004).

[5] See Burgess (2012), de Haas (2007), Leblang (2010), Levitt (1998), O'Mahony (2012), and Newland and Patrick (2004).

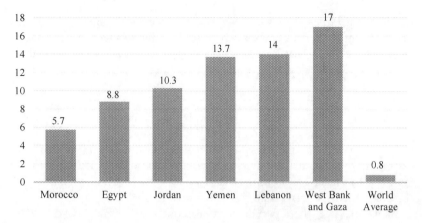

**Fig. 4.1** Remittances as a percentage of GDP across the MENA, 2019 (*Sources:* World Development Indicators, 2022)

The Arab world provides an intriguing scenario to explore the social impact of remittances, since quite a few countries in the region—Morocco, Jordan, Egypt, Lebanon, and Yemen—consistently rank among the world's highest recipients of private transfers from abroad, usually from Western Europe and the Persian Gulf (see Fig. 4.1). Since 2001, remittances have tended to overshadow levels of foreign direct investment (FDI) and ODA across both the Arab world and the rest of the globe.[6] At a record high of $554 billion in 2019, remittances overtook FDI flows as the primary source of investment for low- and middle-income countries (Mohieldin & Ratha, 2020). Outside of the Caribbean and the Pacific Islands, the non-GCC Arab states have the highest average rate of remittances as a percentage of GDP.[7] This trend showed no signs of abating in the near term, as remittances often tend to be counter-cyclical, with emigrant families increasing transfers to their home countries during times of economic and social crises. COVID-19 is proving to represent both types of crises for the region.[8]

---

[6] In 2001, FDI totaled $3 billion while ODA $6 billion. Remittances totaled $15 billion (Kapur, 2003). See Nwanze (2015).

[7] 5.2 relative to the global average of 0.8.

[8] The COVID-19 pandemic has challenged this pattern with an at times forced, at times voluntary mass exodus of labor from host countries. See Aidi et al. (2020).

Women represent fully half of all remittance recipients across the globe—and, more recently, close to half of remittance senders—whereas in the past they were more likely to comprise the majority of those 'left behind' (IOM, 2008). Labor migrants are also increasingly women, which is changing the nature and scope of the remittances sent to home countries; there is some evidence that women send more money, and more often, back to their families, with decidedly different instructions on how that money should be distributed within the family (Ramírez et al., 2005).

In the Middle East, women are still the majority of those left behind, yet these women are often not simply passive recipients of foreign monies. In fact, international remittances may actually enhance women's decision-making power in the home, completely changing familial, and ultimately societal, gender relations as women take on men's traditional roles in households and sometimes even in communities.[9] Remittance funds may also have an indirect impact on women's political mobilization via their impact on women's economic status.[10]

These purported shifts in gender relations within and outside the household occur with women's expanded opportunity to manage household money, but also with shifting attitudes toward appropriate roles for women overall. The MENA region provides an excellent context for such an investigation, partially because Middle East migrants largely tend to send money back from regions (Western Europe and the Persian Gulf) that are ideologically and, in some cases, culturally distinct from their home countries in the Levant and North Africa. The regions where MENA migrants work are also dissimilar from each other to a degree that could easily condition migrant values and even behavior over time, ultimately providing us with a quasi-experiment of sorts. We can imagine migrants living in each region might share distinct political and social sentiments, some based on their experiences in their host countries, others based on the reasons they migrated from their homes in the first place. These same sentiments could also change over time, influencing the instructions migrants give their families for spending the money or determining the individual family members' roles in the household.

---

[9] See Brink (1991), de Haas and van Rooij (2010), Hadi (2001), Hoodfar (1997), Lenoël (2017), Lenoël and David (2019), Menjívar and Agadjanian (2007), Sadiqi and Ennaji (2004), UN INSTRAW (2007).

[10] The work of Rachel Kunz ties this to the neoliberal world order and the gender governmentality implicit within remittances.

100    B. C. WELBORNE

In some cases, diaspora communities may even choose to fund specific political ventures in their home countries, echoing their crystallizing (or shifting) ideological sentiments. This has certainly been the case with proactive dissident diasporas funding the Palestine Liberation Organization (PLO), Berber separatist movements in North Africa, and Amazigh rights movements pressuring Moroccan legislators from abroad.

Extant literature reveals that private transfers from diaspora communities have increasingly political and ideological overtones as migrants play a growing role in politics back home—particularly in countries where remittances support the local economy (Brand, 2018; Leblang, 2010; O'Mahony, 2012). Remittances can directly empower citizens through economic development via an injection of funds that is not entangled in bureaucracy, and so give both diasporas and local populations leverage in demanding social reforms from the government. Yet, remittances could also make dictatorial Arab regimes more resistant to internal and external pressure for social reform, since the funds often serve as a substitute and unconditional sources of foreign exchange for the government (Ahmed, 2012; Ross, 2008; Singer, 2010).

Some see the influence of the diaspora as an important tool for social change, because migrants are less subject to intimidation, bribes, and dishonesty from local politicians or their cronies (Kapur & McHale, 2003). This distance allows the emigrants to express their desire for reform and provide financial support to local revolutionaries or individuals lobbying for social reforms without fear of government reprisal. Because of this, as national economies become increasingly reliant on money sent back by emigrants, politicians in the host state have changed their positions toward diaspora populations from 'benign neglect to active courtship' (Kapur & McHale, 2003; Leblang, 2010).

Obviously, diasporas have complex relationships with their countries of origin and their engagement is multifaceted, ranging from individual family ties to macro-level international financial markets (Leblang, 2010; Newland & Patrick, 2004). For direct engagement, Kathleen Newland and Erin Patrick (2004) find most active diasporas will exert financial pressure through hometown associations, business networks, social capital, and support for or moderation of conflict in their home countries. They venture that hometown associations tend to have the most localized and often more conservative agendas. Business networks tend to have a broader base of action, affecting the transnational realm. The nonprofit Lebanese Business Network exemplifies this type of diaspora activity;

it features an online marketplace geared at matching local Lebanese businesses with expatriate counterparts.

Economic scholarship has also recognized remittances as an overall source of economic stability and poverty alleviation (Adams & Page, 2005; Kapur & McHale, 2003; Singer, 2010), although the empirical link between remittances and other types of societal outcomes is unclear. Conversely, Peggy Levitt (1998) considers the idea of 'social remittances' as a way to channel cultural mores and social capital *from* the receiving country *to* the sending country, as reflected in changing attitudes in the sending country toward an array of human rights and even conditioning new attitudes toward longstanding conflicts in the receiving country.[11] The idea of 'political remittances' has also emerged as a means to transform political identities and practices associated with migration (Kunz, 2008). Since 2005, with the volume of remittances outstripping the volume of ODA and FDI in most Global South economies, migrant workers have been billed as 'agents of change' and development, with governments eager to harness their new skills, monies, and ideas for the 'greater good' (Eade, 2016). Yet, the question remains how deliberate the social impact of remittances might be; this presents a particular difficulty in trying to disentangle their influence on changes in gender norms, as well as their effect on women's broader politicization across the region.

## MIGRANT VALUES AND SOCIAL CHANGE

The bigger conceit underpinning the idea that remittances might unleash *new gender dynamics*, alongside these other effects, is that migrants transfer both money and ideas back to their home countries. However, there is also evidence that substantive ideological shifts can happen in the household, whether through discourse with other family members, changes in overall consumption patterns, or migrants' choice to fund specific social movements and ideologies (Curran & Saguy, 2001). At the household level, transferred monies can serve to lift the standards

---

[11] Newland and Patrick (2004) also highlight the impact of diasporas on domestic conflicts in their roles as conduits for money and arms to internal disputes in Sri Lanka, Eritrea, Somalia, Turkey, Northern Ireland, Spain, and Israel/Palestine. Other groups have a moderating influence on pre-existing conflicts, either by challenging acts attributed to specific insurgent organizations or by withholding monies and vocal support for those activities.

of the household in ways that empower 'left behind' female heads of household or disincentivize women's participation in the labor force by increasing their effective *reservation wage*—the wage at which she perceives a marginal benefit in joining the workforce. Needless to say, the latter two outcomes have distinct impacts on the women's role in their families and their communities.[12]

Michael Ross' (2008) work on the gendered effects of oil rents tangentially posits that remittances could have a similar impact by bolstering domestic incomes, thereby rendering obsolete the need for women to enter the workforce and essentially reinforcing patriarchic norms. Ross finds this to be particularly true for Muslim-majority countries, alongside a host of ethnographic scholarship that confirms these patterns across Muslim-majority states from Albania to Yemen.[13] More generally, research on diaspora communities' exporting of conservative values to their home nations—especially when it comes to gender—lines up with expectations of diaspora conservatism.

For example, Sidney Tarrow's seminal book, *Power in Movement* (2011) documented the increasing conservatism of the Muslim community (among other communities) in the United States. Although this trend may be changing with the promotion of multiculturalism, pluralism, and a renewed commitment to social justice in some American communities,[14] there is not much evidence that diasporas on the whole lean liberal—especially on issues pertaining to gender. In the United States, many Latino and Arab-Muslim diasporas tend to lean conservative on reproductive rights and women's rights more broadly. Overall, the global question remains whether migrants are actually exporting conservative values back to their homelands, or just further reifying them via the decisions made by the household members who remain at home. In many cases, these are other women.

---

[12] This is also partially conditioned by whether they live in urban or rural areas.

[13] Albania (King et al., 2006), Yemen (Myntti, 1984), Morocco (de Haas, 2007; van Rooij, 2000), Turkey (Day & Içduygu, 1997), and Egypt (Taylor, 1984).

[14] There is ample evidence that the Muslim diasporas have become more 'liberal' in terms of their voting preferences over the last twenty years. See Barreto and Bozonelos (2009) and Welborne et al. (2018).

## Promoting Old or New Gender Dynamics?

Does male out-migration lead to 'left behind' women's greater emancipation at home and in the community both economically and politically? Do we see more female-headed households, or do other male family members take over the management of family affairs? In either case—whether women and men are the migrants—can irrevocably change gender relations within a household. This shift can also scale beyond the household.

One of the most basic ways to assess the gendered impact of remittances is to consider them through the lens of who sends and who receives remittances, why they send them, and, most importantly, who decides how they get disbursed once received. Certainly, the gendered nature of the international division of labor also affects how gender plays out in who sends, receives, and spends remittances, alongside the complex within-household negotiations on how the funds are used and distributed. There is also significant research that demonstrates that women remittance senders and recipients behave differently than men in systematic ways. As mentioned earlier, this research reveals that women tend to remit more money than men and, in quite few cases, to make more effective use of remittance money benefiting the broader family when they are the recipients (Kunz, 2008; Sorensen, 2004).

As recipients and managers of remittance funds, women have always played a central role in migration, with an array of social factors—age, education, geographic location, and marriage status—conditioning their roles within migration discourses and realities. Recent scholarship into changing gender roles, and perhaps even women's empowerment, has presumed the changes will occur as male out-migration influences the division of labor across genders in the household and in the public arena by effectively shifting decision-making and management of financial resources to women. There is also a presumption about how men's migration might influence women's choice to engage in paid and unpaid labor—decisions that could ultimately affect women's societal status. If anything, current scholarship has shown that women often do take up the jobs previously performed by men in their households, especially agricultural work such as harvesting crops or caring for livestock (Sorensen, 2004; Steinmann, 1993). However, these notions of household dynamics simplify the power struggles that often occur between women of different generations who live and work under the same roof.

104 B. C. WELBORNE

When women are recipients of remittances, their level of control over the funds varies substantially from person to person and is often demarcated by the level of agency a society affords to women more generally. This is one reason remittances are likely to have a disproportionate impact on women in conservative patriarchic societies, such as those of the MENA, where women's agency is limited, to begin with.[15]

Surprisingly, scholarship on remittance patterns in Egypt and Morocco has shown that women tend to become the heads of their households and primary recipients of remittances after male family members migrate (IOM, 2010; Lopez-Ekra et al., 2011).[16] Further, some research has found that women who are direct recipients of remittances are more likely to experience greater economic empowerment and decision-making power for themselves and their households (Debnath & Selim, 2009). Whether that is true for a given household is often determined by whether a male family member sends money directly to his wife or to his mother— a choice with a substantial impact on family dynamics and potential to shift power in the household. Explicitly, an older matriarch is likely to have different priorities than her daughter-in-law, who may be considered a young interloper with much to prove in her new family.

The global patterns of the 1980s and 1990s, in which men's emigration increased opportunities for women, who picked up the slack in the labor force, hold in Latin America, South Asia, and Sub-Saharan Africa but not so much in the MENA.[17] In fact, there is some evidence that men's migration actually disincentivizes women's participation in the workforce. Deniz Kandiyoti's work offers a possible explanation for why migration dynamics in the MENA may not play out in the same way for women as they do in other cultures—even in some that are equally patriarchic and conservative when it comes to gender relations. She uses the notion of patriarchal bargains, 'a set of concrete constraints that reveal and define the blueprint [that] shapes women's gendered subjectivity and

---

[15] See, for example, Kandiyoti's (1988) discussion of the distinct patterns of 'patriarchal bargains' in the MENA relative to other global regions.

[16] Research in Egypt has shown that in two thirds of households with male migrants, women became the head of the household (IOM, 2010). See also Hoodfar (1997), Hadi (2001), Menjivar and Agadjanian (2007), de Haas and van Rooij (2010), and Lenoël (2017).

[17] See Brink (1991), Chant (1997), Curran and Saguy (2001), Carling (2005), Eade (2016) for more discussion.

determines the nature of gender ideology in different contexts' (1988: 275). Kandiyoti sees the kind of *classic patriarchy* dominant in the Middle East, South Asia, and East Asia as one in which a patrilineal extended household gives senior men singular authority over everyone else:

> Under classic patriarchy, girls are given away in marriage at a very young age into households headed by their husband's father. There they are subordinate not only to all the men, but also to the more senior women, especially their mother-in-law. The extent to which this represents a total break with their own kin group varies in relation to the degree of endogamy in marriage practices and different conceptions of honor. (ibid.: 278)

In other words, these patrilineage-based relationships lock women into a lifecycle in which they can eventually transcend the 'deprivation and hardship' they experience as young brides when they inherit the authority of senior women, which 'encourages a thorough internalization of this form of patriarchy by the women themselves. In classical patriarchy, subordination to men is offset by the control older women attain over younger women' (ibid.: 279). Yet, younger women often have access to the most crucial resource for their autonomy in the household and the one way to circumvent maternal authority—the son. Still, family status has been linked to perpetuating the cycle of subservience, which can be more pronounced for left-behind women who live in multi-generational households or reside in rural areas. The move to the city seems to upend the odds that this kind of familial model perpetuates itself; however the evidence on this is still shaky.[18]

The remittance literature on changing gender relations in Morocco and Egypt from the 1980s and early 1990s largely confirmed the rosy vision of shifting power dynamics within remittance households empowering women (Brink, 1991; Hoodfar, 1997), but scholarship from the new millennium tells a more nuanced story. It seems that whether left-behind women are engaging in remunerated work determines whether remittances expand their opportunities within and beyond the household.[19]

---

[18] See Binzel and Assaad (2011), de Haas (2007, 2009), de Haas and van Rooij (2010) for discussions remittance impact in urban vs. rural contexts within Morocco.

[19] Compare Brink's (1991) accounts of Egypt to Binzel and Assaad (2011) or Lenoël and David's (2019) accounts of Morocco.

In fact, many women—especially older matriarchs—used the remittance money simply to hire domestic labor and decrease the burden of household chores, but did not use remittances to engage in any entrepreneurial activity or to look for work outside the home to supplement remittance income. Paid work outside the home is often perceived as offering women more autonomy and bargaining power within the home (Kabeer, 2012; Malhotra & Schuler, 2005), yet in Egypt and Morocco it has also been construed as the province of 'low-born' or desperate women; no 'reputable' family would let their daughters or wives work if they did not have to (Sadiqi & Ennaji, 2006).

In their work on the public/private dichotomy in Morocco, scholars Fatima Sadiqi and Moha Ennaji describe them as 'two spaces [that] are mutually exclusive … the public space is the street and the marketplace, where men evolve, and the private space is the home, where women live' (ibid.: 88). They describe an 'Arab Muslim patriarchy' in which private space is associated with maleness and power over the state, business, and the economy, whereas the private space is a subordinate domain of women and children. And while this dichotomy has been disrupted and actively challenged since the 1960s, when an increasing number of Moroccan women entered the formal workforce partially due to male out-migration, remittances can also void these progressive trends by raising women's reservation wage.

Christine Binzel and Ragui Assaad (2011) propose that socioeconomic background also has an impact on whether women in households receiving remittances are more likely to work. At low incomes, women are still likely to engage in paid work to bolster family finances, whereas at middle incomes the preference is for women to stay home. In high-income brackets, the 'fashion' for women to work returns. These patterns across social classes often mirror the urban–rural divide (2011: 18). Migration certainly affects the female labor supply in both situations, but the class stratification is often distinct. Binzel and Assaad find that in urban areas, the substitution of women for absent male labor is less likely due to more stringent gender stratification across employment opportunities, while in rural agricultural areas there is much work that men and women are equally equipped to do. Effectively, they find that additional remittance income is more likely to 'kick women out' of the workforce in urban areas than in rural ones, somewhat defying other ethnographic work that claims rural areas are more likely to keep women from working (Joseph, 1996; Lenoël, 2017).

Of course, whether women are employed formally or informally adds nuance to the discussion of what 'work' means in urban versus rural settings, especially since the MENA region as a whole hosts some of the highest rates of women's informal employment in the world—62 percent according to OECD (2020) data. Consequently, although Binzel and Assaad find that rural areas may be more open to women's engaging in agricultural labor side by side with men (especially family members), the narrative shifts if it becomes a question of women working in formal jobs alongside unknown or unrelated men.

In this vein, Audrey Lenoël and Andra David's (2019) work on Morocco and Homa Hoodfar's (1997) pioneering work on Egypt highlight how migrant households are often more scrutinized by their communities and expected to maintain a certain status. Often, this results in left-behind women's being even more hesitant to become financially independent from their husbands, for fear of rumors or accusations of 'un-Islamic' or 'dishonorable' behavior. Neighbors may interpret a woman's engaging in paid work as a sign that her migrant husband has abandoned the family or is not capable of supporting them. In more recent scholarly work, there is limited evidence that left-behind women are seeking employment, precisely *because* incoming foreign currency, alongside social norms, disincentivizes them from looking for work. In other words, there is little recent evidence that remittances are directly empowering Arab women in terms of creating more opportunities for paid labor or for expanding their skills and autonomy outside their immediate households. If anything, remittances seem to incentivize matriarchs and female in-laws alike to stay home and disengage from the workforce, further reifying conservative values across gender and generational lines.

## Does Migration Lead to Emancipation?

In considering the question of whether 'migration leads to emancipation', Hein de Haas and Aleida van Rooij (2010) find that remittances may often engender new inequalities among the already disenfranchised, especially women. Morocco is once more a particularly instructive case, alongside Egypt, here as both have been documented more thoroughly than other countries in the MENA. In Morocco, the larger the extended family, the less likely a migrant's wife will receive remittances directly. More often than not, the in-laws decide how monies are dispersed, a fact

108  B. C. WELBORNE

that creates its own conflicts between young wives and the families they marry into (Hajjarabi, 1988: 180–183).

In-laws are also seen as the caretakers of the wife's chastity while the husband is away, provoking a different but related set of household disputes. However, in situations when wives are able to build a household independent from the in-laws, there is evidence of much more autonomy and personal liberty for women, as well as an escape from supporting extended families (de Haas & van Rooij, 2010; van Rooij, 2000).

De Haas and other migration scholars have also found that remittance-receiving households exhibit higher levels of education for children and women, often spurring a relocation to urban areas where parents can more easily take advantage of educational infrastructure. In fact, one implication of increased migration may be an accelerated breakdown of extended families, with an accompanying increase in female-headed households, though the MENA region is far from being in any danger of such a pattern becoming dominant. A look at the data from the United Nations Department of Economics and Social Affairs (UNDESA) on household size and composition from 2017, shows on average that less than 15 percent of households are female-headed in the MENA in comparison to median proportions of 47 percent in North America, 37 percent in Europe, 34 percent in Latin America and the Caribbean, 33 percent in Oceania, 27 percent in Africa, and 19 percent in Asia (UN DESA - Population Division, 2017).[20]

Historically, only men have been allowed to migrate, as women's migration without a husband or guardian would have been perceived as compromising the honor of the family (Fadloullah et al., 2000). This is often due to the conservative mores of communities that see the largest migration, but could also be because of increasingly conservative values 'sent back' to the household along with foreign monies, not to mention the need to signal virtue and chastity while 'the man of the house' is

---

[20] A quick look at the UN's Household Size and Composition database reveals, if anything, that the collection of female headship statistics has been uneven across the MENA for the better part of the last two decades with the following countries reporting female head of household statistics over that time period: Comoros (39.3 percent in 2012), Egypt (13.45 percent in 2014), the Gaza Strip (9.5 percent in 2017), Iraq (13.45 percent in 2014). Jordan (12.19 percent in 2017), Mauritania (29.1 percent in 2001), Morocco (16.36 percent in 2004), West Bank (11.2 percent in 2017), and Yemen (7.78 percent in 2013). To access the data directly see https://www.un.org/development/desa/pd/data/household-size-and-composition.

away. We will explore how systematic these ideas are across the region in the next section through public opinion data collected from roughly 2010 until 2019 by the Arab Barometer project.[21]

## The Values of Remittance-Receiving Households

My own analysis of public opinion data across the fifth wave of the Arab Barometer survey (2018–2019) reveals that households receiving remittances actually hold slightly *less* conservative values on some of the most salient aspects of gender relations in Arab culture than their non-receiving counterparts (see Table 4.1). I also find that these populations seem to be getting less conservative *over time* through a comparison with results from previous waves of the Arab Barometer starting in 2010 (see Tables A.1–A.3 in the Appendix). To explore the question of how remittances impact individual attitudes toward women, I rely on question Q1017 in the survey, which broadly asks if and how frequently respondents receive remittances:

*'Does Your Family Receive Remittances from Someone Living Abroad?'*

1. *Yes, monthly*
2. *Yes, a few times a year*
3. *Yes, once a year*
4. *We do not receive anything.*

This same question had been asked across three previous waves of the Arab Barometer: wave II (2010–2011), wave III (2012–2014), and wave IV (2016–2017). In the fifth wave, some 12,516 respondents answered it out of a possible 26,564 sampled individuals.[22] I rescale and collapse the categories in the question for easier interpretation, and essentially regress

---

[21] Arab Barometer (https://www.arabbarometer.org/) is a nonpartisan research network surveying a host of Arab nations. The range of years in which they conduct rounds of the survey are called 'waves' and, as of 2022, six waves of the survey have been conducted since the first round of surveys from 2006 until 2009—the first wave.

[22] Importantly, a fraction of the surveyed populations across all four waves that tracked remittance receipts responded to the battery of questions used in this analysis. In the four waves I analyze, between 8000 and 15,000 respondents answered the survey question on remittances, out of a possible 21,000–24,000 respondents in any given wave. See the Appendix for tables depicting the other three waves.

**Table 4.1**  Remittance recipients' attitudes toward women's rights in the MENA, 2018–2019

| Scale: Strongly disagree (1) Strongly agree (4) | A woman can become President or Prime Minister of a Muslim country | In general, men are better at political leadership than women | University education for males is more important than university education for females | It is permissible for a woman to travel abroad by herself | Women and men should have equal rights in making the decision to divorce | Husbands should have final say in all decisions concerning the family | Women's inheritance should be equal to that of men |
|---|---|---|---|---|---|---|---|
| *Coeff/St. Errors/Sig* | | | | | | | |
| Remittance | 0.93 | −0.91*** | 0.36 | 0.25 | 0.72* | 0.04 | 0.80* |
| Frequency | (0.58) | (0.29) | (0.00) | (0.70) | (0.41) | (0.40) | (0.50) |
| Gender | 0.84** | 0.45 | −0.44* | 0.30* | 0.45 | −0.30* | 1.21*** |
| (Women) | (0.43) | (0.42) | (0.29) | (0.14) | (0.35) | (0.18) | (0.44) |
| Age | 0.00 | 0.00 | 0.00 | −0.00*** | 0.00 | −0.00 | 0.00 |
| | (0.00) | (0.00) | (0.00) | (0.00) | (0.00) | (0.00) | (0.00) |
| Education | 0.12 | −0.13 | −0.40 | −0.04 | 0.60 | −0.03** | 0.10 |
| | (0.12) | (0.10) | (0.10) | (0.04) | (0.07) | (0.01) | (0.01) |
| Employed | 0.00 | −0.01* | 0.20 | 0.02 | 0.00 | 0.00 | −0/01 |
| | (0.02) | (0.01) | (0.05) | (0.04) | (0.04) | (0.03) | (0.03) |
| Religiosity | 0.03** | 0.06*** | 0.02** | 0.03* | 0.04** | 0.03** | 0.10* |
| | (0.01) | (0.02) | (0.01) | (0.02) | (0.02) | (0.01) | (0.04) |
| *R-squared* | 0.003 | 0.007 | 0.002 | 0.004 | 0.004 | 0.005 | 0.010 |
| *Obs* | 12,475 | 12,475 | 12,475 | 7382 | 12,475 | 12,472 | 12,473 |

*Source::* Arab Barometer wave 5, 12 countries (Algeria, Egypt, Iraq, Jordan, Kuwait, Lebanon, Libya, Morocco, Palestine, Sudan, Tunisia, Yemen). The questions on attitudes toward women's status, remittances, employment, and religiosity were all rescaled for easier interpretation
Robust standard errors in parentheses: *$p < 0.10$, **$p < 0.05$, ***$p < 0.01$

4 THE GENDER PARADOX OF REMITTANCES    111

it against a battery of public opinion questions that probe attitudes toward the status of women in MENA: from their role in politics and personal mobility to their right to equal inheritance and divorce—the latter of two are the province of the all-important family code and personal status laws that determine much of women's welfare in the region.[23] I also incorporate standard controls capturing gender, age, education, and employment status while including an indicator of self-identified religiosity, which is scaled as 'religious', 'somewhat religious', and 'not religious'. With the religiosity indicator, I control for the type of conservatism, which may have an impact on responses to questions relating to women's status within society.[24] Finally, to adequately capture the in-country variation across the 12 Arab states surveyed in the fifth wave of the survey, all of which have varying levels of out-migration, I used fixed effects regression with robust standard errors.

The findings in Table 4.1 reveal, most recently, a community that is surprisingly progressive as remittance recipients were significantly *more likely* to agree with statements touting equal inheritance and divorce rights for women as men than their non-remittance-receiving counterparts, and to disagree with statements framing men as better political leaders than women. On the whole, they were neutral on the other questions pertaining to women as heads of state and their right to university education, as well as household decision-making.[25] Importantly, this has not always been the case. The previous three iterations of the survey

---

[23] Q601-1 to Q601-18 reflect the questions on women's status within the fifth wave of the Arab-barometer. Previous waves have also hosted a similar battery of questions, but not consistently the same ones. For example, questions pertaining to inheritance laws and divorce have been removed from the most recent surveys in 2020–2021. In terms, of the remittances question Q1017, I collapse the categories presented from frequency of remittance receipt into the simpler receivers (1); non-receivers (0).

[24] Conservatism could also be driven by the rural locations of many remittance-receiving households, although we saw from Binzel and Assaad (2011) that this can be an unfair assumption. In the oft-quoted Moroccan case, as well as other MENA states that have robust agricultural sectors, women have worked side-by-side with men in the fields, albeit informally, for centuries. Unfortunately, this fifth wave of the Arab-barometer did not contain an indicator capturing whether the respondent was from a rural or urban area, though in previous waves rural respondents tended to hold significantly more conservative views on women's right to education, work, and political office (see Tables A.2 and A.3 in the Appendix).

[25] The most recent Arab-barometer survey (2020–2021) actually reveals overwhelming support for women's equal right to university.

reveal a population that was neutral at best initially and has only over time become more sympathetic to basic women's rights (see Appendix Tables A.1–A.3).

When asked over the next three waves to consider equal rights to inheritance, divorce, university education, and access to work, a mixed picture emerges among respondents. While in wave III (2012–2014), remittance recipients agree with university education being more important for men, by wave IV (2016–2017), and wave V (2018–2019) remittance recipients disagree consistently with this sentiment. From wave IV to wave V, we also see remittance recipients agreeing with the idea that men and women should have equal rights to both inheritance and divorce, as well as disagreeing with the sentiment that men make better political leaders than women.

Remittance recipients also consistently disagreed with the notion that husbands should have the final say in family affairs, perhaps precisely because in the absence of the primary male breadwinner, the head of household is often a woman. Furthermore, remittance recipients on the whole tend to be much more open to women traveling abroad and working outside the home than non-recipients.[26]

In general, remittance recipients tended to be more neutral on women's political rights, overall. Perhaps the political result is not surprising since, as mentioned in earlier chapters, Arab households have become conditioned to the idea of women's participation in politics—especially in states that have received copious amounts of foreign aid and adopted gender quotas. At the beginning of the new millennium, hardly any citizens knew what a gender quota entailed, but as we near the third decade of the twenty-first century, knowledge of gender quotas and the need for enhanced women's political participation is widespread, whether disseminated through state press and media or through extensive outreach by women's NGOs operating in the region. Figure 4.2 shows us that even the majority of Arab citizens agree with the imposition of some form of gender quota for women in the fifth wave of the Arab Barometer.

---

[26] Some argue that remittances do, in fact, offer women recipients more freedom and opportunity within their household and the broader community (Aït Hamza, 1988, 1995; Bouzid, 1992; Fadloullah et al., 2000: xix, 130), while other scholarship disputes this notion (Steinmann, 1993; van Rooij, 2000).

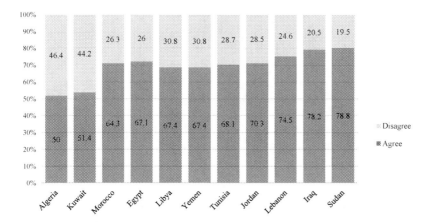

**Fig. 4.2** Arab public opinion: Elected positions should be set aside for women (*Source:* Arab Barometer V [2018–2019], Q601A, categories collapsed)

The statistical results demonstrating diasporas are sympathetic to women's equal personhood when it comes to family code, are not unimportant—especially with the potential political sway of diasporas on the politics back home. As the work of Mounira Charrad (2001, 2011), Suad Joseph (1996), Deniz Kandiyoti (1988), and countless other regional gender experts notes, half the battle in promoting gender equality in the MENA lies in ensuring more equitable outcomes in the enforcement of family law and personal status codes. The increasingly conservative attitudes toward women inheriting equally to men discussed in other work are disheartening, since inheritance and women's access to property and education are often highlighted as the most significant and impactful gender-related reforms that can be passed in Muslim-majority states. Under condition of anonymity, one of my North African academic informants ventured that in the MENA, these gender-related reforms are seen as more powerful in undermining the notion of the family than the push to promote LGBTQ+ rights or even same-sex marriage.

It is no accident that the countries that have experienced the most progress and substantive outcomes for women across a slew of gender indicators are those that have reformed their family codes over the past two decades. Aili Tripp (2019) argues that one key to these countries' ability to enact these reforms is their early embrace of unitary law and many of them enacted unified family codes in the aftermath of colonization.[27] North African states such as Tunisia, Morocco, and Algeria in particular have all adopted unitary law codes and have generally exhibited more progress in terms of the state addressing gender-related disparities and issues related to domestic violence, public health, sexual harassment and rape, and even representation. These also happen to be states with sizable diasporas living abroad—mostly in France—that may have exported more progressive attitudes toward inheritance and divorce to their domestic households and so ensured a peaceful response to gender-related reforms.

## THE INDIRECT POLITICAL EFFECT OF REMITTANCES

From the Arab Barometer survey results, we know that remittance-receiving households are not directly opposed to women in politics—either supporting women's political equality or having neutral responses to it. However, this is, at best, an indirect effect. In remittance-receiving households, women often bear the burden of increased tasks and may long for the days before these new responsibilities. Thus, the dubious 'emancipation' brought about through remittances may not result in any real autonomy or interest in participating more fully in the public sphere, even if there is household support for greater public participation (Hajjarabi, 1995; van Rooij, 2000).

Any specific influence remittances might have on political participation would be conditioned by three possible scenarios:

a. ideas 'sent back' along with remittances;
b. autonomy granted unto women due to their taking control of financial resources of the home; and
c. women's engaging in additional paid work to shore up household revenue while the primary breadwinner is abroad.[28]

Scenario 'a' reflects the most direct potential impact of remittances on political behavior.

---

[27] Importantly, the absence of unified personal status and family laws is partially a byproduct of French and British 'divide and conquer' policies in their Arab colonies (Majed, 2021).

[28] It typically takes a few months for migrants to establish themselves and for the money to begin flowing back home.

As mentioned earlier in the chapter, remittances can also be a proxy for ideological international links. Money is not the only thing that travels across borders; ideas travel, too (Levitt, 1998). As populations communicate with and receive income from family members living abroad, they interact with new ideas and social issues from the migrant's host state. Social networking spread the Arab Spring across the MENA countries with unprecedented speed. This same media is also important for migrant workers wishing to stay in touch with their families, making migrant networks across the region and throughout the world a superhighway for information exchange. Where the information transfer involves social concepts, these linkages throughout the diaspora can become a powerful instrument for policy change, but also social change.

Migrant funds have often been used to bankroll revolutionary or insurgent groups, regional political action committees, and pressure groups that can influence domestic (and, in some cases, international) policymaking. As countries depend on remittance funds for economic stability and poverty alleviation, diaspora communities become politically empowered. Politicians must court and win the support of the emigrant community, who are removed from immediate government control and simultaneously encountering new ideas and systems of governance in their host states. Emigrant communities are in an especially powerful position that enables them to express their desire for reform and influence changes in policy.

The use of remittances to directly fund collective action has been documented in Latin America (Goldring, 2004), with extensive examples in the MENA as well, especially when it comes to funding independence movements.[29] It is less obvious that these funds have ever been used to promote ideologies that might directly empower women, although there is certainly evidence of their use for the promotion of conservative religious movements that would disempower them.

The indirect impact of remittances, illustrated in scenarios 'b' and 'c', has more purchase on the reality of most people living in the region. Remittances provide an extra source of income, usually pushing an

---

[29] See the more recent work of Laurie Brand (2018) for non-insurgent and non-terrorist examples. The more well-known examples extend to the activities of the PLO, the Lebanese diaspora during the civil war, Berber independence activities across North Africa, and Kurdish independence activities led and funded from abroad.

emigrant family's household income well above that of the local population. These funds allow household members to devote more time and resources to participating in social movements or political groups, which can influence policy outcomes. Remittance monies dedicated to household costs also lead to increased expenditures on education, which is known to increase political participation (Edwards & Ureta, 2003).

Changes to household labor dynamics, another result of remittances, can also affect political sentiments. However, more recent research on the gendered impact of male emigration in the MENA has not shown that more women seek out paid work in their absence, nor does it seem to stimulate income-generating activities among women (Lenoël & David, 2019). Binzel and Assaad (2011) and Lenoël and David (2019) have already explored the statistical impact of remittances on women's paid versus unpaid labor force participation in Morocco and Egypt. However, there has not been a cross-regional study that investigates whether these patterns hold in other Arab states. This is a particular challenge for our exploration of how money influences women's political mobilization, since that influence is often mediated through their presence or absence in the workforce.

To assess the impact of remittances—first on women's labor force participation and then on their political representation (as a somewhat imperfect proxy for their political mobilization), I run the two cross-national statistical models featured in Tables 4.2 and 4.3 across 19 Arab League member states from 1994 through 2018. I use data derived from the World Development Indicators (WDI) and estimate my results using Prais–Winston panel-corrected standard errors to control for autocorrelation first for the MENA and then for regional groups based on the WDI regional divisions for Asia, Central Asia, Sub-Saharan Africa, and Latin American and the Caribbean—all regions of the world receiving significant remittances from migrants living abroad. I then run a full model across some 170 countries worldwide for the same period.[30] To capture the impact of remittances, I use a measure of aggregate remittance receipts over GDP that illustrates the depth of the impact of these foreign monies within a given economy and precisely what level of 'rentierism' the state engages in.

---

[30] I use the World Development Indicators' regional categories/definitions in coding regional dummies for Central Asia, East Asia, the Pacific, and Latin America, and combine the European Union with the United States and Canada for OECD states.

**Table 4.2** The impact of remittances on women's labor force participation, world regions, 1994–2019

| | MENA | Africa | Latin America | Central Asia | East and South Asia | World |
|---|---|---|---|---|---|---|
| *Coeff/St. Errors/Sig* | | | | | | |
| Remittances | −0.11 | −0.11*** | 0.12* | −0.56*** | 0.30 | −0.51*** |
| | (0.16) | (0.06) | (0.10) | (0.06) | (0.21) | (0.54) |
| Democracy | 0.53*** | −0.48*** | 0.90*** | −0.07 | −1.30*** | 0.61*** |
| | (0.10) | (0.12) | (0.20) | (0.07) | (0.15) | (0.05) |
| GNI (log) | 10.2*** | −5.00*** | −1.40 | 2.30*** | 1.94* | 2.03*** |
| | (1.10) | (0.10) | (1.12) | (0.36) | (0.62) | (0.24) |
| Rural | 0.18*** | 0.32*** | −0.23*** | −0.10 | −0.04 | 0.24*** |
| Population | (0.10) | (0.02) | (0.20) | (0.10) | (0.05) | (0.01) |
| Fertility Rate | 2.60*** | −1.90*** | −1.01 | −2.60*** | −3.84*** | 0.65*** |
| | (0.32) | (0.35) | (0.72) | (1.00) | (0.53) | (0.13) |
| *R-squared* | 0.43 | 0.36 | 0.19 | 0.73 | 0.19 | 0.12 |
| *Obs* | 337 | 765 | 492 | 244 | 428 | 3109 |

*Source:* World Development Indicators (2022); Polity Project-Systemic Peace (2022)
Robust standard errors in parentheses: $*p < 0.10$, $**p < 0.05$, $***p < 0.01$

Measuring women's labor force participation in the MENA is especially tricky, because of demographic imbalances of both gender and the citizen versus non-citizen labor we see in the workforce composition of the GCC states (see Buttorff et al., 2018). To control for this anomaly, in Table 4.2 I use a measure of women's labor force participation over the total female population, rather than the general population. Finally, Tables 4.2 and 4.3 both incorporate some standard controls others have used to capture factors that might influence women's political and economic participation: regime type captured by Polity IV scores, percentage of rural population over total population, the log of gross national income (GNI) per capita as a measure of income and development, and the total female fertility rate.

When it comes to the impact of remittance on women's labor force participation, Table 4.3 shows us that in many ways, the MENA's patterns are not distinct from the averaged effects across the world. If anything, the negative impact of remittances on global women's workforce participation is more stark and significant, compared with what we see across the MENA countries. This is not completely unexpected, since only a handful

118   B. C. WELBORNE

**Table 4.3**  The impact of remittances on women's political representation, world regions, 1994–2019

| | MENA | Africa | Latin America | Central Asia | East and South Asia | World |
|---|---|---|---|---|---|---|
| *Coeff/St. Errors/Sig* | | | | | | |
| Women's Labor Force Participation | −0.03 (0.07) | 0.20*** (0.03) | −0.10*** (0.03) | 0.20** (0.10) | 0.12*** (0.02) | 0.22*** (0.01) |
| Remittances | −0.60*** (0.10) | −0.05 (0.05) | 0.07 (0.07) | 0.43** (0.10) | 0.80*** (0.11) | 0.17*** (0.03) |
| Democracy | 0.43*** (0.10) | −0.45*** (0.10) | −0.20 (0.20) | −0.70*** (0.10) | −0.61*** (0.07) | 0.02 (0.02) |
| GNI (log) | −1.80 (1.73) | 4.61*** (0.60) | 4.32*** (0.90) | 3.60*** (0.50) | 1.96*** (0.50) | 3.41*** (0.20) |
| Rural Population | −0.16*** (0.06) | 0.30*** (0.03) | 0.10*** (0.02) | 0.10* (0.04) | −0.13*** (0.03) | 0.01*** (0.01) |
| Fertility Rate | 1.55*** (0.56) | −2.73*** (0.30) | −2.30*** (0.60) | −1.53* (0.84) | 3.60*** (0.80) | 0.76*** (0.10) |
| *R-squared* | 0.15 | 0.22 | 0.14 | 0.49 | 0.36 | 0.23 |
| *Obs* | 283 | 644 | 418 | 215 | 365 | 2664 |

*Source:* World Development Indicators (2022); Polity Project-Systemic Peace (2022)
Robust standard errors in parentheses: *$p < 0.10$, **$p < 0.05$, ***$p < 0.01$

of countries in the MENA region are high-level remittance recipients and since the GCC states, in fact, represent source countries for remittances sent to the Levant and North Africa.

In global comparison, we see a significant and strong negative effect of remittances on women's labor force participation in Africa and in Central Asia, suggesting that remittances may indeed reify values that kick women out of the workforce in these regions. Conversely, there is a positive impact on women's labor force participation in Latin America—a region known for sending more female migrant labor abroad, with literature revealing that these remittance-sending women tend to change gender relations for the better in their home countries (Curran & Saguy, 2001).

The findings presented in Table 4.3 hint at the impact remittances have on important aspects of women's formal political participation across a larger sample of MENA countries. Intriguingly, compared to other regions of the world, MENA is the only region in my global analysis where remittances seem to have a negative effect on women's legislative representation. In Central Asian and Asian countries, the effect is positive and significant on women's parliamentary representation, whereas across Africa, the Pacific, and Latin America there are no significant regional effects overall. Yet again, such results hint at a unique context for the MENA states, especially the distinct ways gendered rentierism functions within the region's confines. In other words, the effect may be more political than economic, speaking to the ideological component of sent monies rather than explicitly economic ones.

According to Abdih et al. (2012) and Ahmed (2012, 2013), remittances can mimic the effects of the 'resource curse' in ways similar to foreign aid (Djankov et al., 2008) and oil rents (Gelb, 1988; Ross, 2012), in the sense that they can generate perverse economic and political outcomes. Research on the impact of remittances in Mexico reveals that receiving them may decouple recipients from local economic and political conditions in the same way they insulate the state from public censure, meaning recipients in the home country could also be less politically active and invested in the overall welfare of their fellow citizens (Germano, 2013; Goodman & Hiskey, 2008). Again, this financial buffer means states have reduced incentives to present themselves as accountable to citizens (Ahmed, 2012, 2013).[31] However, Dionne et al. (2014) are ambivalent as to whether they should be considered a 'curse' on par with oil rents and foreign aid, especially since they find the opposite result in their research remittances mobilizing political participation in the African context.[32]

If anything, what we see from the statistical analysis of the impact of the aggregate remittance data on indicators of women's legislative representation and on workforce participation is that remittances have discrete and gendered political effects in the MENA,[33] if not necessarily robust economic effects. Given prior Arab public opinion data showcasing conservative mores related to women's public roles, and controlling for other factors possibly correlated with women's legislative representation,

---

[31] As Dionne et al. (2014) elucidate, remittances' volatility can have a substantial impact on government expectations and spending patterns; they raise real exchange rates through an influx of foreign currency and so undermine the country's other exports and are effectively 'unearned' and 'independent of the citizens' willingness to engage in the economy' (2014: 4).

[32] Tyburski (2012) and Pfutze (2014) have similar findings in the case of Mexico.

[33] This finding is much as Dionne et al. (2014) contend in the African case.

120    B. C. WELBORNE

it is perhaps unsurprising that remittances would have such a negative effect on their formal political mobilization. The effect is more ambivalent on workforce participation. Of course, countries such as Jordan, Lebanon, Syria, and Yemen could confound such results with their distinct gender dynamics, perhaps serving to explain some of the mixed findings we have seen throughout this chapter's discussion.

As should be clear by now, an important issue to consider in moving forward with this line of research is that source countries matter. It makes a difference whether remittances are received from the GCC or from countries in the West. Thus, the attitudes of remittance recipients in Morocco, Algeria, Tunisia, and Sudan overall reflect more progressive values on questions of education, inheritance, women's mobility, and women's access to political office than what we see in Jordan, Lebanon, Egypt, or Iraq when broken down from the Arab Barometer data. This effect, combined with the religiosity of diaspora communities living abroad, can serve to underline the values exported home.

## CONCLUSION

Overall, remittances do not have clear-cut rentier effects, and certainly not the ones expected by those proponing they ellicit the same effects as oil dependency. When it comes to remittances' impact on women's access to the workforce in MENA countries, other factors seem to play a more important role. My own statistical analyses have not revealed a consistent effect of remittances on total women's labor force participation in Arab League member states, contrary to the expectations of longitudinal case studies in high remittance-receiving countries such as Egypt and Morocco. Importantly, averaging the effects of remittances across 19 Arab states would dampen the results.

What we do see is a decisive, unexpected, *and* negative political effect of remittances on women's legislative representation. This raises important questions: Do remittances actually disincentivize women's mobilization into political office or do they incentivize specific groups, such as extreme conservatives and Islamists, that actively lobby against women's presence and participation in politics? Here, the Arab public opinion data muddy the waters further; since remittance recipients have seemingly welcomed women's political participation since the Arab Spring, and in the fifth wave of the Arab Barometer even exhibited support for women's equal rights on key issues pertaining to family code. If nothing else, this analysis reveals that remittances cannot be ignored when considering the political-economic factors conditioning the range of choices afforded to women in Arab society.

## REFERENCES

Abdih, Y., Chami, R., Dagher, J., & Montiel, P. (2012). Remittances and institutions: Are remittances a curse? *World Development, 40*(4), 657–666.

Adams, R. H., Jr. (2009). The determinants of international remittances in developing countries. *World Development, 37*(1), 93–103.

Adams, R., & Page, J. (2005). Do international migration and remittances reduce poverty in developing countries? *World Development, 33*, 1645–1669.

Ahmed, F. Z. (2012). The perils of unearned foreign income: Aid, remittances, and government survival. *American Political Science Review, 106*(1), 146–165.

Ahmed, F. Z. (2013). Remittances deteriorate governance. *Review of Economics and Statistics, 95*(4), 1166–1182.

Aidi, W., Fatai, R., & Karingi, S. (2020, October 26). COVID-19 and migrant remittances: Supporting this essential lifeline under threat. Brookings Africa in Focus Blog. https://www.brookings.edu/blog/africa-in-focus/2020/10/26/covid-19-and-migrant-remittances-supporting-this-essential-lifeline-under-threat/

Aït Hamza, M. (1988). L'Emigration, Facteur d'Intégration ou de Désintégration des Régions d'Origine. Le Maroc et La Hollande. Rabat: Universite´ Mohammed V, 161–175.

Aït Hamza, M. (1995). Les femmes d'emigre´s dans les Societe´s Oasiennes, in: Le Maroc et La Holllande. Une Approche Comparative des Grands Intere´ts Communs. Rabat: Universite´ Mohammed V, 159–169.

Barreto, M. A., & Bozonelos, D. N. (2009). Democrat, Republican, or none of the above? The role of religiosity in Muslim American party identification. *Politics and Religion, 2*(2), 200–229.

Binzel, C., & Assaad, R. (2011). Egyptian men working abroad: Labour supply responses by the women left behind. *Labour Economics, 18*(1), 98–114.

Bouzid, N. (1992). *Espace et Activités au Féminin dans une Vallée Présaharienne du Sud Marocain: La Vallée du Todra*. Université de Rouen.

Brand, L. A. (2018). Expatriates and home state political development. *Mashriq & Mahjar: Journal of Middle East and North African Migration Studies, 5*(1), 11–35.

Brink, J. H. (1991). The effect of emigration of husbands of husbands on the status of their wives: An Egyptian case. *International Journal of Middle East Studies, 23*(2), 201–211.

122   B. C. WELBORNE

Burgess, K. (2012). Migrants, remittances, and politics: Loyalty and voice after exit. *Fletcher Forum of World Affairs, 36*(1), 43–56.

Buttorff, G. J., Al Lawati, N., & Welborne, B. C. (2018, January 18). Measuring female labor force participation in the GCC. Issue Brief 1. https://scholarship.rice.edu/bitstream/handle/1911/99713/bi-brief-011 818-wrme-femalelabor.pdf

Buvinic, M. (2009). *The global financial crisis: Assessing vulnerability for women and children, identifying policy responses.* Presented to UN Commission on the Status of Women, New York. http://www.un.org/womenwatch/daw/csw/csw53/panels/financial_crisis/Buvinic.formatted.pdf

Carling, J. (2005). *Gender dimensions of international migration.* Global Commission on International Migration.

Chant, S. (1997). *Women-headed households: Diversity and dynamics in the developing world.* Macmillan Press.

Charrad, M. M. (2001). *States and women's rights: The making of postcolonial Tunisia, Algeria, and Morocco.* University of California Press.

Charrad, M. M. (2011). Gender in the middle east: Islam, state, agency. *Annual Review of Sociology, 37*, 417–437.

Curran, S. R., & Saguy, A. C. (2001). Migration and cultural change: A role for gender and social networks? *Journal of International Women's Studies, 2*(3), 54–77.

Day, L. H., & Içduygu, A. (1997). The consequences of international migration for the status of women: A Turkish study. *International Migration, 35*(3), 337–372.

de Haas, H. (2007). *The impact of international migration on social and economic development in Moroccan sending region* (International Migration Institute Working Paper 3), 3–45.

de Haas, H. (2009). International migration and regional development in Morocco: A review. *Journal of Ethnic and Migration Studies, 35*(10), 1571–1593.

De Haas, H., & van Rooij, A. (2010). *Migration as emancipation? The impact of internal and international migration on the position of women left behind in rural Morocco.* Oxford Development Studies.

Debnath, P., & Selim, N. (2009). Impact of short term male migration on their wives left behind: A case study of Bangladesh. *Gender and labour migration in Asia* (pp. 121–151). International Organization for Migration (IOM).

Djankov, S., Montalvo, J. G., & Reynal-Querol, M. (2008). The curse of aid. *Journal of Economic Growth, 13*(3), 169–194.

Dionne, K., Inman, K. L., & Montinola, G. R. (2014). *Another resource curse? The impact of remittances on political participation. Afro-Barometer 10 years* (Working Paper No. 145). https://afrobarometer.org/sites/default/files/publications/Working%20paper/Afropaperno145.pdf

Eade, D. (2016). Women, gender, remittances and development in the global south. *Gender and Development, 24*(2), 332–335.

Edwards, A., & Ureta, M. (2003). International migration, remittances and schooling: Evidence from El Salvador. *Journal of Development Economics, 72*(2), 429–461.

Fadloullah, A., Berrada, A., & Khachani, M. (2000). *Facteurs d'Attraction et de Répulsion des Xux Migratoires Internationaux*. Rapport National: Le Maroc. Commission Européenne, Rabat.

Gelb, A. H. (1988). *Oil windfalls: Blessing or curse?* Oxford University Press.

Germano, R. (2013). Migrants' remittances and economic voting in the Mexican countryside. *Electoral Studies, 32*(4), 875–885.

Goldring, L. (2004). Family and collective remittances to Mexico: A multidimensional typology. *Development and Change, 35*(4), 799–840.

Goodman, G. L., & Hiskey, J. T. (2008). Exit without leaving: Political disengagement in high migration municipalities in Mexico. *Comparative Politics, 40*(2), 169–188.

Hadi, A. (2001). International migration and the change of women's position among the leftbehind in rural Bangladesh. *International Journal of Population Geography, 7*(1), 53–61.

Hajjarabi, F. (1988). *Femmes et Emigration: Cas de la Région d'Al Hoceima* (pp. 177–185). Université Mohammed V.

Hajjarabi, F. (1995). *Femmes, Famille et Changement Social dans le Rif. Le Maroc et La Hollande* (pp. 105–110). Université Mohammed V.

Hoodfar, H. (1997). The impact of male migration on domestic budgeting: Egyptian women striving for an Islamic budgeting pattern. *Journal of Comparative Family Studies, 28*(2), 73–98.

Human Rights Watch. (2009, September 3). *Morocco: Lift Restrictions on Amazigh (Berber) Names*. https://www.hrw.org/news/2009/09/03/morocco-lift-restrictions-amazigh-berber-names

Human Rights Watch. (2010, December 14). *Morocco/Western Sahara: More freedom to name their children*. https://www.hrw.org/news/2010/12/14/morocco/western-sahara-more-freedom-name-their-children

IOM. (2008). *World migration report 2008: Managing labor mobility in the evolving global economy*. International Organization for Migration (IOM). https://publications.iom.int/books/world-migration-report-2008-managing-labour-mobility-evolving-global-economy

IOM. (2010). *A study on remittances and investment opportunities for Egyptian Migrants*. International Organization for Migration (IOM). https://egypt.iom.int/sites/egypt/files/Remittances%20and%20Investment%20Opportunities%20for%20Egyptian%20Migrants.pdf

Joseph, S. (1996). Patriarchy and development in the Arab world. *Gender and Development, 4*(2), 14–19.

124   B. C. WELBORNE

Kabeer, N. (2012). *Women's economic empowerment and inclusive growth: Labour markets and enterprise development.* Discussion Paper. London, UK: CDPR-SOAS.

Kandiyoti, D. (1988). Bargaining with patriarchy. *Gender and Society, 2*(3), 274–290.

Kapur, D. (2003). *Remittances: The new development mantra.* Paper prepared for the G-24 Technical Group Meeting.

Kapur, D., & McHale, J. (2003). Migration's new payoff. *Foreign Policy, 139,* 48–57.

King, R., Dalipaj, M., & Mai, N. (2006). Gendering migration and remittances: Evidence from London and Northern Albania. *Population, Space and Place, 12*(6), 409–434.

Kunz, R. (2008). 'Remittances are beautiful'? Gender implications of the new global remittances trend. *Third World Quarterly, 29*(7), 1389–1409.

Leblang, D. (2010). Familiarity breeds investment: Diaspora networks and international investment. *American Political Science Review, 104*(3), 584–600.

Lenoël, A. (2017). The 'three ages' of left-behind Moroccan wives: Status, decisionmaking power and access to resources. *Population, Space and Place, 23*(8), 1–11.

Lenoël, A., & David, A. (2019). Leaving work behind? The impact of emigration on female labor force participation in Morocco. *International Migration Review, 53*(1), 122–153.

Levitt, P. (1998). Social remittances: Migration driven local-level forms of cultural diffusion. *International Migration Review, 32*(4), 926–948.

Lopez-, S., Aghazarm, C., Kötter, H., & Mollard, B. (2011). The impact of remittances on gender roles and opportunities for children in recipient families: Research from the International Organization for Migration. *Gender and Development, 19*(1), 69–80.

Majed, R. (2021, January 27). Towards a feminist political economy in the MENA region. *Women's international league for peace and freedom.* https://www.wilpf.org/towards-a-feminist-political-economy-in-the-mena-region/

Malhotra, A., & Schuler, S. R. (2005). Women's empowerment as a variable in international development. *Measuring Empowerment: Cross Disciplinary Perspectives, 1*(1), 71–88.

Menjivar, C., & Agadjanian, V. (2007). Men's migration and women's lives: Views from rural Armenia and Guatemala. *Social Science Quarterly, 88*(5), 1243–1262.

Mohieldin, M., & Ratha, D. (2020, June 11). *How to keep remittances flowing.* Brookings Future Development Blog. https://www.brookings.edu/blog/future-development/2020/06/11/how-to-keep-remittances-flowing/

Myntti, C. (1984). *Yemeni Workers Abroad. Merip Reports, 124,* 11–16.

Newland, K., & Patrick, E. (2004). *Beyond remittances: The role of diaspora in poverty reduction in their countries of origin*. Migration Policy Institute.

Nwanze, K. (2015, July 8). *Empowering families to finance development with remittances and diaspora savings*. Brookings: Future Development Blog. https://www.brookings.edu/blog/future-development/2015/07/08/empowering-families-to-finance-development-with-remittances-and-diaspora-savings/

O'Mahony, A. (2012). Political investment: Remittances and elections. *British Journal of Political Science, 43*(4), 799–820.

OECD. (2020, June 10). *COVID-19 crisis in the MENA region: Impact on gender equality and policy responses*. Tackling Coronavirus (Covid-19): Contributing to a Global Effort. https://www.oecd.org/coronavirus/policy-responses/covid-19-crisis-in-the-mena-region-impact-on-gender-equality-and-policy-responses-ee4cd4f4/

Pfutze, T. (2014). Clientelism versus social learning: The electoral effects of international migration. *International Studies Quarterly, 58*(2), 295–307.

Ramírez, C., Domínguez, M. G., & Morais, J. M. (2005). *Crossing borders: Remittances, gender and development* (UN INSTRAW Working Paper).

Ross, M. L. (2008). Oil, Islam, and women. *American Political Science Review, 102*(1), 107–123.

Ross, M. L. (2012). *The oil curse*. Princeton University Press.

Sadiqi, F., & Ennaji, M. (2004). The impact of male migration from Morocco to Europe on women: A gender approach. *Finisterra: Revista Portuguesa de Geografia, 39*, 59–76.

Sadiqi, F., & Ennaji, M. (2006). The feminization of public space: Women's activism, the family law, and social change in Morocco. *Journal of Middle East Women's Studies, 2*(2), 86–114.

Singer, D. A. (2010). Migrant remittances and exchange rate regimes in the developing world. *American Political Science Review, 104*(2), 307–323.

Sorensen, N. N. (2004). *Migrant remittances as a development tool: The case of Morocco*. International Organization for Migration (IOM).

Steinmann, S. H. (1993). Effects of international migration on women's work in agriculture. *Revue De Géographie Du Maroc, 15*(1–2), 105–124.

Tarrow, S. G. (2011). *Power in movement: Social movements and contentious politics*. Cambridge University Press.

Taylor, E. (1984). Egyptian migration and peasant wives. *Merip Reports, 124*, 3–10.

Tripp, A. M. (2019). *Seeking legitimacy: Why Arab autocracies adopt women's rights*. Cambridge University Press.

Tyburski, M. D. (2012). The resource curse reversed? Remittances and corruption in Mexico. *International Studies Quarterly, 56*(2), 339–350.

UN INSTRAW. (2007). *Gender, remittances and development: Feminization of migration* (United Nations INSTRAW Working Paper 1).

UN DESA, Population Division. (2017). Household size and composition around the world 2017—Data Booklet (ST/ESA/ SER.A/405).

van Rooij, A. (2000). *Women of Taghzoute: The effects of migration on women left behind in Morocco* (IMAROM Working Paper Series No. 12). Amsterdam, The Netherlands: University of Amsterdam.

Welborne, B. C., Westfall, A. L., Russell, Ö. Ç., & Tobin, S. A. (2018). *The politics of the headscarf in the United States*. Cornell University Press.

CHAPTER 5

# Independents, Women's Work, and Oil Rents

Jordanian activist and the President of Sisterhood is Global Institute (SIGI), Asma Khader, recently stated, 'Economic empowerment is the basis for every subsequent empowerment, and the political participation of Jordanian women will not progress unless their economic participation also increases …'.[1] The academic literature agrees with her that 'the more access women have to outside income, the more influence they wield within the home and the political arena' (Iversen & Rosenbluth, 2006; Schlozman et al., 1999). Our discussion of remittances from Chapter 4 illustrates this aptly. When women in Morocco and Egypt received remittances directly, especially young wives, household gender dynamics changed. Families moved to cities; wives were more likely to pursue higher education for themselves and their children. The type of remittances further influenced both women's willingness to work and their broader access to independent monies, perhaps even conditioning their interest in political office.

---

Partially reprinted with permission from Brill Publishers/ Welborne, B. C. (2020). On Their Own? Women Running as Independent Candidates in the Middle East. *Middle East Law and Governance, 12*(3): 251–274.

[1] SIGI (2020).

© The Author(s), under exclusive license to Springer Nature Switzerland AG 2022
B. C. Welborne, *Women, Money, and Political Participation in the Middle East,*
https://doi.org/10.1007/978-3-031-04877-7_5

Curiously, we also saw in Chapter 4 that remittances specifically correlate with fewer women in office in the MENA region, whereas the extant literature discussed in Chapter 3 has shown that foreign aid tends to increase the number of female office-holders the world over and in the MENA. This reveals a key difference between top-down foreign financial incentives (aid as a form of public money) and bottom-up ones (remittances as private money) in determining women's path and access to power and influence.

Most research in the Global North and the Global South has focused on women's entry into the workforce as a catalyst for political change, following the standard tropes of modernization theory.[2] Yet, the Arab world has always represented somewhat of an outlier to this line of scholarship. Mainstream pundits and scholars alike presume religious proscription would mean women were not present in the workforce, precluding that path to their increased political mobilization. Although this point is certainly salient, religion and tradition are not consistent in their effects, nor are they overwhelming barriers to women's political or even economic participation in the MENA. In Al Lawati and Buttorff's (2020) review of copious public opinion polls surveying working women in the GCC states, most respondents indicated that family and culture, and not so much religion, were keeping women from working. Still, MENA states overall have some of the lowest formal rates of women's workforce participation relative to the rest of the world—a feature of the region that needs to be addressed head-on.

Between 1996 and 2020, the average rate of women's labor force participation as a percentage of the total workforce was 17–20 percent in the MENA, compared to the world average of 47 percent (Buttorff et al., 2018). A recent UN Women study (2020) forecast a further decline in those already low numbers, predicting some 700,000 women would lose their jobs due to the COVID-19 epidemic. These economic statistics stand in stark contrast to the region's numeric progress in increasing the number of women in its national assemblies, which experienced a 300-percent jump from 2000 to 2020, largely through the spread of gender quotas and government appointments (IPU, 2020; also Welborne, 2020).

---

[2] See Lipset (1959) for a general discussion of modernization theory and its ties to democracy.

These low workforce statistics do not reveal the true variation in women's work-lives across subregions of the MENA. Certain subregions may actually offer enough lucrative professional job opportunities and experience, creating a mix of incentives that can allow women to seriously consider running for office without institutional support in environments where political parties do not extensively field or fund female (or even male) political candidates (Shalaby, 2016).

In this chapter, we will build on our discussions of women in the workplace in previous chapters, exploring how one of the most overt forms of rentierism—oil dependency and oil-dependent investment— plays into unexpected work, political opportunities, and pitfalls for women who choose to run for public office. The discussion in previous chapters has focused on aid- or remittance-dependent states in the MENA, which tend to be poorer than their oil-wealthy GCC counterparts. But not all oil-wealthy states are created equal, as Michael Herb (2014) points out in his seminal analysis of resource-abundant versus dependent states. Where gendered rentierism becomes notable here is in the discussion of women's path to political influence and its dependence on the mechanisms undergirding the distribution of oil rents throughout society.

We will look at the role of oil windfalls in creating better-paying job opportunities for potential female candidates—particularly those who opt to run as independents for political office. We will give special attention to the cases of female candidates in the GCC, where women enjoy some of the highest rates of citizen-based labor force participation across the MENA but simultaneously low rates of political representation (short of government appointment). We will consider how women's workplace connections—both local and international—allow them to bankroll campaigns in ways similar to their male counterparts. Specifically, we will compare the experience of Bahraini and Omani women to that of Lebanese and Jordanian women running for office as independents, contrasting the latter two groups with their counterparts in other parts of North Africa, who tend to obtain office through political party backing. Finally, we will look at the role of partisanship in women's entry into politics and what this trend of more successful women independents' acceding to legislatures bodes for the region.

130    B. C. WELBORNE

## The Emergence of Women Independents

Women have successfully run for office as independent candidates in seven Arab states: Algeria, Lebanon, Oman, Jordan, Bahrain, Kuwait, and Egypt.[3] As a region, most recently the MENA led the world in the number of states with independent female Members of Parliament (MPs) in their national legislatures (see Table 5.1; Welborne, 2020). I classify as 'independent' women MPs or political candidates operating without explicit political party support for their campaigns, and without party support or affiliation once they enter office (Brancati, 2008; Weeks, 2016, 2018).[4] Such a phenomenon runs counter to expectations, especially considering these are transitioning or straightforwardly authoritarian states where funds are already limited for anyone running for public office. Yet, we have seen a cadre of independent women candidates emerge, often as a result of the particular combination of their inclusion in the professional labor force, their social networks, and, of course, the institutional presence of gender quotas. That combination is not the same across contexts; so, whereas gender quotas happen to be essential for female independents in the Levant and Egypt, they are irrelevant to women running for office in the GCC states—at least until recent changes in the UAE.

In the 2018 Lebanese parliamentary elections, for example, most of the final 82 women who ran for office were independents (Hamdan, 2018). Of the six winners, one classified herself as an independent; this was veteran journalist Paula Yacoubian, who won Beirut's first electoral district despite the ubiquity of regime-backed candidates (Astih, 2018). Many of these women independents also ran on lists affiliated with civil society

---

[3] Countries such as the UAE and Saudi Arabia are not included in this list because female MPs are effectively state appointments and/or these countries do not have elected (or lower) houses of Parliament.

[4] Irish scholar Liam Weeks defines an independent as 'someone who is neither a member of, nor affiliated with, a political party' effectively campaigning 'on their own' (2016: 582). This simple definition belies the complicated ways 'independence' can manifest in nonpartisan politics in the Global North and Global South. Many nominal independents still have ties to political parties (for example, Joe Lieberman in the United States) or connections to the government in power. See the work of Grigorii Golosov (2003) on Russia. However, there is limited evidence that these ties *by default* prevent independents from engaging in autonomous agenda-setting within parliamentary assemblies; rather, 'programmatic autonomy' varies from context to context as well as on the kinds of issues individual MPs choose to promote.

## 5 INDEPENDENTS, WOMEN'S WORK, AND OIL RENTS 131

**Table 5.1** Women independents in global assemblies, 2015–2018[5]

| Global Region* (number of countries) | Percentage of countries with female independents (%) | Countries with female independents |
|---|---|---|
| Middle East and North Africa (19) | 36** | Algeria, Oman, Jordan, Bahrain. Egypt, Kuwait, Lebanon*** |
| Europe (42) | 14 | United Kingdom, Croatia, Ireland, Slovenia, Lichtenstein, Romania |
| Latin America and Caribbean (33) | 14 | Panama, Chile. Honduras, Guyana |
| South Asia (8) | 12 | Bangladesh |
| Central Asia (11) | 9 | Armenia |
| East Asia (16) | 6 | Myantnar |
| Pacific (12) | 8 | Australia |
| Sub-Saharan Africa (45) | 6 | Uganda, Eswatini, Cape Verde |
| North America (3) | 33 | Canada |

*The World Bank's regional descriptors were used for filtering 186 countries into global regions. A different ordering of the countries in each world region can yield slightly different results, but overall the unique status of the MENA holds.
**With the results of the May 2018 elections in Lebanon, the country was dropped from this list, bringing the new percentage total to 32%.
***The number of female independents relative to partisan women in elected assemblies across the the MENA for 2017: Algeria (5 /119); Oman (1/1); Jordan (17/20); Bahrain (3/3); Egypt (12/89); Kuwait (2/2); Lebanon (1/4)

organizations and movements, such as the *Kulluna Watani* movement, aiming to challenge status quo politics in Lebanon.[6]

Yacoubian herself ran under the *Kulluna Watani* banner, resigning in August 2020 along with other members of the civil society movement in protest of a failing Lebanese government, which had neglected to fully address a slew of crises that beset the nation. Despite her affiliation with the movement, Yacoubian saw herself as an independent candidate lucky enough to snag an Armenian Orthodox seat in the legislature, but also

[5] Featured in Welborne, B. C. (2020). On their own? Women running as independent candidates in the Middle East. *Middle East Law and Governance, 12*(3): 251–274.

[6] *Kullouna watani* is Arabic for 'We are all for the nation'. The movement fielded some 66 candidates in nine voting districts (Cohen, 2018).

## 132    B. C. WELBORNE

adamant she would not be joining any blocs within it—the typical strategy of Lebanese politicians[7]:

> Which bloc can I join? None. Bloc members always follow the directives of the bloc leader. I may be closer to certain blocs on certain issues — I can lobby with the various blocs on specific topics — but not be part of them. (*Arab Weekly*, 2018)

Yacoubian spoke about two important ingredients in her 2018 win—professional status and class—in an interview with the *Cairo Review*:

> I was the famous figure of Kulluna Watani, and I think I campaigned on a different agenda than the rest. I also think that my region [Achrafieh, an old and upper-class district of Beirut] is the region that can bring change to Lebanon. Its residents are both highly educated and liberal ... which is why it was easier for us to make it there. (Cohen, 2018)

Yacoubian's description of the urbane socioeconomic class that elected her dovetails with the success of female independent politicians in other Arab countries with smaller, more professionalized, and urbanized populations such as Bahrain, Kuwait, the UAE, and Oman. Smaller district size also enables vote-buying, and political reach does not require an extensive party network so much as robust traditional social connections. These independent candidates tap into old and new patronage networks for their campaigns. Some stem from the traditional power-brokers in a given Arab society (from tribal elders and royal sponsors to regime-backed political parties); others have emerged with the international community's political and, more importantly, financial commitment to women's empowerment as part of broader efforts at democratization (Bush, 2011; Carapico, 2002; Welborne, 2010). In some cases, women are also embracing non-traditional feminist transnational networks to obtain the support they need, whether looking to other Arab women's movements or international advocacy networks (Tripp, 2019).

In Jordan, former MP Falaak Jamani reflected this blend of public and private experience in her military and medical background. As we saw in Chapter 3, her cross-cutting professional experience, mixed with personal *wasta*, granted her the rare ability to place people in jobs across two key

---

[7] In some respects, the Armenian Orthodox seat functions as a de facto quota.

sectors and win the favor of local tribes, to the point where they invited her to participate in their *diwans* (tribal councils) as a full member.[8] The Arabic term *wasta* captures 'an implicit social contract, typically within a tribal group, that obliges those within the group to provide assistance (favorable treatment) to others within that group' (Barnett et al., 2013). Stephanie Nanes' research highlights how this ability to engage in 'public service provision' is imperative to wielding any political influence in Jordan, which applies equally to women (and men) in other Arab states (David & Nanes, 2011; Nanes, 2010, 2015). A hallmark of this phenomenon was women's increasing ability to parlay a wide variety of social networks toward political campaigns—reminiscent of the idea of *wasta* among men.

Through our analysis of Arab Barometer survey data, my colleague Gail Buttorff and I found that Arab countries where women reported having levels of *wasta* similar to men tended to have more women serving in political office. Essentially, these women had comparable ability to provide services and access intercessory networks as their male counterparts in the political arena.[9] Certainly, it is not unexpected for women in the MENA to rely on tribal or sectarian affiliation as mechanisms for political promotion, but many of the women who ran for office had *wasta* in their own right, often from work in the private sector. This was clear in Jordan, at times in Lebanon, and particularly in the GCC states. Consider Reem Badran's direct parliamentary win in the 2010 Jordanian elections. Badran's background hints at her impressive ability to fundraise and organize largely honed working for local and international banks. She was the second deputy to the president of the Amman Chamber of Commerce and previously executive director of the Jordan Investment Board. Her connections to the Jordanian political establishment via her father, an ex-prime minister, certainly helped her bid for a seat in Amman's rich third district, but the ability to bankroll her own campaign was also essential.

---

[8] Falaak Jamani won her first mandate through the quota for governorate of Madaba in 2003 and was later re-elected in a landslide victory in 2007.

[9] This is a particularly striking development since most male independent candidates in the region are typically seen as emblematic of the political establishment, rather than disruptors of the status quo. In Lebanon, women reported having the same levels of *wasta* as men, but still had low levels of legislative representation relative to their counterparts in North Africa who also benefit from parliamentary gender quotas (see Buttorff & Welborne, 2015).

Access to the public and private economic spheres—as well as opportunities beyond traditional, often gendered, work—can generate private wealth for women that, in turn, they can use to fund political campaigns in the absence of government funds. Lucrative employment also provides potential women candidates with skills and experience, such as networking and public speaking, that they can parlay into running successful political campaigns at national and municipal levels. Private wealth and skills acquired in professional, salaried employment may also open up the political sphere to women independent of the political party system, which may be unwilling to promote women because of cultural or other strategic calculations. Private wealth also avails women with the money necessary to buy votes where and when necessary. As we have seen, it is likely not an accident that female independents tend to emerge in Arab countries with smaller populations, where vote-buying and political reach are less dependent on the larger political party networks than they are in the more populous North African states.

Mainstream literature still focuses on political parties as the primary conduit for women's political participation and inclusion in local and national legislatures worldwide, regardless of regime type (Wängnerud, 2009). Nonetheless, many candidates run for national office without political party support, especially in transitioning regimes or countries where party organizations are weaker than in OECD democracies (Brancati, 2008; Norris, 2006; Weeks, 2018). The MENA countries reflect this trend at the national and local levels, in countries where political parties are banned and where parties are regular features of the political landscape. Certainly, parties can provide men and women alike with an immediate source of funds and campaign support, as well as built-in networks of potential constituents in democratic and authoritarian regimes. However, political parties are fairly weak across most of the MENA region and we find an entire sub-region—the GCC—that effectively bans political parties as a form of socio-political organization (Langohr, 2004; Lust, 2009; Shalaby, 2016).

The GCC countries represent somewhat unique cases since these bans effectively turn everyone into an independent. In fact, there is some evidence that GCC governments are actively encouraging men and women to run exclusively as independents, rather than partnering with sanctioned 'political associations', as the national governments hope to 're-orient parliamentary life … away from religious-based groups' (England & Kerr, 2018). Until recently, none of the GCC states had broached the subject of parliamentary gender quotas as a real possibility, despite the existence of quotas for certain sectors of the labor force, often in the guise of labor nationalization policies, in Kuwait and the UAE (Rutledge et al., 2011; Willoughby, 2004). The UAE recently embraced what is essentially a gender quota in its 2019 parliamentary elections, and so increased women's representation in the National Assembly to 50 percent. Per Sharifa al-Barami, an Omani women's activist quoted in the Muscat Daily (2015), women's campaigns often center narrowly on individual communities necessitating a quota if they are to have broader appeal:

> There is also a need for a quota for women because men tend to campaign as representatives for their tribes and regions ... These are important, but don't get votes. This discourages women for entering the elections.

This may also explain why women seem to do better campaigning at the municipal (*wilayat*) level in Oman than at the national level (Hasan, 2016).[10]

Despite the lack of political parties, we still see women largely elected, not appointed, to national assemblies. Male and female candidates alike rely on private funds and networks to secure office, a fact that would lead us to expect no women at all in the political arena, except for those who rise to political positions through executive appointment. In the last decade, with suffrage extended across almost all GCC states, this has actually not been the case. Although the number of women winning seats directly is still small, it is surprising that they can win seats at all, considering the unpopularity of gender quotas and the lack of any other real form of party-like support. Furthermore, there is limited international NGO or associational presence, with the organizations that often provide leadership training and campaign workshops for women in the Levant and North Africa either banned or heavily circumscribed.[11]

---

[10] Two of the women who ran successfully at the local level were members of the Omani Women's Association—Rahma al-Ghufailiyah (Liwa municipality) and Rahma al-Noufli (Mussanah municipality)—the only NGO allowed in the country to represent women's interests.

[11] American development contractors such as the NDI, the IRI, the International Foundation for Electoral Systems (IFES) do much of this work alongside similar government-sponsored European organizations (see Bush, 2015).

136    B. C. WELBORNE

Meanwhile, GCC women are winning political office; and while most come from notable families, there are surprising outliers to this trend. Part of the reason may be their ability to independently fund campaigns, either through family connections or their own income. Here, directly elected women politicians tend to come from economically enfranchised background and well-connected families, so clientelist political parties (whether pro or anti-regime) are not part of the party-gatekeeping mechanisms that often undergird political office, as is the case in North Africa. Rather, tribal clout, private economic wealth, or access to independent sources of funds through work or family enable women to overcome initially high barriers to entry without having to work through political parties.[12]

As Gail Buttorff, Nawra Lawati, and I have shown in prior work, when taking women's labor force participation in the GCC states as a percentage of the women's population and not the inflated male population (an artifact of non-citizen migration trends from South Asia), GCC women do much better in terms of incomes adjusted for purchasing power parity and even type and level of employment, with many working in professional, white-collar jobs (see Fig. 5.1). This is doubtless a byproduct of the push by current GCC regimes in many a state to educate their populations and build human capital, often for nationalist reasons— that is, to undercut the dependence on foreign labor (Buttorff et al., 2018).

## GENDERED RENTIERISM IN OIL-DEPENDENT VERSUS OIL-ABUNDANT STATES

I and others have already challenged the Michael Ross (2008) thesis that oil wealth is necessarily compromising of women's workforce and political participation. But, it is also worth exploring how this form of rentierism

---

[12] It is also important to reiterate that electoral systems play a role in whether states incentivize the creation of parties or MPs run as independents outside the doctrines of the state. Parties function differently in authoritarian settings, including most of the countries of the Middle East. Amal Sabbagh (2005) argues that female tokenism is actually more pronounced within the region's political parties than in many government institutions, with many state policies appearing to be 'more gender sensitive' than normal party messaging. In her case comparison of Lebanon, Yemen, and Jordan, support for women's political participation came from very different actors—major political parties in Yemen, prominent politicians in Lebanon, and the monarchy in Jordan (Sabbagh, 2005: 65).

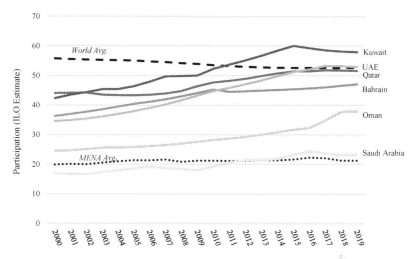

**Fig. 5.1** Women's labor force participation in the GCC, 2000–2019 (*Source:* World Development Indicators, 2022)

seems to have benefited GCC women, albeit in very specific contexts, and perhaps to see how it may have even played into women's election to political office in the new millennium. As Miriam Cooke aptly states, 'women in the workplace signal their nations' modernity; women in 'abayas perform their countries' authenticity' (2014: 141). Gendered rentierism has been a particular component of GCC states that rely on image, one way or the other, to promote an array of businesses beyond oil, although oil wealth is what has universally allowed other sectors to flourish in the first place—as with finance and construction in the UAE and Kuwait, and media in Qatar.

Al Lawati and Buttorff (2020) presciently note the importance of oil prices in determining women's status—creating opportunities in some cases, limitations in others—since it is so closely linked to the windfalls from oil rentierism. They observe how some of the most significant changes for women in Saudi Arabia—from lifting the driving ban to reducing the impact of guardian consent laws—occurred during periods of oil-price crisis. In Bahrain, this galvanized women's entry into startups, with the kingdom hosting more female startup founders than London or the Silicon Valley. However, the Omani case is also indicative of what we might expect from fluctuating oil prices, with many women

138    B. C. WELBORNE

fearing they would lose their jobs in bouts of public sector downsizing, due to waning revenue from oil, and with the majority of women working for the state across all GCC countries.[13]

The recent push to expand labor nationalization policies in the GCC has somewhat allayed these fears, with a significant reduction in the issuance of expatriate worker visas, even allowing women to gain access to jobs in workspaces from which they were previously barred, such as tourism in the Omani case. Legislation in Bahrain has gone one step further in its labor nationalization requirements for foreign companies, mandating that one local employee must be hired for every four foreign employees—and that employing a Bahraini woman counts as two local employees.

The depth of these changes for women and how they fare when oil prices are high versus when they are low somewhat dovetails with whether oil producers are 'abundant' (rents per capita) or 'dependent' (rents as a percentage of GDP) on oil rents in the first place. And, it is certainly related to how fearful a given state is of the 'restive' potential of its population—female or male—in a crisis. In his work on extreme versus mid-tier rentier states, Michael Herb (2014) highlights how Kuwait, Qatar, and the UAE tend to have higher rents per capita, and so he classifies them as resource-abundant, largely due to their small citizen populations and the extreme economic windfalls the state garners and can distribute from oil rents. This has allowed these states to host the MENA's highest percentages of citizen women in the workforce. Herb makes no bones about how these workforce statistics are a byproduct of women's educational achievements, which have largely been paid for by oil wealth (2014: 22–23).

The oil-abundant states of Kuwait and UAE have given more women opportunities to work in an array of professional sectors than what we see in their other GCC counterparts. In fact, Kuwait has more citizen women in the workforce than men (Toumi, 2016). We also see some of the highest rates of women's participation in the banking and finance sectors of these extreme rentier states, constituting in some cases more than half of the employee base, as in the Emirate of Dubai. Still, only a

---

[13] Kuwait, Qatar, Saudi Arabia, and the UAE in the majority of their female citizens working in the public sector, at 92 percent, 87.3 percent, 81 percent, and 75 percent, respectively, in 2016 (Al Lawati & Buttorff, 2020: 249; GCC Statistical Center, 2016: Table 12).

fraction of these working women are in executive roles, although yet again the UAE and Kuwait have the region's highest percentages of women managers (Kemp et al., 2015).

But what of Saudi Arabia, Oman, and Bahrain—GCC states that might be mid-tier rentier states and so borderline oil-dependent, due to a combination of large population (Saudi) and waning oil rents (Bahrain and Oman)? All three of these states are rich in resources but have female workforce participation rates below the extreme GCC rentiers and the overall MENA average. The current overtures being made to women in these mid-rentiers may be indicative of concerns about dissatisfied citizens in states that are more dependent than abundant in oil rents, revealing where the ability to co-opt restive citizens may be limited—as hard as that may seem to fathom. And so, we see a picture in which oil prices are increasingly decoupled from expected behavior, with oil-dependent states fearful of revolution (such as Saudi Arabia, Oman, and Bahrain) reaching out to women when oil prices are *down*, whereas oil-abundant states (such as Kuwait and the UAE) expanding women's and men's opportunities when oil prices are *up*.

The outlier to this pattern is Qatar—an extreme rentier monarchy that, due to more conservative mores, has fewer women managers and fewer women in the workforce overall, with numbers more akin to Saudi Arabia than its counterparts Kuwait and the UAE. Much as in Saudi, Qatari society frowns on gender mixing at work (Salem & Yount, 2019). We also see this translate into a consistent lack of women's political representation in the Qatari national legislature, up until the recent executive appointments of four women to the Shura Council in 2017—not unlike Saudi Arabia's appointment of 30 women to their Consultative Assembly. By contrast, women have been directly elected since the turn of the millennium in the rest of the GCC, first in Bahrain, then Kuwait, the UAE, and Oman. As stated before, the highest number of female MPs is actually in the UAE assembly which recently adopted what is a de facto quota system. Kuwait has had up to four female MPs elected and is one of the few GCC states to host a more robust homegrown feminist movement. Oman recently expanded its numbers as well.

## The Political Economy of Women's Legislative Representation

### The Bahraini Case

The Bahraini regime's quelling of political societies (and direct banning of the oppositional Islamist *al-Wefaq* and secular *al-Wa'ad* societies) since the Arab Spring has made it difficult for candidates to run under the auspices of a social movement. Thus, the majority of MPs in the national assembly are now independent, meaning that women have had to launch their own campaigns for these positions without the external political affiliations that would have elevated their bids for office. And, of course, this is occurring in an atmosphere where political opposition—often Shi'a—is not tolerated.

In the Bahraini parliamentary elections of November 2014, a record number of Shi'a women were directly elected to the *Majles An-Nawab*. In fact, all three women elected to the Parliament—Fatimah al-Asfour, Rula al-Haiki, and Jamila a-Sammak—were Shi'a.[14] Their success in Bahrain's first post-Arab Spring elections is particularly interesting, since the Shi'a community in Bahrain is economically and politically marginalized from the regime (Wehrey, 2014). Yet, these women were also well-known acolytes of the regime (a surprise to no one who follows Bahraini politics more closely). Furthermore, significant wealth was concentrated in the hands of these new female MPs, with rumors abounding that they were effectively royal appointments.

Importantly, all three were professional women—a lawyer, a businesswoman, and a doctor.[15] The interplay of socioeconomic status, private economic wealth, public sector connections, and political representation is clear. MP al-Haiki was chief executive officer of the ADAMOV Management and Consulting Group, and Jamila a-Sammak had been a dominant force in Bahrain public health, most recently serving as the administrative manager for government hospitals across the kingdom. A quick look at Bahrain's Majles a-Shura (the upper house) in 2014 revealed a majority of its female members had connections to international business networks,

---

[14] The first Shi'a woman directly elected to Bahrain's parliament was Sawsan Taqawi, who won by default (she was the only candidate in the district) in the 2011 by-elections.

[15] In Bahrain, political parties are referred to as political societies. The 1989 Law of Associations, which was revised in 2007 and, most recently, in 2012, regulates the formation of political associations—effectively political parties. See Kasoolu et al. (2019).

most prominently deputies Hala Ramzi Fayiz Qurisa, Samya al-Moayyed, and Dalal al-Zayed.

With the 2018 elections, the number of women in the Majles doubled to six, with a newly appointed female speaker of the house in Fawzia bint Abdullah Zainal.[16] Yet the 2018 Majles continued to reflect the trends of 2014 in terms the elite backgrounds and social networks of the women representatives. Fawzia and MP Zainab Abdel Amir both work in media, MP Kaltham al-Hayki has worked in the financial and telecommunications sectors, and two other women MPs, Drs. Sawsan Kamal and Masouma Abdel Rahim, are otherwise employed as psychiatrists. Zainab and Kaltham are on the Economic and Financial Affairs Committee.

On the whole, this cohort of women is better educated and connected than many of their male counterparts in the Majles—squarely playing into the stereotypes that have become the rule, that female MPs across the region often outpace their male colleagues in education and even professional connections, if not political experience. Most of the male MPs have honed their craft in the trenches of municipal office, which is uncommon for Bahraini women. Gender segregation has been an issue for women campaigning, although there has been a slow yet steady shift in the expectations of men and women mixing at campaign events, as illustrated with Fawzia Zainal's welcome of men and women into her events during her campaign.

In some respects, these women's background makes sense in a state that has long allowed women to pursue education—the first in the GCC—and one in which close to 70 percent of university students are female. More striking is the fact that many seek and find employment in the private sector; this is an anomaly in the Arabian Gulf where women are most likely to work in public sector jobs for the benefits and security and are often actively shunned and discouraged from the private sector for a variety of reasons. As of 2016, though, the majority of Bahrain's women (57.2 precent) worked in the private sector. This also means women in Bahrain are more likely to have access to the types of money that make campaigns viable, even if their public sector social networks are invaluable as well.

---

[16] Sawsan Kamal, Zainab Abdul Amir, Massoma Abdul Raheem, and Kaltham Al Hayki joined Fawzia Zainal and Fatima Al Qatari, who were previously in the Parliament.

142    B. C. WELBORNE

## The Omani Case

In Oman, Nemah bint Jamiel bin Farhan al-Busaidiya, was the female political stalwart of the sultanate's Parliament until the 2019 elections (Muscat Daily, 2015; Vela, 2015). Al-Busaidiya was elected for a second term as a representative for Seeb district—a locality that has also elected a female municipal councilor in the past. An elementary school teacher, Busaidiya allegedly won her second-term seat by stumping door-to-door in her neighborhood and through her reputation in the community as an educator. Omani political analyst and journalist Ahmed Ali Mukheini claimed she had led a 'clean campaign' that appealed to her community.[17]

Mukheini was also the primary advisor to Tawasul, an organization that attempted to offer political training to female candidates in the 2015 election cycle. He observed that most female candidates actually came from middle-class backgrounds, often working in low- to mid-level jobs in education or other branches of the public sector—a departure from the typical male candidate profile (Al-Balushi, 2014). Mukheini believed these women were largely motivated by a wish to hear more women's voices in the system but did not display much knowledge on how to campaign for office or on the intricacies of the political process.[18] Yet, Omani women's activists have lamented the low showing of women in the 2016 elections.

The Omani case may seem a strange selection, considering the dearth of women in the political system, but the presence of Al-Busaidiya and the insights behind the way she ran her campaign are trenchant. A woman winning without party or tribal backing, without a gender quota in place to facilitate her entry into Parliament, in a male-dominated majoritarian electoral system, is not insignificant. Her win hints at not only the new social networks women can tap into, but also the power of a female personalism even within plurality systems.

While economic associations and non-partisan social networks may play a key role in women's ability to run for office as independents in the GCC, as we have seen in Bahrain and Oman, institutional mechanisms play a more important role in other states—especially the mechanism of gender quotas. Jordan and Lebanon still have some of the lowest rates of women's employment in the MENA region as we saw in Fig. 5.1,

---

[17] Author interview in Muscat, Oman. January 2016.

[18] In contrast, it is an open secret that Omani men use parliamentary office as a way to set up lucrative business arrangement during and after their tenure.

although the countries' standard of living has certainly grown over the last twenty years and we do see many female professionals. Yet, both states host political parties run by women and have, on average, more directly-elected women in their legislatures than their GCC counterparts.

### *The Jordanian Case*

It is no accident that women who attain posts in the Jordanian Majles an-Nawab tend to be well-connected and often independently wealthy, with close ties to the international NGO and business community, not unlike the story of women politicians in the GCC. This was indeed the case for Reem Badran and Falaak Jamani, the only two women elected outside of the gender quota before the 2013 national elections. Yet, not all successful independent women candidates are similarly well-heeled. In the 2013 parliamentary elections, retired schoolteacher Mariam Losi won her seat outright because she was perceived 'as a decent, traditional Jordanian women living the same life as other Jordanians' (Christophersen, 2013: 29). Losi's story in Jordan, as Busaidiya's in Oman, hints that the social networks on which independent female candidates rely are not always tribal (as in Jordan) or sectarian (as in Lebanon), but can sometimes relate to the women's professions. Teachers' unions, for example, have a history of politicization across the MENA, so it is not surprising to see women and men from teachers' ranks successfully entering politics.[19]

By the snap elections of 2013, with worries of the Arab Spring destabilizing Jordan, women became regular fixtures of the country's politics. Some 121 ran for national office, especially with the 2012 shift to electoral law guaranteeing 15 spots in the Majlis-al Nawab to women candidates, up from 10 in 2010.[20] As before, however, women were not limited to

---

[19] See the work of Fida Adely (2012) and others for additional insight.

[20] Although the quota for women in the Parliament has risen steadily—from 6 to 12 and to 15 in the current law, or 10 percent of the seats in the lower chamber—this is below the 20.4 percent global average for female participation in parliamentary governments. The women's quota works as a 'first loser' mechanism, in which the woman who receives the highest percentage of votes in her district among all female candidates but does not get enough votes to win a seat outright against male competitors, gains a seat in Parliament. In practice, some smaller tribes that have struggled to win seats outright have used the women's quota to gain parliamentary representation by putting forward female candidates in small districts, where just a few voters can sway election results. See IRI (2013).

the quota and could compete directly with their counterparts at the local and national level, and increasingly did so successfully. More than half of voters in the snap elections were female (51.8 percent), as were 16 percent of the candidates.[21]

Alongside regular seats, the advent of national lists with the reforms of 2013 increased the number of women (and candidates overall) running for office, since more funding was tied to running on a candidate list. Many in the popular community figured this was yet another mechanism for political elites and tribes to solidify their hold on politics, while offering the illusion of emergent party platforms. In total, women won 18 seats, three more than the quota, with two women winning outright in their districts and one winning a seat as the head of a national list. Candidates registering to run were often required to put down JD 500–JD 4000 JD depending on the size of the municipality they intended to run in for post-campaign clean-up, putting women yet again at a disadvantage.[22] IRI interviews with female candidates noted that many complained of similar obstacles, especially 'lack of funding for their campaigns, as it is rare for men within the family, or husbands, to finance their campaigns' (IRI, 2013: 26).

### *The Lebanese Case*

Until the 2018 parliamentary elections in Lebanon, Nayla Tueni, the youngest and 'most silent' Lebanese MP, was 'technically' the first woman independent in the Lebanese Parliament. Tueni was one of four women at the time and had the distinction of being the only one not directly affiliated to a political party. She came into office in 2009 under the wings of the March 14th bloc, but never fully committed to joining the movement, much to its members' chagrin, and retained her seat through the debacle of the postponed 2014 general elections.

Tueni's outspoken stance against Hizbollah gleaned her support from the Christian right (Lebanese Forces and Kataeb). However, she was

---

[21] Jordanian Embassy data. IRI claims 14 percent of the candidates were female (2013).

[22] These were deposits with the municipality where they registered to ensure candidates would clean up campaign materials after the elections. Although not stipulated under the election law, candidates were asked to volunteer information on their campaign's funding sources, to be posted publicly by the Independent Election Commission (IEC). Follow up on this request, however, varied from one district electoral commission to another.

an avowed secularist whose controversial marriage to a Shi'a Muslim somewhat weakened relations to the aforementioned groups. Importantly, she also won her seat representing Ashrafiyeh through a de facto quota earmarked for Greek Orthodox Christians. In many respects, her experience is similar to Toujan Faisal's in Jordan, the MP who won through a Circassian quota, although Toujan cultivated an 'activist' reputation that eventually got her marginalized from Jordanian political life.

Tueni's surprising independent status owes itself to an ability to balance sectarian politics (perhaps through silence in situ) and a familial political brand that transcends standard party allegiances. Similar to the female Jordanian MPs who ran successfully as independents and were not strategically fielded by small tribes, Tueni also came from a politically established family; her father was slain former MP Gebran Tueni. Tueni is also the heir to the An-Nahar newspaper dynasty, formed by her great-grandfather Gebran Tueni, and is a member of the Board and a deputy manager for the paper. Her work as a political journalist gave her additional prominence and reach that many other female candidates did not have without party backing, although this has also put her in the line of tabloid fire due to her controversy-stirring marriage.

Tueni is not the only Lebanese woman whose extensive ties to rich patrons have enabled her to establish herself. Certainly, Bahiya Hariri's ties to the Hariri empire helped her secure a continued role in Lebanese politics. But, other, more independent political personalities also owe a debt to their ties to the international and local community, as the experience of Paula Yacoubian highlights. Another political woman with a background in journalism, Yacoubian has a prominent role in Lebanese daily television through the Hariri-backed Future TV stations, and on the Saudi-sponsored MBC channel and other pan-Arab channels.

### The Egyptian Case

What we observe in parts of the GCC and the Levant stands in stark contrast to trends in North Africa, Europe, and North America, where women's political participation often occurs via political parties, partially due to a long history of party development via French colonial influence. The one exception here is Egypt, where changes to the electoral law in 2015 incentivized more women to run as independents.

Amidst much turmoil, Egypt's post-Arab Spring electoral engineering has offered more opportunities for women to enter politics, though often through the direct patronage of the Sissi administration. In 2015, a spate of laws restructured the electoral recruitment process establishing a mixed electoral system with 448 members elected as independents (some 80 percent), 120 as party-based candidates, and 28 (or five percent) as presidential appointees. Article five and 27 of the law effectively stipulated a gender quota for candidate lists requiring some 56 women to be placed on electoral lists, while also introducing a clause mandating that 50 percent of presidential appointments must be female (WUNRN, 2016). Consequently, a record-breaking 89 women entered the parliament in January 2016 with 75 of them directly elected, while the remaining 14 were appointed (Ibid.). Though the largest number of the 75 women who ran for office ran under the flag of a political party (in particular, the al-Wafed Party), 12 of them succeeded as independents (ECWR, 2016). In a country dominated for decades by the National Democratic Party's (NDP) political apparatus, parties are still a primary mechanism through which women enter politics. However, the success of female independents speaks to some shifts in Egyptian women's paths to political office.

As in other countries, women independents face many unique challenges: first and foremost, the issue of obtaining campaign funds. The current female MP, Mona Mounir, observed: 'Political money plays a central role in campaigning, media and publicity, which constitutes a financial burden for women, especially those running for independent seats' (Mecky, 2015). Furthermore, Egyptian women are stymied in their access to the political arena by their limited ability to engage in vote-buying; a byproduct of a lack of funding alongside cultural expectations of 'appropriate' female behavior when campaigning. In an interview with the al-Ahram newspaper Salma al-Naqqash, director of the Women Political Participation Academy at Nazra, noted:

> I personally attribute this [low numbers of women winning office] to the majority-based system in elections, that lead to the control of political capital in elections as it was quite evident in the field that a lot of candidates relied on buying votes...such a system never really gives space for diverse political groups to participate equally in elections and the less empowered groups such as women are less visible. (Mecky, 2015)

While many male independents were accused in the media of using their financial and political capital to muscle into the parliament, this same accusation was not lodged against any women—many of whom ran shoe-string campaigns canvassing their communities door-to-door. Dina Abdel-Aziz—the youngest MP in the 2016 parliament—largely adopted this strategy in her district. Zeinab Abdel-Rahman, another independent candidate who campaigned in Cairo, noted that her campaign volunteers were largely female and supported her because they wanted to see a woman entering politics. However, she also observed this might have been specific to the more 'privileged classes' in her district stating, 'Among the less privileged, political capital [wasta] is the key player' (Mecky, 2015). In the Egyptian case, a combination of appointments and a de facto candidate (electoral list) gender quota led to more women entering the national assembly overall. Consequently, much as in Jordan, a mixed system with a gender quota paved the way for the few independent candidates that made it into the parliament; though in contrast to Jordan, the majority of female MPs in Egypt are actually still partisan and, arguably, partisanship is still an integral part of Egyptian parliamentary politics.

In contrast to the Egyptian case, virtually no MP (male or female) won as an independent in Djibouti, Iraq, Mauritania, Morocco, or Yemen, since the electoral processes in these states are exclusively dominated by political parties with closed-list districts. Women were present in the legislatures of all these countries, but the majority gained their position via parties taking advantage of gender quotas. Tunisia and Algeria are somewhat outliers in this list because despite their closed-list proportional representation systems, women independents have managed to inject themselves into the parliamentary system, although they usually had prior party affiliations or signaled party affiliations.

Yasmine Berriane's work on Morocco also hints at another reason why there may be fewer women running as independents in North African states. Parties often snap up potentially promising women who work with NGOs or run local associations before they decide to run for local office in Morocco, especially since the adoption of gender quotas (Berriane, 2015: 436–437). Importantly, we generally see more diversity in the economic background of female candidates when political parties are doing the recruiting, especially in Tunisia, Morocco, and Egypt—countries with more robust labor and Islamist social movements.

In previous research, I found evidence that electoral systems were largely responsible for incentivizing men and women to campaign as independents, due to waning or non-existent party strength, although this may yet shift with Lebanon and Jordan newly embracing list-PR systems

(Welborne, 2020). The embrace of gender quotas combined with mixed and plurality systems tended to yield more independent women in Parliaments. I also found only a limited number of women running successfully as independents at the national level in North African states.[23] This was certainly due to dominance of partisan politics in these states, but also to the size and scale of North African countries, which make it difficult and potentially compromising for women to mobilize constituents. There is some evidence of smaller district sizes working in women's favor, as in the Tunisian elections (Clark et al., 2018, 2021). Thus, campaigning is not as daunting of a task for women in the comparatively small countries or localities of the GCC and the Levant, as the Tunisian case also illustrates.

Another explanation for the lack of female independents in North Africa may arise from the more limited earning potential of North African women. Women in North Africa earn comparatively less than their counterparts in the Gulf and the Levant—a byproduct of their higher presence in low-paid agricultural work than in the more lucrative service sector. According to a 2012 ILO report, some 36.2 percent of women in the Middle East worked in agriculture, compared with 40 percent in North Africa, while 56.7 percent of women in the Middle East were employed in the service sector, compared with only 48 percent in North Africa (ILO, 2012). More recent World Bank statistics reveal that 15–30 percent of women participate in the labor force in North Africa, compared with a striking 30–50 percent on average for citizen women in the GCC states (see Buttorff & Welborne, 2015). Simply put, North African women may need to rely on the financial apparatus of political parties when personal incomes are small and access to the labor market is structured in ways that confine them to non-lucrative sectors. This would most certainly affect their ability to launch independent political campaigns.

### *The Moroccan Case*

This reality became palpable in the results from open-ended questions to a late-2018 survey I conducted in conjunction with the National Democratic Institute (NDI) with female candidates who had run in Morocco's 2015 local and regional elections and the 2016 national elections. NDI had organized informational events on women campaigning

---

[23] The story is very different at the municipal level, where many women run without party backing.

in the northern provinces of Morocco that summer with some 300 attendees give or take and kindly offered to send out a quick open-ended survey to the women who participated in an event that winter. Of some 50 responses, about 25 were complete enough to interpret, if not to generalize from.

A majority of the respondents were Amazigh—not uncommon for candidates from the central north but no less fascinating and reflective of an internal push by Amazigh CSOs to get more of their candidates on the ballot.[24] They represented a mix of women who had campaigned in the 2015 municipal elections and 2016 national elections, with both winners and losers in the fray. Some were fully employed, a few with doctorates; others were unemployed. Considering these women were attracted to an NDI event at a swank hotel in Rabat, it is unsurprising that the majority of my respondents had university degrees—fairly rare in a country where some 50 percent of the population is illiterate.

Age-wise, the surveyed sample comprised women who were mostly in their 20s and 30s and single, along with married or divorced women between the ages of 40 and 60; all of the married women had children. All of the women who responded were affiliated with political parties, mostly with the Party of Progress and Socialism, but also with the reigning Islamist Party of Justice and Development, the Authenticity and Modernity Party, the Popular Movements, and the stalwart Socialist Union of Popular Forces. Only one response was unaffiliated with any political party—a woman out of Tangier who had run at the local level and been elected as an independent affiliated with a party list. This was also the only respondent who did not use social media in her campaign.

About half of the participants were aware, at the time, that Morocco had a dedicated fund out of the Ministry of Interior to help women run for office; the rest were ignorant of this opportunity, as the ministry had not readily advertised it and my contacts at NDI confirmed as much. Responses from candidates who ventured an estimate of how much it took to run a campaign varied from about 300,000 dirham ($32,700) to 3 million ($327,000) depending on whether the campaign was national or local, with some observing the amount would vary from province to province.

---

[24] Beni Mellah, Beni Mellal, Rabat, Meknes, Tetouane, Larache, Sale, Kenitra, and El Jadida were represented—but also Tiznit, Casablanca, and Agadir in the South and Tangier in the North.

About half of the respondents had relied on their own finances and the help of their family, while the other half were funded by political parties. The half who had received help from parties were mostly grateful for money and staff for their campaign; for example, some 30,000 dirhams for a municipal candidate in Kenitra, while one more established candidate in the same party complained about the lack of flyers and direct monetary support for her national bid for office in Casablanca. It was shocking that the majority of the women affiliated with political parties did not report receiving any kind of financial or other official help from those parties.

Most of the women declined to respond to questions about whether there was a difference between men and women related to campaigning. Those who did respond noted a need for 'more confidence in the abilities of women candidates' and pointed out the necessity for 'moral and financial support'. A candidate from Sale observed a need for more training for women to appear before the media. I was struck by how many of the candidates noted the need for moral support, and not just enhanced access to material resources, or intervention from the state to 'promote parity'.

The limited nature of my survey does not allow us to draw broad conclusions, but it does illustrate the difficult position women find themselves in when mounting political campaigns—even those who are supported by a political party. It is no accident that in all but four cases, the women who filled out the survey were employed; otherwise, they would have been hard-pressed to find the funds to campaign.[25]

Although women are more likely to work in North Africa than in the Levant, they still have trouble cracking into higher-paying jobs, especially in the private sector. That said, the public sector affords many women across the MENA the benefits and experience via working for the government. Public sector work can be a boon for political office in terms of party recruitment and community recognition, not to mention institutional knowledge, but may not represent an advantage when one's own funds are necessary to seal the deal on campaigning.

In general, it has been hard to track where women work in North Africa, especially in Morocco, where the culture of gathering data on women's labor force participation is relatively new and women's presence in the labor force is more often than not characterized by informality, with

---

[25] Two 'unemployed' respondents were university students; the two others were retired.

UN Women projecting that women comprise 61.8 percent of informal workers in the region (UN ILO, 2018; Women, 2020). A gender-mainstreaming coordinator for GTZ that I spoke with had this to say about her sense of Morocco and its ability to gather gender-disaggregated labor force statistics:

> Morocco does not have a culture of gathering statistical data so it's highly problematic to craft policy based on this type of information. For example the Ministry of Employment, after our recommendations, is considering tallying women laboring as housemaids ... They openly admitted not having any idea of how many people may be employed in this way.

In follow-up interviews I conducted in 2017 with officials from the Ministry of Solidarity, Women, Family, and Social Development and the Ministry of Justice, I found many of the same issues in collating consistent data over time.

## CONCLUSION

Back in 2010, noted Jordanian journalist and activist Rana Husseini found that Jordanian women contributed only 8 percent to the country's GDP in 2007, constituting 37 percent of the workforce in the public sector and 12 percent in the private sector, but overall comprising a very low proportion (14.7 percent) of the total labor force. At the time, according to Freedom House data (2010), most of these women were employed in low-paying 'social professions' such as education (41 percent), health and social work (15.1 percent), and the broader service sector (5.7 percent). Today, their overall labor force participation has barely crept up to 15 percent (Kasoolu et al., 2019).

The Jordanian results are striking in comparison with the more conservative GCC countries' labor force participation average, which is closer to 30 percent, and even 50 percent in some countries. While these statistics represent significant gains in the past decade from the single-digit numbers characteristic of the 1990s in the MENA, they are also suggestive of the financial restrictions women face in actively contesting political seats without significant, often inherited, wealth. Surprisingly, GCC women who run as independents may have more resources to rally than their counterparts in Jordan, Lebanon, or Egypt—states with a longer history of women running for office although not necessarily as

152    B. C. WELBORNE

lengthy a history of women occupying more lucrative professional jobs (even though women may have been active in the workforce longer).

Campaigning is an expensive endeavor. Given the still-low rates of labor force participation among women in the Middle East overall, independent female candidates running for office may also bode limited representation of women across the socioeconomic spectrum. This seems to be the case in plurality and mixed regimes, since many independents in the Levant and GCC tend to be better-heeled. However, even affluent women face significant challenges in obtaining campaign funding. Wijdan Talhouni Saket, a former Jordanian Senator and wealthy businesswoman in her own right, recalled almost being denied a loan because her husband was not with her during the application process, echoing the same problems Saudi women faced back in 2015 in obtaining campaign funds under strict guardianship laws.

> Despite the fact that I inherited significant money, property and shares from my parents—and under Islamic law this remains mine—when I applied for a bank loan for my already established and successful antique business, the banker still insisted I get my husband to sign as guarantor on the loan. Why? Just because he is male. My husband is a government employee and would never be able to pay back the loan on his salary. It's ridiculous. The same would never happen if the sexes were reversed. If a wealthy, established businesswoman like me still faces discrimination in access to credit, imagine how much harder it is for other women in business. (USAID, 2007: 9)

Yet, there are reasons to be hopeful. A 2008 study funded by the World Bank conducted by MENA expert, Nadereh Chamlou, found that even though there were fewer women-owned firms in the MENA relative to other developing regions, they were larger (more than 50 employees) and tended to hire women. This research found that such women-owned firms were 'as old, large, diversified, productive, and sophisticated as the male-owned firms' (Chamlou, 2008). Egypt, Saudi Arabia, and Morocco in particular had more large-scale women-owned firms in operation. Of course, ownership is not the same as running a business, but the study also points out that an increasing number of women are doing both.[26] There

---

[26] If anything, high barriers to entry may be discouraging more women from running small businesses, which are still more likely to be owned by men.

are obviously women with the means, and increasingly the inclination, to run. Thus, unsurprisingly, GCC women have the income advantage here, even though they may not have the mobility advantage of the women in the Levant and North Africa. As we have seen throughout this chapter, part of this advantage can be tied to the economic windfalls generated by oil rents, especially in extreme rentier states.

Foreign direct investment may also play an as yet underexplored role in empowering women for political office by providing interested individuals with the means and the skills to fund and organize successful campaigns in political environments where formal support is lacking or where local private firms hesitate to hire female talent for cultural reasons. These ties between the foreign business community and female candidates are more salient in countries, where political parties are less established and cannot be relied on to fund expensive electoral campaigns.

Ultimately, reviewing cases such as those of Bahrain and Jordan suggests that the link between economic and political participation is more nuanced than simple participation in the labor force. That said, the recent success of independent, wealthy, and professional female candidates in both these countries suggests that socioeconomic status may also translate into access to political office, given the lack government support available to fund campaigns. But a growing trend in the GCC for women to run as independents and the most recent electoral results in Egypt may bode for new trends in women's political access—especially as their presence in the labor force changes in its scope and substance.

At a time declining trust in the political party apparatus when the popular press, even in the West, is increasingly questioning the role of parties, the emergence of parallel structures for political recruitment and mobilization—even in authoritarian regimes—is a point of interest. Political participation and representation exclusively through parties is often billed as a uniquely Western conceit, usually spread through colonial or neocolonial rule. But, the vectors for 'political access' and even 'independent agenda-setting' may look very different in non-European contexts where other organizational mechanisms abound. Especially in states where political parties are completely co-opted by the regime, alternate modes of political mobilization may be the only real tools for change—or at least for representation, if not always in the active voice.

When it comes to agenda-setting, women who opt to promote more radical gender-related reforms may fare better when elected through non-partisan mechanisms. It might not be an accident that some of the

## 154    B. C. WELBORNE

most far-reaching changes in rape legislation—specifically, the repeal of the laws allowing the acquittal of rapists who marry their victims—have been pushed forward by independent female MPs in Jordan, alongside the activism of feminist organization such as Sisterhood is Global (Al-Atiyat, 2019; Husseini, 2019; Tahhan, 2017). Similar changes to 'rape laws' in Algeria, Lebanon, and Tunisia were also the product of decades of lobbying from grassroots feminist organizations (Alqawasmi, 2017; Darhour & Dahlerup, 2020). Overall, the jury is still out as to whether these independent women are clients of the state or genuine pioneers, but their ability to successfully contest male-dominated electoral regimes in both partisan and non-partisan or settings signals an important shift in cultural and institutional understandings of the seat of authority and service provision in the Middle East.

## REFERENCES

Adely, F. (2012). *Gendered paradoxes: Education Jordanian women in nation, faith, and progress*. University of Chicago Press.

Al Lawati, N., & Buttorff, G. J. (2020). Working women in the oil monarchies. In *Routledge handbook of Persian Gulf politics* (pp. 248–261). Routledge.

Al-Atiyat, I. (2019). Repealing Jordan's rape Article 308. *Confluences Méditer-ranée, 3*, 99–111.

Alqawasmi, A. (2017). *Sposa il tuo stupratore! Cambiamenti nelle legislazioni dei Paesi arabi: riformare le culture o riscoprirle?* Dialoghi Mediterranei 28. https://boa.unimib.it/retrieve/handle/10281/240155/347634/Marry%20your%20rapist%20laws%20changing%20in%20Arab%20countries%3a%20reforming%20cultures%2c%20or%20exploring%20others%20%7c%20Dialogh.pdf

Al-Balushi, F. (2014). *The role of social institution in supporting Omani women political candidates: 'A case study of Majlis A-Shura elections (1998–2011)* [Master's Thesis presented to Sultan Qaboos University].

*Arab Weekly*. (2018, May 27). Leading media figure Paula Yacoubian, a new face in Lebanon's parliament. https://thearabweekly.com/leading-media-figure-paula-yacoubian-new-face-lebanons-parliament

Astih, P. (2018, May 8). Six women represent Lebanese females in 2018 parliament. *Asharq Al-Awsat*. https://english.aawsat.com//home/article/1261566/six-women-represent-lebanese-females-2018-parliament

Barnett, A., Yandle, B., & Naufal, G. S. (2013). Regulation, trust, and cronyism in Middle Eastern societies: The simple economics of 'wasta.' *The Journal of Socio-Economics, 44*(February), 41–46.

Berriane, Y. (2015). The micropolitics of reform: Gender quota, grassroots associations and the renewal of local elites in Morocco. *The Journal of North African Studies, 20*(3), 432–449.

Brancati, D. (2008). Willing alone: The electoral fate of independent candidates worldwide. *The Journal of Politics, 70*(3), 648–662.

Bush, S. S. (2011). International politics and the spread of quotas for women in legislatures. *International Organization, 65*(1), 103–137.

Bush, S. S. (2015). *The taming of democracy assistance.* Cambridge University Press.

Buttorff, G., & Welborne, B. C. (2015). *Working those connections: Exploring Arab women's differential access to opportunity in the Middle East and North Africa* (Issue Brief No. 09.25.15). Rice University's Baker Institute. https://www.bakerinstitute.org/media/files/files/0669afc2/BI-Brief-071715-WRME_Wasta.pdf

Buttorff, G. J., al-Lawati, N., & Welborne, B. C. (2018). Cursed no more? The resource curse, gender, and labor nationalization policies in the GCC. *Journal of Arabian Studies, 8*(suppl. 1): 65–86.

Carapico, S. (2002). Foreign aid for promoting democracy in the Arab world. *The Middle East Journal, 56*(3), 379–395.

Chamlou, N. (2008). *The environment for women's entrepreneurship in the Middle East and North Africa.* The World Bank. https://openknowledge.worldbank.org/bitstream/handle/10986/6479/448240PUB0Box310only1 09780821374955.pdf?sequence=1&isAllowed=y

Christophersen, M. (2013, March). *Jordan's elections: A further boost for tribes* (NOREF Report). Norwegian Peacebuilding Research Center. https://www.files.ethz.ch/isn/162496/3cfcb191c3644dd32cda0c2c3431d149.pdf

Clark, J., Şaşmaz, A., & Blackman, A. (2018). *List fillers or future leaders?* Female candidates in Tunisia's 2018 municipal elections. Democracy International. http://democracyinternational.com/media/Policy%20Brief_Gender.pdf

Clark, J. M., Blackman, A. D., & Sasmaz, A. (2021). *What men want: Politicians' strategic response to gender quotas.* CEU events. https://events.ceu.edu/sites/default/files/media/attachment/blackman-gender_quotas_april2021.pdf

Cohen, L. (2018, Fall). Lebanon's black sheep. *The Cairo Review of Global Affairs.* https://www.thecairoreview.com/q-a/lebanons-black-sheep/

Cooke, M. (2014). *Tribal modern: Branding new nations in the Arab Gulf.* University of California Press.

Darhour, H., & Dahlerup, D. (2020). Introduction: The Arab uprisings and the rights of women. In *Double-edged politics on women's rights in the MENA region* (pp. 1–46). Palgrave Macmillan.

David, A., & Nanes, S. (2011). The women's quota in Jordan's municipal councils: International and domestic dimensions. *Journal of Women, Politics and Policy, 32*, 275–304.

156    B. C. WELBORNE

ECWR. (2016, February 16). Egyptian women in 2015 parliamentary elections. *Egyptian Center for Women's Rights (ECWR) reports.* http://ecwron line.org/?p=6788

England, A., & Kerr, S. (2018, October 21). Bahrain's Shia loath to give Sunni rulers election credibility. *Financial Times.* https://www.ft.com/content/f96 91dac-bb64-11e8-94b2-17176fbf93f5

Freedom House. (2010, March 3). *Women's rights in the Middle East and North Africa 2010—Jordan.* https://www.refworld.org/docid/4b9901227d.html

Golosov, G. V. (2003). The vicious circle of party underdevelopment in Russia: The regional connection. *International Political Science Review, 24,* 427–444.

GCC Statistical Center. (2016). *Labour statistics in GCC countries 2016, Table 12: Employed (15 years and above) by nationality, gender and work sector in GCC countries.* https://gccstat.org/en/statistic/statistics/labour

Hamdan, H. (2018, May 31). Lebanese women determined to continue fight for more political representation. *Al Monitor.* https://www.al-monitor.com/pulse/originals/2018/05/lebanon-2018-election-women-in-parliament-obs tacles-quota.html

Hasan, D. (2016, December 27). Oman polls: The women who stood for election to make a difference-and won. *Times of Oman.* http://timesofoman.com/article/99395

Herb, M. (2014). *The wages of oil: Parliaments and economic development in Kuwait and the UAE.* Cornell University Press.

Husseini, R. (2019, May 20). Rape cases drop, thanks to abolishment of Article 308-activists. *Jordan Times.* https://jordantimes.com/news/local/rape-cases-drop-thanks-abolishment-article-308-%E2%80%94-activists

ILO. (2012). *Global employment trends for women report.* International Labour Organization (ILO). http://www.ilo.org/wcmsp5/groups/public/---dgrepo rts/---dcomm/documents/publication/wcms_195447.pdf

ILO. (2018). *Women and men in the informal economy: A statistical picture.* International Labour Organization. https://www.ilo.org/wcmsp5/groups/public/---dgreports/---dcomm/documents/publication/wcms_626831.pdf

IPU. (2020). *Women in national parliaments* (Statistical archive). Inter-Parliamentary Union. http://archive.ipu.org/wmn-e/world-arc.htm

IRI. (2013, January 23). *Jordan parliamentary elections report.* International Republican Institute (IRI). https://www.iri.org/sites/default/files/fields/field_files_attached/resource/jordan_january_2013_parliamentary_election_r eport_-.pdf

Iversen, T., & Rosenbluth, F. (2006). The political economy of gender: Explaining cross-national variation in the gender division of labor and the gender voting gap. *American Journal of Political Science, 50*(1), 1–19.

Kasoolu, S., Hausmann, R., O'Brien, T., & Santos, M. A. (2019). *Female labor in Jordan: A systematic approach to the exclusion puzzle* (Center for International Development Working Paper No. 365). Harvard University. https://growthlab.cid.harvard.edu/files/growthlab/files/2019-10-cid-wp-365-female-labor-jordan.pdf

Kemp, L. J., Madsen, S. R., & Davis, J. (2015). Women in business leadership: A comparative study of countries in the Gulf Arab states. *International Journal of Cross Cultural Management, 15*(2), 215–233.

Langohr, V. (2004). Too much civil society, too little politics: Egypt and liberalizing Arab regimes. *Comparative Politics, 36*(2), 181–204.

Lipset, S. M. (1959). Some social requisites of democracy: Economic development and political legitimacy. *American Political Science Review, 53*(1), 69–105.

Lust, E. (2009). Democratization by elections? Competitive clientelism in the Middle East. *Journal of Democracy, 20*(3), 122–135.

Mecky, M. (2015, November, 18). Egyptian women in parliament polls: Hopes and hurdles. *Al Ahram English.* http://english.ahram.org.eg/NewsContent/1/164/166619/Egypt/Egypt-Elections-/Egyptian-women-in-parliament-polls-Hopes-and-hurdl.aspx

Muscat Daily. (2015, October 27). Lack of trust in Majlis a'Shura hindering women, say activists. *Muscat Daily.* http://www.muscatdaily.com/Archive/Oman/Lack-of-trust-in-Majlis-A-Shura-hindering-women-say-activists-4dv6

Nanes, S. (2010). *Regime stability in the face of global economic crisis: Cosmetic reform and a municipal quota for women.* Annual Meeting of the American Political Science Association.

Nanes, S. (2015). The quota encouraged me to run: Evaluating Jordan's municipal quota for women. *Journal of Middle East Women's Studies, 11,* 261–282.

Norris, P. (2006). Recruitment. In R. S. Katz & W. Crotty (Eds.), *Handbook of party politics.* Sage.

Ross, M. L. (2008). Oil, Islam, and women. *American Political Science Review, 102*(1), 107–123.

Rutledge, E., Al-Shamsi, F., Bassioni, Y., & Al-Sheikh, H. (2011). Women, labour market nationalization policies and human resource development in the Arab Gulf states. *Human Resource Development, 14*(2), 183–198.

Sabbagh, A. (2005). The Arab states: Enhancing women's political participation. In J. Ballington & A. Karam (Eds.), *Women in parliament: Beyond numbers.* International Institute for Democracy and Electoral Assistance (IDEA).

Salem, R., & Yount, K. M. (2019). Structural accommodations of patriarchy: Women and workplace gender segregation in Qatar. *Gender, Work and Organization, 26*(4), 511.

Shalaby, M. (2016). *Women's political representation and authoritarianism in the Arab world, prepared for the women and gender in Middle East politics workshop.* Project on Middle East Political Science

(POMEPS). https://pomeps.org/2016/04/14/womens-political-represent
ation-and-authoritarianism-in-the-arab-world/#_ftnref14

Schlozman, K. L., Burns, N., & Verba, S. (1999). 'What happened at work today?': A multistage model of gender, employment, and political participation. *The Journal of Politics, 61*(1), 29–53.

SIGI. (2020, May 11). "عين على النساءعين على النساء" : واحدة من كل ثلاث مترشحات تعرضت دعايتها الانتخابية للتعدي الكتروني أو تقليدياً برنامج[Where are the women?]. http://www.sigi-jor dan.org/?p=9171

Tahhan, Z. (2017, August 4) Meet the woman who pushed to repeal Jordan's rape law. *Al Jazeera Online—Women's Rights*. http://www.aljazeera.com/ind epth/features/2017/08/meet-woman-pushed-repeal-jordan-rape-law-170 803111944315.html

Toumi, H. (2016, April 8). Kuwait leads Gulf states in women in workforce. *Gulf News*. https://gulfnews.com/world/gulf/kuwait/kuwait-leads-gulf-states-in-women-in-workforce-1.1705940

Tripp, A. (2019). *Seeking legitimacy: Why Arab autocracies adopt women's rights*. Cambridge University Press.

UN Women. (2020). *The impact of Covid-19 on gender equality in the Arab region policy brief 4*. https://www2.unwomen.org/-/media/field%20office% 20arab%20states/attachments/publications/2020/04/impact%20of%20c ovid%20on%20gender%20equality%20-%20policy%20brief.pdf

USAID. (2007). *Jordan gender assessment*. United States Agency of International Development (USAID). http://pdf.usaid.gov/pdf_docs/Pnadm944.pdf

Vela, J. (2015, October 26). One woman elected in Oman's Shura Council elections. *The National*. http://www.thenational.ae/world/middle-east/one-woman-elected-in-omans-shura-council-elections

Wängnerud, L. (2009). Women in parliaments: Descriptive and substantive representation. *Annual Review of Political Science, 12*, 51–69.

Weeks, L. (2016). Why are there independents in Ireland? *Government and Opposition, 51*(4), 580–604.

Weeks, L. (2018). *Independents in Irish party democracy*. Manchester University Press.

Wehrey, F. (2014, March 10). *A new US approach to Gulf security*. Carnegie Endowment for Peace. https://carnegieendowment.org/2014/03/10/new-u.s.-approach-to-gulf-security-pub-54853

Welborne, B. C. (2010). *The strategic use of gender quotas in the Arab world*. International Foundation for Electoral Systems; http://www.ifes.org/Con tent/Publications/White-Papers/2011/The-Strategic-Use-of-Gender-Quo tas-in-the-Arab-World.aspx

Welborne, B. C. (2020). On their own? Women running as independent candidates in the Middle East. *Middle East Law and Governance, 12*(3), 251–274.

Willoughby, J. (2004). *A quiet revolution in the making? The replacement of expatriate labor through the feminization of the labor force in the GCC countries* (American University Department of Economics Working Paper No. 2004–18). https://www.researchgate.net/publication/277221553_A_Q uiet_Revolution_in_the_Making_The_Replacement_of_Expatriate_Labor_t hrough_the_Feminization_of_the_Labor_Force_in_GCC_Countries

WUNRN. (2016). Egypt-women in 2015 parliamentary elections – Overview and Analysis. *Women's united nation's report network.* http://wunrn.com/2016/02/egypt-women-in-2015-parliamentary-elections-overview-analysis/

CHAPTER 6

# Gendered Rentierism—A Curse or an Opportunity for Women?

Adeel Malik maintains that relying on rents as external windfalls is in reality 'the original sin of development in the Middle East and North Africa'—that the region is not so much plagued by a 'resource curse' as a 'rent curse' (2017: 42). But has it been an unequivocal curse for women? I argue the intersection of neoliberal capitalism and state feminism undergirded by *rentierism* led to distinct political-economic outcomes for gender relations, that have often proved quite transformational for women. In many respects, *gendered rentierism* sheds light on how and when rentier states blend state feminism with neoliberal 'authoritarian upgrading' in a bid to sell themselves as 'reformers' to the international community without necessarily committing to substantive changes. However, this same strategy has also allowed savvy activists to hold governments publicly accountable for promises they have made through conditional aid agreements. Foreign aid as a form of rent when used to target women's issues can lead to tangible political outcomes and agency for women agitating for social reforms on the ground. This has been the case with groups lobbying to criminalize marry-your-rapist laws, as well as those agitating for reforms to laws addressing domestic violence and sexual harassment. Much of this 'success' has been predicated on including more women in positions of executive and legislative power, with gender quotas an oft-embraced entry-point for the latter.

© The Author(s), under exclusive license to Springer Nature Switzerland AG 2022
B. C. Welborne, *Women, Money, and Political Participation in the Middle East,*
https://doi.org/10.1007/978-3-031-04877-7_6

161

Furthermore, there is a very robust literature connecting gender quota adoption to foreign aid. In previous work I have demonstrated that external funds, especially gender-related conditional foreign aid can facilitate grassroots action and semi-autonomous agenda-setting for individual women and women's political organizations in the face of government opposition and limited domestic sources of financial support (Welborne, 2016). Aid conditionality also alerts women's organizations to a source of financial leverage vis-à-vis their governments for enhanced inclusion into the system. This reveals an unexpected facilitator of political agency and autonomy for marginalized communities even in autocratic regimes. It should also encourage policymakers and women's advocates not to 'throw the baby out with the bathwater' in excoriating women-friendly foreign aid as it represents an important accountability tool for many grassroots women's movements in non-democratic contexts.

The extant literature on financial investment and women's associated opportunities has largely focused on foreign direct or oil-related investment's role in structuring women's place in the international division of labor—usually presuming that relationship to be exploitative. My own analysis demonstrates that oil-related investment and associated oil rents have a much more complex relationship with women's political inclusion in the Middle East. This is partially the case because the GCC region hosts more citizen women in professional-level jobs than other parts of the MENA. Investigating the background of successful female candidates in legislative elections reveals their ties to the foreign and local business community and access to lucrative jobs, which allow many of them to independently fund their political campaigns and, in some cases, to run without the endorsement of a political party or through formal government selection. Essentially, many of these women are running as 'independents'—an unlikely scenario in a region normally deemed to disincentivize women's political activity. Even with regime support, where there are limited mechanisms of or interest in executive appointment, since the social and economic hurdles for women running without the support of a formal network such as a political party or association are quite daunting. One only need to compare this to women running as independents in democratic states with a robust political party culture— it's difficult enough for women to win even with political party support and a legislative gender quota present. While the ability to run as an independent often re-affirms the difference between the haves and the have-nots in Arab society, the capacity for women to negotiate independent campaigns successfully across partisan settings signifies an important shift in what used to be a very gendered, institutionalized, and exclusive path to political access in the MENA. It also allows the reader to reimagine the types of social networks and connections that might help women achieve political office across Arab states in the future.

While foreign investment and foreign aid often reflect *corporate* or *state-level* goals and interests, remittances are more likely to capture *individual* emigrant as well as remittance recipient interests and objectives. Current research on remittances suggests they may have gendered social effects that vary across cultural contexts. In some global regions, remittances encourage more female out-migration, entrepreneurship, and political mobilization by bolstering domestic incomes. In others, the boost to incomes renders the need for women to enter the workforce obsolete and thereby reinforces existing patriarchic norms. A host of ethnographic scholarship confirms the latter patterns in Muslim and, specifically, Arab nations, which directly contrasts the often-rosy view of the overall welfare-benefit of remittances highlighted in the economic scholarship. I find Arab diasporas may export and consolidate *more progressive values* related to gender in their home communities through remittances in the MENA. However, this attitude on the part of remittance receivers does not translate into mobilizing women to run for office. My analysis comparing the MENA states to the rest of the world reveals that aggregate remittances channeled to the region have limited effect on women's labor force participation, but contribute to *even lower* levels of women's legislative representation—a finding unique to the Arab world in comparison to other remittance-receiving regions such as South Asia, Latin America, and Sub-Saharan Africa. Existing scholarship confirms these regional patterns and highlights the importance of who is emigrating (men vs. women), where they are emigrating from (i.e. the degree of patriarchic values in sending states), and which values emigrants choose to prioritize when sending money back home. This is especially important in terms of who spends the funds (left-behind spouses or other male family members) and in what way. Naturally, this decision-making impacts the gender dynamics of the household in profound ways. However, Chapter 4 also shows these attitudes may not translate into anything more than a change in household relationships in the short term. Importantly, individual remittance senders may be fairly conservative, and when sending money back to the home country could choose to

164    B. C. WELBORNE

back more conservative, traditional political movements that aim to curtail gains achieved on women's rights—something aggregate public opinion data in the home country would not capture.

## Patriarchal Bargains Across Rentiers

The set of choices women negotiate across different rentier ecosystems—ones characterized by aid, oil rents, and/or remittances—harken back to Deniz Kandiyoti's (1988) work on patriarchal bargains and reflect the scope of opportunities women enjoy given societal gender relations. The lens of gendered rentierism adds a political-economic flavor to these considerations. As more women enter the public sphere for work, either due to the failure of alternate welfare-providing institutions such as the family, tribe, and mosque/church, or because some of them are directly incentivized by the state, their set of options changes in unpredictable ways. But so do the state's options for a benign paternalism depending on its access to and generosity with rents. Yet again, it is not an accident that we have encountered women-centered agenda-setting most explicitly in high and mid-level rentier states centered around oil rents and foreign aid rents. These rent-dependencies have both increased women's political participation by virtue of foreign aid as well as increased women's economic participation through distributional incentives generated by oil rents in a portion of oil-rich states. While oil rents in high-rentier states are used to co-opt women into the workforce (but, importantly, not into politics), states dependent on foreign aid actively promote women's political inclusion through gender quotas, but often stymie their economic inclusion. The social outcomes created by gendered rentierism are not always so clear-cut in terms of their benefits for women. It is also not clear what impact these dependencies have on non-elite, uneducated women—especially those working in the informal sector, a sizable population in the MENA.

One thing is certain, it pays for Arab governments to promote women's empowerment in countries that receive significant financial inputs through development projects, whether humanitarian or corporate in nature. Local policymakers are keenly aware of this (see Chapter 3) and manipulate gender-related political reforms in the hope that they translate into greater donor and investor confidence, often through improved performance on global development rankings—essentially, scorecard diplomacy. Even though these reforms may be adopted for material reasons, there are still surprising spillover benefits for women and, in particular, women's movements who wish to wield some political influence. Gender-based 'scorecard diplomacy' prioritizes a variety of signals of 'modernity' and 'stability' that, in connection with states' neoliberal dependency, on external rent sources can galvanize enormous change. With so many external quantitative mechanisms used to vet 'progress' based on gender indicators, many a CSO, NGO, and IGO can now rely on a surprising outside source of accountability for the otherwise 'errant' state. Even if these are just the latest trappings of 'authoritarian upgrading', the court of public opinion has now extended beyond internal audiences to the world with social media—something that certainly benefits any local women's movements with ties to transnational women's advocacy networks. Promoters of state feminism now have to reckon with transnational feminist advocacy and an environment in which local actors can often bypass the state to reach supranational actors and so agitate for change.

## The Problem of Rents Depoliticizing Women's Empowerment

Sarah Ababneh (2020) speaks eloquently to the problem of women's empowerment and broader gender-related issues being depoliticized in the MENA precisely at a time when there is so much interest in addressing them. Importantly, the modalities the state embraces—especially those spearheaded by systems steeped in market feminism and gendered rentierism to shore up their image abroad—often seem to be geared at a type of compromise which neutralizes, co-opts, and, ultimately, commodifies women's activism. As Arab women seek to bypass government censure and effectively work with the state as well as IGOs and corporate actors promoting women's issues, they sacrifice promoting independent, authentic, and crucial socioeconomic agendas for what are often limited and largely symbolic political gains. Furthermore, these gains are usually only accessible to a very small subset of elite women in any given country. Some of this is even evident in the more generic language of states addressing 'women's issues' rather than promoting 'women's rights'. The incentive for states and for women's NGOs and CSOs to center their efforts around attractive sound-bites and scorecards is high, while limiting actual, but often controversial, legally-binding interventions that might benefit women on the ground. The flip side of course is the problem of the state imposing any one vision of 'benefit' on women—especially in countries with weak institutional infrastructure to begin with.

As highlighted throughout this book, most of the MENA states are rentier economies. Overall, this has led to insufficient investment in productive sectors that would employ both men and women, and women remain disproportionately represented in bloated and flagging public sectors. This lacking investment means that in most cases these economies are importing more goods than they are exporting. The region's current path is doomed to increasing unemployment, characterized by high rates of informality and exacerbated by the COVID-19 pandemic, which has gutted the formal workforce and work-related opportunities for both genders. In one positive trend, the pandemic renewed the focus on labor nationalization efforts in subregions of the MENA and perhaps created an environment more opportune to future women's labor recruitment. However, this 'silver lining' is the product of a zealous pandemic-based xenophobia intensifying existing racial and class tensions between citizen and non-citizen labor. It is also questionable whether it will make up for the pandemic-related economic precarity of women, which has coincided with increased domestic violence, decreased access to healthcare, and a de-prioritization of women's needs, rights, and wants.

Ultimately, I conclude that the states' dependence on a variety of external rents has a key impact on the strength and scope of the existing partriarchal bargains conditioning women's economic and political incorporation into public life. Many of the more substantive efforts to change women's status in the MENA by grassroots and transnational actors alike were put on hold due to COVID-19. Much like the Arab Spring of 2011, political uprisings in 2019 seemed to usher in a tide of change from Sudan to Lebanon with women actively participating in a wave of renewed protest across the region with a sense of fresh possibility for more accountable and representative government. COVID-19 effectively quashed those stirrings. As the world recovers from the pandemic's effects, it is worth considering its long-term impact on women's economic and political opportunity—especially as so many women are essential workers in the health sector or primary caregivers within the region. If anything, COVID-19 allowed the state to reconsolidate its hold on MENA societies, and it remains an open question as to how women will fare in the future because of it.

## REFERENCES

Ababneh, S. (2020). The time to question, rethink and popularize the notion of 'women's issues': Lessons from Jordan's popular and labor movements from 2006 to now. *Journal of International Women's Studies, 21*(1), 271–288.

Ennis, C. A. (2019). Rentier-preneurship: Dependence and autonomy in women's entrepreneurship in the Gulf. *The Politics of Rentier States in the Gulf, 33,* 60–66.

Kandiyoti, D. (1988). Bargaining with patriarchy. *Gender & Society, 2*(3), 274–290.

Malik, A. (2017). Rethinking the rentier curse. *International Development Policy/Revue Internationale de Politique de Développement, 7.*

Welborne, B. C. (2016). No agency without grassroots autonomy: A framework for evaluating women's political inclusion in Jordan, Bahrain, and Morocco. In *Empowering women after the Arab Spring* (pp. 65–90). Palgrave Macmillan.

# APPENDIX

See Tables A.1, A.2, and A.3.

© The Editor(s) (if applicable) and The Author(s), under exclusive
license to Springer Nature Switzerland AG 2022
B. C. Welborne, *Women, Money, and Political
Participation in the Middle East,*
https://doi.org/10.1007/978-3-031-04877-7

# 170 APPENDIX

**Table A.1** Attitudes toward women among remittance receivers in MENA, 2010–2011

| Scale: Strongly disagree (1) Strongly agree (4) | A woman can become President or Prime Minister of a Muslim country | In general, men are better at political leadership than women | University education for males is more important than university education for females | It is permissible for a woman to travel abroad by herself | Women and men should have equal rights in making the decision to divorce | Married women should be permitted to work outside the home | Women's inheritance should be equal to that of men |
|---|---|---|---|---|---|---|---|
| *Coeff/St. Errors/Sig.* | | | | | | | |
| Remittance | 0.08 | 0.04 | 0.04 | 0.08 | 0.02 | −0.01 | 0.05 |
| Frequency | (0.10) | (0.04) | (0.08) | (0.08) | (0.01) | (0.05) | (0.06) |
| Gender | 0.45*** | −0.26*** | −0.30*** | 0.46*** | 0.43*** | 0.38*** | 0.32*** |
| (Women) | (0.08) | (0.07) | (0.06) | (0.06) | (0.07) | (0.06) | (0.06) |
| Age | 0.00 | 0.00* | 0.00* | 0.00 | −0.00 | 0.00 | 0.00 |
| | (0.00) | (0.00) | (0.00) | (0.00) | 0.00 | (0.00) | (0.00) |
| Education | 0.02 | −0.02** | −0.10*** | 0.03** | 0.02* | 0.04*** | −0.03* |
| | (0.01) | (0.01) | (0.03) | (0.01) | (0.01) | (0.01) | (0.02) |
| Employed | 0.00 | −0.03 | −0.05* | 0.02 | −0.07 | 0.00 | −0.00 |
| | (0.02) | (0.02) | (0.03) | (0.03) | (0.04) | (0.02) | (0.03) |
| Rural | 0.08 | 0.00 | 0.00 | −0.00 | −0.04 | −0.01 | −0.03 |
| | (0.03) | (0.03) | (0.05) | (0.10) | (0.07) | (0.06) | (0.08) |
| Religiosity | 0.01 | 0.02 | 0.05** | 0.03* | 0.03 | 0.00 | 0.04*** |
| | (0.02) | (0.01) | (0.02) | (0.02) | (0.02) | (0.01) | (0.01) |
| *R-squared* | 0.02 | 0.01 | 0.03 | 0.03 | 0.04 | 0.04 | 0.02 |
| *Obs* | 10,135 | 10,386 | 10,386 | 10,386 | 10,386 | 10,386 | 10,386 |

*Source* Arab Barometer wave 2, ten countries (Algeria, Egypt, Iraq, Jordan, Lebanon, Palestine, Saudi Arabia, Sudan, Tunisia, Yemen). The questions on attitudes toward women's status, remittances, religiosity, and employment were all rescaled for easier interpretation
Robust standard errors in parentheses: $*p < 0.10$, $**p < 0.05$, $***p < 0.01$

APPENDIX 171

**Table A.2** Attitudes toward women among remittance receivers in MENA, 2012–2014

| Scale: Strongly disagree (1) Strongly agree (4) | In general, men are better at political leadership than women | University education for males is more important than university education for females | Married women should be permitted to work outside the home |
|---|---|---|---|
| *Coeff/St. Errors/Sig.* | | | |
| Remittance | 0.02 | 0.05* | 0.04*** |
| Frequency | (0.05) | (0.03) | (0.01) |
| Gender (Women) | −0.38*** | −0.34*** | 0.41*** |
| | (0.05) | (0.08) | (0.07) |
| Age | 0.00 | −0.00 | −0.00 |
| | (0.00) | (0.00) | (0.00) |
| Education | 0.00 | −0.00* | −0.00 |
| | (0.0) | (0.00) | (0.00) |
| Employed | −0.00 | −0.06** | 0.06*** |
| | (0.04) | (0.03) | (0.02) |
| Rural | 0.04 | 0.07** | −0.06* |
| | (0.06) | (0.03) | (0.04) |
| Religiosity | 0.01 | 0.02 | −0.05*** |
| | (0.04) | (0.02) | (0.01) |
| *R-squared* | 0.03 | 0.04 | 0.06 |
| *Obs* | 8479 | 8479 | 8479 |

*Source* Arab Barometer wave 3, 12 countries (Algeria, Egypt, Iraq, Jordan, Kuwait, Lebanon, Libya, Morocco, Palestine, Sudan, Tunisia, Yemen). The questions on attitudes toward women's status, remittances, employment, and religiosity were all rescaled for easier interpretation

Robust standard errors in parentheses: $*p < 0.10$, $**p < 0.05$, $***p < 0.01$

172 APPENDIX

**Table A.3** Attitudes toward women among remittance receivers in MENA, 2016–2017

| Scale: Strongly disagree (1) Strongly agree (4) | A woman can become President or Prime Minister of a Muslim country | In general, men are better at political leadership than women | University education for males is more important than university education for females | Husbands should have final say in all decisions concerning the family | Women's inheritance should be equal to that of men | A married women can work outside of the home if she wishes |
|---|---|---|---|---|---|---|
| *Coeff/St. Errors/Sig.* | | | | | | |
| Remittance | −0.00 | −0.01* | −0.00* | −0.01 | 0.01 | 0.01* |
| Frequency | (0.01) | (0.01) | (0.00) | (0.01) | (0.01) | (0.00) |
| Gender | 0.76*** | 0.72*** | −0.38** | −0.15 | 0.10 | 0.40*** |
| (Women) | (0.14) | (0.28) | (0.14) | (0.11) | (0.15) | (0.10) |
| Age | 0.00* | 0.02 | −0.00 | −0.00 | 0.00 | −0.00 |
| | (0.00) | (0.02) | (0.00) | (0.00) | (0.00) | (0.00) |
| Employed | 0.11 | 0.13 | 0.12 | 0.12 | −0.01*** | 0.13 |
| | (0.14) | (0.14) | (0.15) | (0.14) | (0.00) | (0.15) |
| Rural | 0.38* | 0.52*** | 0.29 | 0.14 | 0.04 | −0.13 |
| | (0.23) | (0.16) | (0.16)* | (0.19) | (0.15) | (0.14) |
| Religiosity | 0.01 | −0.02** | −0.01 | 0.03** | −0.00* | 0.01 |
| | (0.02) | (0.01) | (0.01) | (0.01) | (0.00) | (0.01) |
| *R-squared* | 0.005 | 0.005 | 0.004 | 0.005 | 0.0004 | 0.007 |
| *Obs* | 8700 | 8700 | 8700 | 8700 | 8700 | 8700 |

*Source* Arab Barometer wave 4, seven countries (Algeria, Egypt, Jordan, Lebanon, Morocco, Palestine, Tunisia). The questions on attitudes toward women's status, remittances, employment, and religiosity were all rescaled for easier interpretation. *Education* dropped because variable split into two samples rendering comprehensive analysis problematic
Robust standard errors in parentheses: *$p < 0.10$, **$p < 0.05$, ***$p < 0.01$

# Index

**A**
Al-Sissi, Abdel Fatteh, 31
  President of Egypt, 31
Arab Barometer
  waves 1,2,3,4,5, 10, 109, 112, 120
Authoritarian, 5, 7, 11, 13, 15, 20,
    46, 60–62, 73, 77, 130, 134,
    136, 153
  neoliberalism, 16
  upgrading, 5–7, 18, 161, 165

**B**
Beblawi, Hazem, 16, 36–38
Beijing Conference
  1995, 77
  UN Women, 77
Bourguiba, Habib
  President of Tunisia, 30
Brand, Laurie
  neoliberalism, 74
  remittances and migration, 100
  state feminism, 6, 13

Bretton Woods Institutions, 11, 62
  IMF, World Bank, 12, 63

**C**
Campaigns, 2–5, 19, 65, 67, 77, 129,
    132–136, 141, 142, 144,
    146–150, 152, 153, 162, 163
  independents, women, 130, 140,
    147
  Saudi women, municipal elections,
    3
Candidates, 1, 2, 28, 45, 78,
    129–131, 134, 140, 143, 144,
    146, 149, 150
  female, 1–4, 19, 45, 65, 67, 129,
    135, 142–145, 147, 148, 152,
    153, 162
  independents, 130–133, 147
Capability Theory
  Nussbaum, Martha, 59
  Sen, Amartya, 59
Capitalism

© The Editor(s) (if applicable) and The Author(s), under exclusive     173
license to Springer Nature Switzerland AG 2022
B. C. Welborne, *Women, Money, and Political
Participation in the Middle East,*
https://doi.org/10.1007/978-3-031-04877-7

174 INDEX

neoliberal, 5, 15, 16, 18, 31, 35, 161
Conditionality, aid, 46, 49, 59, 62, 162
COVID-19, 20, 84, 98, 128, 166

**D**
Dependency, 9, 165
 oil, 19, 20, 120, 129
 resource, 16
Development, 12–14, 16–19, 32, 33, 37, 43–49, 59, 61–63, 65, 67, 68, 75–77, 96, 97, 100, 101, 117, 133, 135, 145, 161, 164
Dutch Disease, 41
 rentierism, 37
 resource curse, 37

**E**
Egypt, 7, 32, 34, 39, 46, 50, 51, 60, 62, 65, 74, 78, 80, 81, 98, 102, 104–108, 116, 120, 127, 130, 145, 147, 151–153
Elections
 municipal (Saudi), 1, 28, 149
 parliamentary (MENA), 31, 61, 65, 78, 130, 135, 140, 143, 144
 women's political participation, 29

**F**
Family code/law, 10, 30, 32, 34, 78, 83, 111, 113, 120
Feminism
 Islamic, 18
 market, 17, 20, 33, 35, 36, 72, 165
 neoliberal, 33
 secular, 31, 32, 73
 state, 5–7, 9, 16, 17, 31–33, 35, 47, 67, 71, 74, 161, 165
Feminist movements, 80, 139

First ladies, 7, 34
Foreign Aid, ODA, 50, 62, 76, 78, 83, 97, 98, 101
Foreign direct investment (FDI), 49, 98, 101

**G**
GCC (Gulf Cooperation Council), 2, 6, 9, 12, 14, 15, 19, 27, 28, 34–39, 41–43, 46, 48–51, 61, 62, 76, 117, 118, 120, 128–130, 133–139, 141–143, 145, 148, 151–153, 162
Gender
 empowerment, 7, 11, 12, 14–19, 28, 32, 33, 36, 42–45, 47, 48, 60–63, 65, 68, 71, 76–78, 84, 103, 132, 164, 165
 equality, 8, 9, 11, 13, 20, 27, 29, 35, 40, 41, 44, 47, 48, 60, 62–64, 73, 76, 77, 113
 gap, 13, 20, 45, 60
 mainstreaming, 12, 28, 44, 63–65, 71, 77, 151
 rentierism, 15–20, 27, 36, 40, 47, 51, 72, 119, 129, 137, 161, 164, 165
GONGOs (Government Sponsored NGOs), 6, 7, 13, 34, 48, 65, 67, 68, 74

**H**
Hatem, Mervat
 state feminism, 7, 32, 33, 74
Herb, Michael, 42, 138
 oil abundant vs. dependent, 42, 129
Heydemann, Steven
 authoritarian upgrading, 6

**I**
Independence, 30, 33, 115

colonial, 32
Independents, 17, 19, 20, 37, 49, 76, 107, 108, 127, 129
  campaigns, 147, 148, 152, 163
  women, 130, 131, 134, 143, 144, 146, 148, 153, 154, 162
International Monetary Fund (IMF), 46, 47, 84
Islam
  Islamic feminism, 18
  Islamic fundamentalism, 45
  Islamism, 30, 43

**J**
Jordan
  Asma Khader, 127
  Falaak Jamani, 4, 79, 132, 143
  female MPs, 147, 154
  foreign aid, 9, 38, 47, 48, 60, 68, 74
  GONGOs, 7, 74
  MCC, 74
  Nuha Maita, 4

**K**
Kandiyoti, Deniz, 7, 104, 105, 113, 164
Kelley, Judith, 8, 9, 27, 71

**L**
Labor force participation, female, 14, 41, 43, 50, 116–118, 120, 128, 136, 150, 152, 163
Left-behind women, 105, 107
Liberalization, 6, 8, 16
  neoliberal economic policy, 12
  neoliberalism, 6

**M**
MENA (Middle East and North Africa), 4–7, 10, 12, 13, 15–20, 27, 28, 30, 31, 33, 36–39, 41–43, 46, 48–51, 60–64, 68, 72, 75–77, 80, 82–85, 96, 97, 99, 104, 107, 108, 111, 113, 115–120, 128–130, 133, 134, 138, 139, 142, 143, 150–152, 162–166
Millennium Challenge Corporation (MCC)
  Jordan, 74
Millennium Development Goals (MDGs), 11, 12, 44, 64, 77
Modernization, 14, 33, 34
  theory, 128
Mohammad VI
  King, Morocco, 31, 74
Morocco, 2, 8, 9, 18, 19, 27, 29, 30, 32, 41, 45, 48, 50, 60, 62, 65, 67, 69–71, 74–76, 78, 81, 82, 95, 96, 98, 102, 104–108, 114, 116, 120, 127, 147–152
*Moudawana*, 75, 95
  family code, 30

**N**
Neoliberal, 6, 9, 12, 14–18, 20, 31, 33–36, 46, 47, 62, 74, 99, 161, 165
  actors, 33
  feminism, 33
Ngo-ization, 33, 48, 68

**O**
Oil abundance vs dependence, 42, 129, 136, 138
  development, 43

176  INDEX

**P**
Patriarchal bargains, 7, 10, 20, 41, 104, 164
Patriarchy, 105
Personal status laws/codes, 5, 10, 30, 32, 34, 78, 111, 113
Privatization, 33

**Q**
Quota, gender, 4, 5, 8, 9, 11, 13, 29–31, 43, 60, 61, 65, 67, 70, 71, 73–78, 80, 84, 85, 112, 128, 130, 133, 135, 142, 143, 146–148, 161, 162, 164

**R**
Rape laws, 81, 82, 154
Remittances, 5, 14–17, 19, 20, 38–40, 42, 46, 49–51, 76, 78, 84, 85, 96–112, 114–121, 127, 128, 163, 164, 170–172
Rents
    gender rentierism, 15–18, 20, 36, 40, 47, 51, 72, 119, 129, 137, 161, 164, 165
    rentierism, 5, 15–19, 36–40, 116, 129, 136, 137, 161
    rentier state, 18, 36–40, 47, 52, 139, 161, 164
        extreme, 43, 138, 153
    rentier state theory, 20
Reputation, 62, 75, 77, 81, 142, 145
    international, 8, 9, 71
    reputational benefits, 7, 8
Resource curse, 51, 119
    rent curse, 37, 161
Right-based development, 59
Ross, Michael, 14, 16, 37, 39, 41–43, 50, 51, 100, 102, 119, 136

**S**
Sabbagh, Amal, 64, 65, 67–69, 74, 136
Saudi Arabia, 3, 5, 11, 62, 82, 137, 139, 152
    Lama Suleiman, 3
    municipal elections, 1, 28
    Rasha Hefzi, 1, 3
    women candidates, 3
Scorecard diplomacy, 9, 27, 71, 164, 165
September 11th, 45, 46, 49, 59
Sexual violence, 80
Social contract, 5, 33, 37, 38, 40, 42, 46, 51, 133
State feminism, 5–7, 9, 13, 16, 17, 31–33, 35, 47, 67, 71, 74, 161, 165
Structural Adjustment Agreement (SAA), 46, 47, 84
Sustainable Development Goals (SDGs), 44, 64, 82

**T**
Tunisia, 29–32, 38, 39, 41, 65, 70, 74, 75, 78, 81, 82, 114, 120, 147, 154

**U**
United Nations
    UNDP, 65, 66
    UN Women, 11, 128, 151
    USAID, 9, 11, 12, 66, 74

**V**
Virtue signaling, 5, 7, 18, 62, 71

**W**
World Bank

Bretton Woods, 11, 12, 62, 63
Development Indicators, 116

MDGs, 11, 12, 44, 64, 77
SDGs, 44, 64, 82

Printed in the United States
by Baker & Taylor Publisher Services